INSTITUTIONAL REFORM AND ECONOMIC DEVELOPMENT IN THE CHINESE COUNTRYSIDE

Edited by

Keith Griffin
Magdalen College, Oxford

M. E. Sharpe, Inc.
Armonk, New York

Published in the United States by M. E. Sharpe, Inc.,
80 Business Park Drive, Armonk, New York, 10504

Published in Great Britain by The Macmillan Press Ltd

Printed in Hong Kong

Library of Congress Cataloging in Publication Data

Main entry under title:

Institutional reform and economic development in the Chinese countryside.

Includes index.
1. China—Economic conditions—1976– —Addresses, essays, lectures, 2. China—Rural conditions—Addresses, essays, lectures. 3. Agriculture—Economic aspects—China—Addresses, essays, lectures. 4. Communism—China—Addresses, essays, lectures. I. Griffin, Keith B.
HC427.92.157 1984 338.951′009173′4 84–5335
ISBN 0–87332–285–1
ISBN 0–87332–286–X (pbk.)

Contents

Preface

Most of the material used in preparing this book was obtained by the seven of us during a three-week field trip in rural China in July and August 1982. Financial assistance was provided by the British Academy/Social Science Research Council, the Chinese Academy of Social Sciences, the ILO's Asian Regional Team for Employment Promotion (ARTEP), Oxford's Webb Medley Fund and the Institute of Social Studies in The Hague. We are most grateful for this assistance.

Five of us made a return visit to China in September 1983 when we presented our findings to our colleagues at the Institute of Agricultural Economics in Beijing and gave them an opportunity to comment on our facts, methods of analysis and conclusions. During the course of a three-day seminar there was a lively exchange of views which it is safe to predict will lead some of us to reassess our position on some points in future writings. The essays published here, however, were not revised after the seminar because we thought it best to present the picture as we saw it in the summer of 1982 without much benefit of hindsight. Instead it was decided to write an Epilogue which would contain the highlights of the 1983 trip.

The return visit to China, including additional field work in Shaanxi and the Chongqing municipality, was financed in large part by a grant from ARTEP. Further help was provided by the Institute of Social Studies in The Hague. Again, we are most grateful for this generous assistance.

Parts of Chapter 2 were published in the *Oxford Bulletin of Economics and Statistics* and in *China Quarterly*. An earlier version of Chapters 3 and 4 was published by ARTEP as *Agrarian Policies and Institutions in China after Mao*.

We are deeply grateful to Mr Wang Geng Jin, our host at the Institute of Agricultural Economics, and to Mr Ni Xinyi, also of the Institute, who accompanied us on the field trip and did much to facilitate our research. Our interpreter was Mr Ruan Kehung, without whose constant help nothing would have been possible. We are indebted, too, to the regional offices of the Chinese Academy of Social Sciences in Sichuan and Yunnan, to numerous ministries and government agencies in Beijing and perhaps above all to the leaders and ordinary members of the communes we visited.

The final typescript was prepared for publication by Mrs Iris Patrick. Her skill, patience and good humour are much appreciated.

Magdalen College
Oxford

KEITH GRIFFIN

Units of Measurement

1 mu (or mou)	0.1647 acre 1 ≃ 1/6 acre
	0.0667 hectare
1 jin	0.5 kg
1 yuan	10 jiao = 100 fen
1 US $	1.71 yuan in 1981

Notes on the Contributors

John Enos, Fellow and Tutor in Economics, Magdalen College, Oxford; co-author (with Keith Griffin) of *Planning Development* (1970) and of numerous articles in professional journals.

Ajit Kumar Ghose, Economist, International Labour Office, Geneva; co-author (with Keith Griffin) of 'Rural Poverty and Development Alternatives in South and South-east Asia: Some Policy Issues', *Development and Change* (1980) and editor of *Agrarian Reform in Contemporary Developing Countries* (1983).

Keith Griffin, President, Magdalen College, Oxford; author of *The Political Economy of Agrarian Change* (1974); *Land Concentration and Rural Poverty* (1976) *International Inequality and National Poverty* (1978); and (with Jeffrey James) *The Transition to Egalitarian Development* (1981).

Kimberley Griffin, Research Economist, Central Bank of Botswana; formerly teacher at the Institute of Finance and Economics, Tianjin.

Azizur Rahman Khan, Economist, World Bank, Washington, DC; author of *The Economy of Bangladesh* (1972); co-author (with Dharam Ghai) of *Collective Agriculture and Rural Development in Soviet Central Asia* (1979); co-editor (with three others) of *Agrarian Systems and Rural Development* (1979).

Eddy Lee, Director, Asian Regional Team for Employment Promotion, Bangkok; author of 'Egalitarian Peasant Farming and Rural Development: The Case of South Korea', *World Development* (1979); editor, *Export-led Industrialisation and Development* (1981); co-author (with Rizwanul Islam and Azizur Rahman Khan) of *Employment and Development in Nepal* (1982).

Ashwani Saith, Professor, Institute of Social Studies, The Hague; author of 'Production, Prices and Poverty in Rural India', *Journal of Development Studies* (1981) and (with Keith Griffin) *Growth and Equality in Rural China* (1981).

1 Introduction

KEITH GRIFFIN

China is by far the world's largest underdeveloped country. The census completed in July 1982 revealed that there are 1008 million Chinese living on the mainland. This is half again as many as India's 673 million, the next most populous country. It is nearly double the size of the other thirty-one countries classified by the World Bank as low-income economies, with a combined population of 511 million, and it is almost as large as all sixty-three middle-income economies put together, with their combined population of 1139 million. In global terms, nearly a quarter of mankind lives in the People's Republic of China.

According to conventional measures of national income, China is also one of the poorest countries on earth. Its average income is a bit higher than that of India but slightly lower than that of Pakistan. Moreover, China is noticeably poorer than many of the other large underdeveloped countries such as Indonesia, Egypt, Nigeria or Brazil. Thus by reason of her size and poverty, China deserves the attention of everyone interested in the economic development of underdeveloped countries.

The Chinese economy, as is well known, is organised along socialist principles. All large industrial enterprises belong to the state or to its decentralised organs, private property in most productive assets has been abolished and the rural sector has been organised into collective or co-operative institutions known as communes. Indeed, the socialist agricultural sector in China is by far the largest in the world. The second largest socialist economy, that of the Soviet Union, contains an agricultural labour force of only 25 million persons whereas in China the agricultural labour force is about 458 million, i.e. eighteen times as large. Furthermore, the institutional arrangements in rural China, centred on the people's commune, are distinctive and are currently going through a period of major reform. Hence a knowledge of contemporary China, and particularly of Chinese rural development, is important to everyone interested in the economics of socialist countries.

Our main purpose in this book is to report on research undertaken in the rural areas of China in the summer of 1982. The objectives of our research were to assess the likely impact of the economic reforms on production, efficiency and accumulation in the country side; to consider the possible impact of institutional change on the distribution of income at the local level and to examine the present role of commune and brigade level enterprises in promoting rural development. Field work was concentrated in two provinces, Sichuan and Yunnan, and data gathered there plus additional material obtained in Beijing constitute the raw material on which our conclusions are based.

Our findings and interpretations are presented in the chapters that follow. In order to understand our findings, however, it is necessary to place them in the wider context of China's overall development and then to compare China with the rest of the Third World. In making these comparisons we shall rely on data assembled by the World Bank and shall refer to the decade ending in 1980.

Let us begin with growth and accumulation. As can be seen in Table 1.1, the average annual rate of growth of gross domestic product in China was 5.5 per cent during the period 1970–81. This exceeds by a considerable margin the rate of growth achieved in India and the other low-income countries and is about the same as the rate of growth of the middle-income countries. What is true of aggregate output is true also of the two most important sectors of agriculture and industry. Chinese agriculture grew 2.8 per cent a year, half a percentage point faster than the low-income economies as a whole and nearly as fast as the growth in middle-income economies. As a result, food production per head in China was 16 per cent higher at the end of the decade than at the beginning, compared to 3 per cent in India, 11 per cent in the other low-income countries and 10 per cent in the middle-income countries. In industry, China grew nearly twice as fast as India, 2.6 times as fast as the other low-income countries and 22 per cent faster than the middle-income countries. Thus the growth performance in China compares very favourably indeed with the rest of the Third World.

Some of the reasons are not hard to find. First, China devotes a larger share of its domestic product to investment than other underdeveloped countries, that is, 28 per cent in 1981 as compared to 23 per cent in India, 14 per cent in other low-income economies and 25 per cent in the middle-income economies. Secondly, the rate of growth of investment in China is high: in fact, it is much higher than in the other low-income countries and not too much below the rate currently achieved in the middle-income countries. Moreover, if one takes a longer view than a decade, the rate of growth of investment in China has been faster than in the middle-income countries.

Not only has production increased more rapidly in China than in most other Third World countries, but the population has increased significantly less rapidly than the average. As a result, output per head has tended to rise much faster in China than elsewhere. The recent census indicates that the rate of demographic expansion in China is about 1.5 per cent a year and falling. In Table 1.2 we reproduce a number of estimates used by the World Bank. It can be seen that China compares very favourably with population growth rates in India (2.1 per cent), other low-income countries (2.6 per cent) and the middle-income countries (2.4 per cent). Indeed, combining the estimates of the rates of growth of GDP and the population yields estimates of the rate of growth of GDP per head during 1970–81 of 4 per cent a year in China, 1.5 per cent in India, 1 per cent in other low-income countries and 3.2 per cent in the middle-income countries. Clearly, China has done much better than the great majority of underdeveloped countries.

The birth rate in China, at 21 per thousand, is only half or two-thirds as high as in most other Third World countries. Similarly, the death rate

TABLE 1.1 *Growth and accumulation*

	China	*India*	*Other low-income economies*	*Middle-income economies*
1. GNP per head, 1981 (US dollars)	300	260	240	1500
2. Percentage annual rate of growth, 1970–81				
GDP	5.5	3.6	3.6	5.6
Agriculture	2.8	1.9	2.3	3.0
Industry	8.3	4.4	3.2	6.8
Investment	6.0	4.9	3.7	7.9
3. Gross domestic investment as per cent of GDP, 1981	28	23	14	25
4. Food production per head, 1979–81 (index: 1969–71 = 100)	116	103	111	110

SOURCE IBRD, *World Development Report 1983*, World Development Indicators, Oxford University Press, 1983.

in the other Third World countries is 50 to 100 per cent higher than in China. For example, India's death rate, at 13 per thousand, is 62 per cent higher than China's death rate of 8 per thousand. Evidently, China has been unusually successful both in regulating fertility and in reducing mortality. The latter is reflected, too, in the very low infant mortality rate of 71 per thousand. This is only about 59 per cent of the rate in India and other low-income countries and significantly below the average rate in the middle-income countries. Indeed, China enjoys a demographic profile more like that of a rich country than a poor. As a result, a large fraction of the country's population is economically active and the dependency ratio is correspondingly low.

The benefits of growth have been spread widely in China. Life expectancy is sixty-seven years compared to only fifty-two in India and even less in the majority of the other low-income countries. The adult literacy rate is nearly double that of the low-income countries and marginally higher than that of the middle-income countries.

Equally significant is the secondary school enrolment ratio. In China, about one out of three children of secondary school age are in school; in India, just over one in four; in the other low-incomes economies, less than one in five; and in the middle-income economies, two in five. These differences in enrolment ratios underline in the most vivid way possible the differences in development priorities between China and most of the rest of the Third World.

TABLE 1.2 *Demographic and social indicators*

	China	*India*	*Other low-income economies*	*Middle-income economies*
1. Population growth rate, 1970–81	1.5	2.1	2.6	2.4
2. Crude birth rate, 1981	21	35	44	35
3. Crude death rate, 1981	8	13	17	11
4. Infant mortality rate, 1981	71	121	124	81
5. Life expectancy (years)	67	52	50	60
6. Adult literacy (%)	69	36	40	65
7. Secondary school enrolment, 1980 (per cent of age group)	34	28	19	39

SOURCE IBRD, *World Development Report 1983*, World Development Indicators, Oxford University Press, 1983.

This general picture should not be forgotten when considering the specific aspects of Chinese rural development discussed in this book. Our views on, say, institutional change, the population programme and policies for rural industry should be kept in their proper global, national and historical contexts. If the context is ignored our views are likely to be misunderstood. Equally, it is important to recognise that we were able to visit only a small number of units and most of these were fairly accessible from major cities and towns, were considerably more prosperous than the average and hence were not representative of the full range of economic circumstances that can be encountered in rural China. This does not mean that no general conclusions can be drawn from our work – far from it – but it does mean that inferences must be drawn with due regard to the local context of our observations.

During the three weeks we were in China we were able to visit fourteen units and collect a great deal of quantitative and qualitative material. The units visited are listed in Table 1.3 along with some of the special features and the distributed collective income per head of each.

The first communes visited were in the Beijing municipality and are among a handful of communes accustomed to receiving large numbers of visitors both foreign and local. In particular, one commune visited, Evergreen People's Commune, is very exceptional in that the basic accounting unit is the commune rather than the team. The 'production responsibility system' at Evergreen takes the form of contracts between the commune and the various teams, whereas in much of the rest of China it takes the form of contracts between the production team and individual households or individuals or work groups. Evergreen Commune, in a sense, represents the type of commune advocated by the now much maligned Gang of Four. Over half its total income originates in the industrial sector and its distributed collective income per head of 606 yuan was the highest of any unit visited. The second commune visited, Yellow Sands Commune, also is heavily industrialised and is very prosperous.[1] It is distinctive in that all accumulation in the commune occurs at the level of the brigade although distribution is at the level of the team. These two communes obviously enjoyed an enormous advantage in being located close to Beijing. Transportation costs were low, there was a ready market for manufactured products and high value vegetables and fruits could be grown for the inhabitants of the capital city. Yellow Sands even had a profitable sideline activity of cultivating cut flowers and decorative plants for sale in Beijing.

Six units were visited in Sichuan province. The Phoenix Corporation was a radical experiment in which the teams largely disappeared after

TABLE 1.3 *List of units visited*

Unit	*Distributed collective income per head*	*Features*
Beijing municipality		
1. Evergreen Commune	606	Commune is basic accounting unit. Industry accounts for 55% of total income.
2. Yellow Sands Commune	409	Accumulation entirely at brigade level. Industry accounts for 60% of total income.
Sichuan province		
3. Brigade No. 17 (Phoenix Corporation), Zhan Xiang Commune, Qionglai county	502	Corporation divided into four companies; 87.8% of income originates at corporation (brigade) level. Teams have largely disappeared.
4. Brigade No. 9, Zu Chiao Commune, near Chengdu	235	Contracts largely based on work groups; 57.1% of income originates in commune and brigade level enterprises.
5. Jinan Joint Corporation Guanghan county	n.a.	Commune decapitated; industry hived off to a separate corporation which issues shares.
6. Co-operative No. 7, Heping Village, Dong Nan Xiang, Guanghan county	286	Teams transformed into autonomous co-operatives; commune dissolved. Responsibility system based on work groups.
7. Mi Mu Commune, Xindu county	152	Teams enter into contracts with households and individual workers.
8. Chao Tan Brigade, Yuan Men Ko Commune, near Chengdu	367	Teams enter into contracts with work groups. Specialises in vegetables.
Yunnan province		
9. Team No. 1, Gao Chang Brigade, Gao Chang Commune, Yu Xi county	401	Richest team in the county. Team contracts with small work groups and individual workers.
10. Team No. 7, Xiang Sui Brigade, Xiao She Qiao Commune, Yu Xi county	120	Located in the mountains. Practises contracts with households (*bao gan dao hu*).

TABLE 1.3 (*Contd.*)

Unit	*Distributed collective income per head*	*Features*
11. Team No. 8, Long Xu Brigade, Gao Chang Commune, Yu Xi county	323	Located in the hills. Practises contracts with households (*bao chan dao hu*). Shifting cultivation; land not a constraint. Yi nationality.
12. Sun Jin Brigade, Chun He Commune, Yu Xi county	263	Teams enter into contracts with workers.
13. Gao Chio Team, Pu Chao Brigade, Ala Commune, near Kunming	127	Samei people. No brigade enterprises; team's assets being sold off (buffaloes); contracts with households. Commune disintegrating.
14. Fu Bao Brigade, Liu Jia Commune, near Kunming.	320	Contracts with work groups. Industry accounts for 75% of output.

being absorbed into the brigade. The brigade then became an instrument for rapid industrialisation. The experiment appeared to have been a great success and per capita distributed collective income was very high, being midway between Yellow Sands and Evergreen Commune. At the other extreme, and equally radical, was the experiment in Guanghan county with the dissolution of the commune system and the transformation of production teams into autonomous co-operatives, of which Co-operative No. 7 of Heping village was a good example. Brigade- and commune-level enterprises were hived off to a separate Jinan Joint Corporation which issued shares to the collective units which formerly owned the enterprises. Also visited were two prosperous units – Brigade No. 9 of Zu Chiao Commune and Chao Tan Brigade of Yuan Men Ko Commune – which practised a form of the 'responsibility system' in which teams entered into contracts with work groups. The sixth unit studied in Sichuan was Mi Mu Commune where teams had contracts either with households or individual workers.

In Yunnan we visited a very rich team (Team No. 1 of Gao Chang Brigade) and a relatively poor team in the mountains which practised the most common form of the 'responsibility system', *bao gan dao hu* (Team No. 7 of Xiang Sui Brigade). We also visited two units composed mostly of people from one of the many minority nationalities of the province, namely, Team No. 8 of Long Xu Brigade and Gao Chio Team of Pu Chao Brigade. The latter was a relatively poor team with a distributed collective income per head of 127 yuan. It was distinctive in that there were signs that it was entering a process of cumulative disintegration. In contrast, Fu Bao Brigade was prosperous, heavily industrialised and wished to maintain strong collective units by organising collective agriculture largely around work groups rather than households. Finally, there is Sun Jin Brigade, which also maintained a strong collective identity although farming was organised on the basis of individual workers (*bao chan dao lao*).

It should be evident from this brief description of the communes visited that we were able to observe at first hand units which differed both in the circumstances in which they found themselves and in the policies which they chose to adopt. Indeed the variation that can be found from one commune to another is one of the most lasting impressions of our trip. The policy framework is of course the same for all communes except those which have been given explicit permission to conduct radical experiments. Within the policy framework, however, there is ample latitude for local differences in judgement, interpretation and methods of implementation. And there is no doubt that local leaders do exercise their discretion on a wide range of issues, for example, the criteria used in allocating collective land to those who will farm it, the persons entitled to cultivate collective land under contract (work groups, households or individuals), the conditions specified in the contract, the size of the private plot, the methods of recruiting labour to commune and brigade level enterprises, the proportions of income to be set aside for collective accumulation, the types of industrial activity to be undertaken, etc.

Given the varying practices from one team to another, let alone from one commune to another, it is not always easy to discern the underlying trends or to predict with confidence future developments. People who have been to the same places at the same time, spoken to the same informants, seen the same things and examined the same data may nonetheless reach different conclusions about such fundamental issues as whether the commune system is disintegrating and being abandoned, whether income inequality is likely to increase or whether the long-run rates of growth of output and capital accumulation are likely to increase or decline. Disagreement about such things may in part reflect differences in ideological predispositions, since all of us are inclined to see what we are looking for, but more important, I think, it reflects an inherent difficulty of doing research in the social sciences, where so much depends on weighing one piece of fragmentary evidence against another and then assessing its impact on the behaviour of an economy which is itself changing over time.

The reader of this book will find more than one point of view represented. Although we have shared a common experience, we are not of a single mind and we think it more instructive that our differences should be exposed openly rather than hidden behind verbal foliage. Both in China and afterwards there were animated discussions among ourselves about the significance of recent changes in the rural areas of that vast country. Our initial views have been refined and although they are far from being definitive we are ready to present them to a wider public. In doing so, however, we hope our readers will regard this book as a report on a conversation, a conversation indeed in which they are welcome to participate.

OUTLINE OF THE BOOK

In the next chapter the recent reforms are viewed in an evolutionary perspective. The household economy is regarded as the fourth tier of a four-tiered commune system and the new policies are interpreted as representing essentially a shift in the locus of cultivation from the production team (the third tier) to the household (the fourth tier). Empirical evidence is presented which suggests that so far at least the introduction of the production responsibility system has not resulted in an increase in inequality in the distribution of income at the local level. Indeed, some evidence indicates that inequality actually has diminished.

The empirical evidence is fragmentary and the period of time covered is very short and hence no firm conclusions can be drawn from these results. There is reason to believe, however, that in principle the responsibility system should produce a more equal distribution of income than the work point system it has largely replaced.

Under the work point system a household's collective distributed income depends upon the number of workers it contains and the average number of work points earned by each worker. In practice there is relatively little variation in the number of work points earned by a worker: differentials are narrow and each worker receives an income corresponding roughly to the average productivity of labour. Under these conditions, collective income per head within, say, a production team would vary inversely with the dependency ratio. For example, if one household has a dependency ratio of four and another of two, per capita income in the former would be only half as large as per capita income in the latter.

Under the production responsibility system, in contrast, a household's income from the collectively owned land it cultivates depends on the number of mou farmed and on yields per mou. As a first approximation it is reasonable to assume that within a team output per mou would vary relatively little from one household to another. Under these conditions, 'collective' income per head would vary directly with the number of mou per head. If all of the team's land were allocated strictly on a per capita basis, income per head would be virtually identical in all households.

Given our assumptions, the ratio of highest to lowest per capita incomes within a team would be equal to the ratio of highest to lowest dependency ratios under the work point system, whereas under the responsibility system it would be equal to the ratio of the highest to lowest mou per head. Provided only that the range of dependency ratios is greater than the range of mou-per-head ratios, the responsibility system will produce a more equal distribution of income within a team than the work point system.

In Table 1.4 we attempt, with an arithmetic example, to demonstrate the strongly equalising tendencies implicit in the responsibility system. For simplicity we assume (i) that total output is constant whichever system is used, (ii) that output (or work points) per worker is the same for all workers under the work point system, and (iii) that output per mou is the same in all households under the responsibility system regardless of the size of household and the number of workers it contains.[2]

Let us now compare the average for an entire team with the outcome obtained by a representative labour-weak household consisting of one worker and three dependents. Under the work point system our worker received the same as all other workers, but because the household's dependency ratio is twice as high as the average, output per head (or collective distributed income per capita) is only half the average. Consider next Case *A*, one variant of the responsibility system under which 40 per cent of the land is allocated on a per capita basis and 60 per cent on a per worker basis. Applying this rule means that the labour-weak household is entitled to cultivate 2.8 mou or 70 per cent of the average number of mou per head for the team as a whole. As a result, income per capita in the household rises by 40 per cent (from 50 to 70 yuan) to a level only 30 per cent below the average. Finally, in Case *B* we illustrate another variant of the responsibility system in which all the land is divided in equal amounts per head. In this case, income per capita in the labour-weak household doubles to 100 yuan and attains a level equal to the average for the team.

Evidently reality is more complex than the simple model in Table 1.4, and it is possible to think of many disequalising tendencies that could emerge, but the model has the virtue of demonstrating clearly that the immediate consequence of switching from the work point to the production responsibility system could be an improvement in the distribution of income.[3]

In Chapter 3 Azizur Rahman Khan examines the responsibility system in great detail. He regards the changes that have been introduced since 1978 as revolutionary and argues that change may still be accelerating. The system of contracting with households is said to be, in effect, a form of peasant farming, albeit an extraordinarily egalitarian form. Nonetheless, there are features of the contracting system which could well lead to greater inequality in future.

Khan argues that the new incentive system for households can be expected to raise production. This increased production will accrue as a bonus to those households which succeed in raising output above the norm, and since the bonus typically is 100 per cent, and tax and other levies are fixed amounts, the incidence of the tax, procurement and bonus arrangements will be highly regressive: the higher the level of output produced by a household, the lower the average rate of taxation. The effect of this, in turn, is to reward households more than proportionately for increases in productivity. That is, on the margin, net household incomes rise faster than output, with the result that as output increases inequality in the distribution of income will tend to rise.

Moreover, where political and economic functions have been separated by transferring administrative responsibilities to the *xiang*, Khan argues that the communes have been weakened to such an extent that for all practical purposes they have ceased to exist. Where the linkages between the three tiers of the commune have been severed, the possibility of achieving high rates of collective accumulation has been reduced and this may have unfortunate implications for the long-run rate of growth in rural areas.

In Chapter 4 Eddy Lee discusses the effects of the reforms on employment and the allocation of labour between (i) collective agriculture, (ii) commune and brigade enterprises, (iii) capital accumulation and (iv) private sector activities. His point of departure is an analysis of the effect of the work point system on labour incentives. He concludes that the old system resulted in a high degree of equality but it may have

TABLE 1.4 *Distributive implications of the responsibility system*

	Production team	*Representative labour-weak household*		
		Work-point system	*Case A*	*Case B*
1. Population	100	4	4	4
2. Workers	50	1	1	1
3. Cultivated area (mou)	100		2.8	4
4. Dependency ratio [(1)/(2)]	2	4	4	4
5. Mou per head [(3)/(1)]	1		0.7	1
6. Output per worker	200	200		
7. Output per mou	100		100	100
8. Output per head [(6)/(4) or (7) × (5)]	100	50	70	100

NOTE In Case A, 40 per cent of the land is distributed on a per capita basis and 60 per cent on a per worker basis; in Case B, all of the land is distributed on a per capita basis.

had some negative consequences for labour productivity and the efficiency of labour allocation.

Turning to the recent changes, he underlines the importance of distinguishing between the administrative reform and reforms in the payment system. The former is concerned primarily with decentralising decision-making from the production team to the household, whereas the latter is concerned with changing the incentive system away from work points towards one in which income is closely related to individual work effort. Lee argues that the reforms mean that the commune system no longer acts as a guaranteed source of employment. On the other hand, the reforms should lead to an expansion in the level of employment for three reasons. First, the improved terms of trade have raised the returns to labour and this will increase both the demand and supply of labour. Second, the expansion of the private sector will lead to greater absorption of labour in the household economy. Third, the rapid growth of commune and brigade enterprises will generate increased demand for labour in the industrial sector.

As regards the distribution of income, Eddy Lee believes that on balance the effects may be favourable, primarily because much of the land under the responsibility system is allocated on a per capita basis. The cost of even greater equality, however, may be a slower rate of accumulation. The reason for this is that the reforms have weakened collective accumulation in agriculture and it remains to be seen whether household savings and investment increase sufficiently to offset the decline in collective investment.

In Chapter 5 Ashwani Saith reflects on China's population policies. He shows that since 1969 the birth rate has fallen steadily and the overall rate of growth of the population now is rather slow. Hence from a macroeconomic perspective China would not appear to have a demographic problem. It can be argued, however, that there is a serious sectoral imbalance in the sense that given the population growth rate and the rapid increase in per capita income, the rate of growth of food output is too low. The obvious solution of accelerating food production is being attempted but agriculture suffers from diminishing returns to material inputs and consequently it will not be easy to increase the rate of growth of food production markedly. In this context the possibility of further reducing the rate of demographic expansion has obvious attractions.

The current policy is to encourage all families to have only one child. This policy, unfortunately, is in partial conflict with the institutional reforms that have been introduced after 1979. Saith argues that the reforms are likely, at least in the short run, to increase the demand for labour within the household and hence to increase the average number of children desired by parents. More important, he believes that to the extent that the reforms weaken collective institutions, parents will have to place greater reliance on their children, particularly on their male children, for security in old age, and this will further increase the demand for children. Thus the reforms will make it more difficult to implement the single child family programme and pressure on local leaders to attain the demographic objectives means that local leaders in turn are likely to become more authoritarian in their dealings with the peasantry.

Quite apart from this, the single child family programme is likely to increase inequalities between rural and urban areas (since the latter will have a higher rate of adoption and hence a higher level of benefits) and between Han and minority nationalities (since the programme is not implemented in minority areas). If the programme is successful in rural areas, parents are likely to become increasingly reluctant to send their only child to school (particularly secondary school) because an extra pair of hands under the responsibility system will have great economic value. In the cities, in contrast, the economic return on a young child is low whereas the return on an educated child is high, and consequently parents will have a strong incentive to send their child to school. The net effect will be to widen educational inequalities between the city and the countryside.

Saith is particularly concerned about the consequences of the single child family programme for women. On the whole he believes that the programme in combination with the production responsibility system represents a backward step. Women are likely to find themselves relegated to the household economy and the private plot and therefore to experience greater 'domestication'. He foresees a return to 'traditional' values and the associated subordination of women, while the premium now placed on male offspring may result in a sharp rise in the incidence of female infanticide. Thus according to this analysis the possible benefits of the single child family programme are unlikely to exceed the probable social and political costs.

Attention shifts in Chapter 6 to a consideration of the role played by commune- and brigade-level enterprises. There are more than 1.3 million such enterprises in rural China employing more than 30 million people, or about 9 per cent of the rural labour force. These enterprises already account for about a third of collective income and are growing rapidly. It is argued in the chapter that commune- and brigade-level enterprises have multiple advantages for rural development. Because of their low average capital–labour ratio, they create jobs at low cost.

Because of their low capital–output ratio, they represent an efficient use of capital. Because of their small scale – they employ only twenty-three persons on average – they can be widely dispersed and used to industrialise the countryside. Finally, because of the high rate of profit they enjoy, commune- and brigade-level enterprises are an important source of funds for capital accumulation in rural areas. That is, they are the engines of growth in many communes.

John Enos examines a few specific commune- and brigade-level enterprises in Chapter 7, illustrating the variety of activities in which they are engaged, and thereby manages to put some flesh on the bones presented in the previous chapter. His conclusions are based on a sample of twenty-three industrial enterprises which he visited as a member of the delegation.

He shows that commune- and brigade-run industries are no longer always small in scale, simple in technology and restricted in the markets they serve. Many now serve markets throughout China and even abroad. Technologically, they are becoming increasingly sophisticated and in the richer communes the rural industries may soon become as technologically advanced as the state enterprises. There has been a blossoming of commune- and brigade-level enterprises in the last five years which has led to a great expansion in the variety of products manufactured, the size of new firms and the degree of capital intensity. On the whole these industries have performed well. In comparison with state enterprises, commune- and brigade-level activities are notable for the speed of construction (and the correspondingly short gestation period) and for the high degree of capacity utilisation of installed capital equipment (two and even three shifts being common).

John Enos speculates that commune- and brigade-level enterprises may be subject to fewer allocative distortions than state industries. On the other hand, because of their rising fixed or 'sunk' costs, they may be less flexible in future than they have been in the past. That is, the mobility of capital may decline as rural industry finds it less easy to change the composition of output in response to changing circumstances. Even so, the share of industry in total commune income can be expected to continue to rise rapidly. This rising income, however, may be unevenly distributed because the more prosperous communes are likely to be in a better position than the relatively backward communes to preempt the most profitable investment opportunities. If this turns out to be the case, it may be necessary for the central authorities to intervene to prevent inter-commune and inter-regional inequalities from becoming unacceptably wide.

In Chapter 8, the penultimate chapter, Ajit Ghose places the recent rural reforms within a national development perspective. The old development strategy reflected Mao's determination to provide a minimum standard of living and economic security for everyone and to ensure that social inequalities did not become too wide. These objectives, by and large, were achieved but only at the cost of a slow rise in consumption, some allocative inefficiency and a low productivity of investment. High rates of capital accumulation were attained by using the price mechanism to extract resources from the countryside to finance the expansion of heavy industry. No more than 17 per cent of the state investment budget was allocated to agriculture and supporting industries, and the communes were expected to be self-reliant and mobilise their own resources for capital construction projects.

The new development strategy entails a shift of emphasis from accumulation in favour of higher consumption; from productive to non-productive investment, e.g. in housing; and from heavy industry in favour of agriculture and light consumer goods industries. The price structure has been altered in order to provide a stimulus to agricultural production, but higher producer prices have not been reflected in higher retail prices in urban areas. As a result, basic foods and clothing are being heavily subsidised and this may undermine the capacity of the state to finance its own investment programme. There is a hint here that a reform of urban prices may soon become urgent.

In the short run Ajit Ghose believes that the reforms will lead to greater production efficiency, but the longer-run prospects are less clear, above all because the reforms undermine the capacity of the commune system to mobilise labour for capital construction. Moreover, in practice the reforms are likely to result in greater peasant differentiation. Land is unlikely to remain evenly distributed, reallocation of land holdings are likely to be infrequent and informal labour hiring practices are likely to emerge on a significant scale. Intra-regional inequalities may well increase. On the other hand, both inter-regional and rural–urban inequalities may diminish, labour mobility and migration will increase and there will be a sharper division of labour within the countryside. Hopefully poverty will diminish.

THE INCIDENCE OF POVERTY AND MALNUTRITION

Although China has done exceptionally well in comparison with most of the other Third World countries, it nevertheless remains very poor.

Furthermore, virtually all the serious poverty in China is located in the rural areas. This should not be overlooked when assessing the developments reported in this book. The Chinese themselves, of course, are well aware of the problems they confront and have recently adopted a poverty standard, or poverty line, to enable the incidence of poverty to be monitored. The standard has been set at 50 yuan per capita and is designed to reflect an income just sufficient to prevent malnutrition. That is, the standard provides for about 1600 calories per person per day in the rice-consuming regions and about 1400 calories per day in the wheat-consuming regions.

Using this poverty line, the Chinese have identified 221 counties as those which had an average distributed collective income per head of 50 yuan or less in each of the three years 1977–9. These are designated as chronically poor counties. The geographical distribution of these counties is indicated in Table 1.5. As can be seen, nearly 65 per cent of the chronically poor counties are concentrated in five provinces, of which Yunnan is one, and nearly 64 per cent of the 87.9 million people living in the chronically poor counties are in these same provinces. It should be noted, however, that Tibet is not included in the official estimates and thus the number of poor counties is understated somewhat.

The data in Table 1.5 constitute the empirical basis for the frequently made claim that there are about 100 million people in China, or 10 per cent of the entire population, who suffer from malnutrition. This figure should be interpreted with caution, however. First, one should take into account the distribution of household income around the county average. Most of the counties in Table 1.5 had a distributed collective income per head that was very close to the cut-off point of 50 yuan, and hence something like a half of the households in those counties must have received a collective income in excess of the poverty minimum. We know that in the period 1977–9 there were 1539 observations of counties with a per capita distributed collective income of less than 50 yuan.[4] Some of these counties fell below the poverty line in all three years (and hence formed the group of 221 counties) while a majority fell below the line in only one or two of the three years. The important point, however, is that 76.6 per cent of all 1539 observations were of counties with an average income between 40 and 50 yuan; in only 23.4 per cent of the cases was average income less than 40 yuan. It is only in this second group of counties where it would be reasonable to suppose that a significant majority of households received less than 50 yuan per head in the form of collective income. Of course, some counties with incomes

TABLE 1.5 *The distribution of chronically poor counties*

Province	*Number of counties*	*Percentage of total*	*Population (thousands)*	*Percentage of province's total population*
1. Guizhou	43	19.6	13 730	61.1
2. Gansu	26	11.8	6610	41.2
3. Henan	26	11.8	17 320	27.0
4. Shandong	24	10.9	12 820	19.7
5. Yunnan	23	10.4	5480	20.0
6. Shaanxi	11	5.0	1820	7.7
7. Fujian	11	5.0	4560	22.6
8. Hebei	11	5.0	3180	7.1
9. Anhui	10	4.5	9440	22.4
10. Shanxi	8	3.6	1180	5.8
11. Xinjiang	8	3.6	1110	16.3
12. Giangxi	5	2.3	1620	5.4
13. Guangdong	3	1.4	1650	3.9
14. Ningxia	3	1.4	920	32.4
15. Zhejiang	3	1.4	1340	4.2
16. Jiangsu	2	0.9	1980	4.1
17. Sichuan	2	0.9	1630	1.9
18. Inner Mongolia	1	0.4	60	0.4
19. Jiangxi	1	0.4	1420	5.4
Total	221	100.3	87 870	11.2

SOURCE Nicholas Lardy, *Agriculture in China's Modern Economic Development*, Cambridge University Press, 1983, Table 4–9, p. 173, based on data released by the Ministry of Agriculture, Commune Management Bureau, 1981.

above 50 yuan had households with incomes below the poverty line, but the number of households in this category almost certainly was much lower than the number of households in poor counties with incomes above the poverty line.

Secondly, the number of counties with an average income below the poverty minimum has fallen rapidly. Between 1979 and 1981 the number of counties with a distributed collective income per capita of less than 40 yuan fell by 55.5 per cent and the number between 40 and 50 yuan fell by over a third. Thus the data for 1977–9 do not describe accurately the situation today.

Thirdly, income generated in the private sector is ignored, yet it is known that private sector income now accounts for well over a third of household income and in many cases the proportion is much higher than this. Moreover, a large fraction of private sector income consists of food grown on the private plots and animal products derived from poultry and pig raising. It is likely, hence, that families with a distributed collective income per capita of 40 yuan would have an additional 10–15 yuan per head from the private sector and consequently their combined collective and private incomes would be at least 50 yuan per person. That is, the great majority of households classified as poor would have an income sufficiently high to prevent malnutrition. They wouldn't eat well, but it is improbable that they would suffer from hunger.

In the next chapter it is argued that the lower is collective income per head, the higher tends to be the share of private sector income in the total. If this hypothesis is confirmed by further research, still more households would be raised above the poverty line by their private sector activities. In this event, a nutrition-based poverty line centred on distributed collective income would greatly exaggerate the number of households suffering from malnutrition.

Finally, if one also takes into account other sources of family income arising outside the commune, for example wages earned from employment in state enterprises and remittances plus other intra-family income transfers, it seems likely that relatively few families would have a living standard equivalent to less than 50 yuan per person. In the present state of knowledge it is not possible to quantify the extent of malnutrition, but when everything is taken into account it would be surprising if as much as 3 per cent of the population, i.e. 30 million people, suffered from chronic malnutrition. If in fact the figure turns out to be as low as this, China will have gone a long way towards eliminating one of the most disturbing features of underdevelopment.

NOTES AND REFERENCES

1. A book about the commune was written by an earlier visitor. See A. Z. M. Obaidullah Khan, *The Yellow Sand Hills* (Comilla, Bangladesh: Bangladesh Academy for Rural Development, 1975).
2. The third assumption would be valid if the marginal product of labour in farming were zero in all households, or if households with an above average number of workers allocated a relatively high proportion of labour to non-agricultural activities, or if labour-weak households substituted material inputs for labour in farming.
3. A similar conclusion is reached by C. H. Chai in his 'Changes in Property Rights and Income Distribution Under China's Baogan Daohu System', paper presented to a conference on Development and Distribution in China, University of Hong Kong, 14–17 March 1983.
4. Nicholas Lardy, *Agriculture in China's Modern Economic Development* (Cambridge: Cambridge University Press, 1983) table 4–8, p. 172.

2 Institutional Change and Income Distribution

KEITH GRIFFIN and
KIMBERLEY GRIFFIN

The rural areas of China are going through a period of major institutional reform.[1] The Chinese People's Commune, one of the great social inventions of the twentieth century, is being radically transformed in directions which only now are beginning to become clear. In assessing this transformation, however, it is important to maintain an historical perspective.

Institutional change is not new to the people of China. Indeed, the commune system as we know it today can be regarded as the outcome of a rapid sequence of institutional reforms that began around the time of liberation in 1949. The sequence started with a redistributive land reform and the creation of small family farms. This was complemented by the formation of mutual aid teams consisting of small groups of three to five households in a village neighbourhood, the purpose of which was to facilitate sharing in the use and purchase of agricultural implements.[2] Thus even in this early period, long before mechanisation was significant, it was efficient and mutually beneficial for small farmers to work together and pool the tools that were then in very short supply.

The mutual aid teams, in turn, paved the way for more complex forms of collective organisation. They evolved first into lower-level or elementary agricultural co-operatives and later into higher-level or advanced agricultural co-operatives.[3] In 1958, when the Great Leap Forward was launched, the co-operatives were merged into very large communes in which an attempt was made to apply communist principles of production and distribution. As early as August 1959, however, it was evident that this attempt had not succeeded and it was therefore necessary once again to reconstruct China's rural institutions. That reconstruction produced the commune as we knew it until about 1979. That is, the arrangements made after the failure of the Great Leap Forward survived with relatively modest modifications for about two decades. Now, of course, major modifications are again underway.

The point we wish to emphasise, however, is that the commune was not a single, once-for-all invention; rather, it was the product of experimentation and adaptation. The commune, to repeat, was the product of a process, not the consequence of an ephemeral happening, or one man's imagination or even of a unique momentous event. The commune system has a history, a history of change and transformation, and the mutations that have recently captured so much attention are evidence that the process of experimentation continues. This feature of the Chinese style of rural development, namely its encouragement of experimentation, is highly distinctive and helps to ensure that institutional arrangements are responsive to the wishes of the peasantry and the needs of the economy.

The institutional changes in post-liberation China occurred with the agreement and active co-operation of the great majority of the rural population. The commune system was not imposed from above upon a hostile, unwilling or reluctant populace. Apart from the initial land confiscation which accompanied the triumph of the revolution and which abolished the landlord class, the changes introduced into the rural areas usually were made voluntarily, after much consultation between the peasantry and local government and party officials. The institutional transformation of rural China was not accompanied by massive violence, widespread passive resistance or by a sharp fall in output. This is not to say that there were no cases of violence, intimidation, coercion, intense social pressure, or of officials exceeding their authority; similarly, it would be untrue to imply that every innovation was greeted with enthusiasm by the peasantry and that no resistance ever was encountered anywhere; but on the whole, change occurred with the consent of those affected, peacefully, rapidly and effectively. It was a remarkable achievement.

This is widely agreed. The initial land redistribution was accomplished by the rural people themselves, through their Peasant Associations.[4] When the time came to form co-operatives the vast majority of the rural population, namely the poor and lower–middle peasants, joined them voluntarily, although there was some resistance from middle and rich peasants and some coercion. The formation of advanced co-operatives was achieved 'with neither the violence nor the massive sabotage characteristic of Soviet collectivisation'[5] and the 'Party never accepted the use or threat of force against the mass of peasantry as either legitimate or, in the long run, functional.'[6]

Nonetheless, it is true that many ordinary members of communes did experience during the periods of the Cultural Revolution and the Gang of Four an intolerable degree of coercion from local officials and a tendency on the part of some party leaders to issue commands from the top down. The result was some loss of confidence by the peasantry in the party and this has been accompanied by greater reluctance to follow the leadership of local officials. This, in turn, has made it more difficult to mobilise collective effort and has made it politically necessary, perhaps, to place greater reliance on material incentives and individual initiative. It would perhaps be a mistake, however, to believe that there is a widespread wish in the Chinese countryside to abandon collective institutions and disband the commune system.

The new reforms, which we shall discuss in detail below, have been accepted voluntarily and in many places with enthusiasm. But three points should be noted. First, the reforms are not uniform. They are of many kinds and vary considerably from one area to another; even where broadly similar systems have been introduced, reforms can differ significantly in detail.

Second, many communes have resisted all attempts at reform. This is especially true in prosperous and well-organised communes where the collective economy is strong. Conversely, in the poorer communes where the collective economy tends to be relatively weak households have responded to the reforms with alacrity. Third, the reforms are concerned primarily with decentralising decisions about agricultural production to the level of the household. Industrial production within the commune, however, remains an important part of the collective economy and, indeed, commune and brigade-level enterprises continue to grow at a very rapid rate.[7] There are few signs here of a wish to abandon collective institutions.

On the contrary, China's collective institutions are deeply rooted. The reason for this is that the commune system has grown organically out of the pre-revolutionary settlement pattern and consequently rests upon a cohesive social foundation (see Table 2.1). At the apex of the system is the commune itself. A commune normally consists of a cluster of villages around a traditional market town or county township and may contain as few as 15 000 persons or as many as 50 000. The present day communes typically were formed through the amalgamation of several higher-level or advanced co-operatives.

Table 2.1 *Characteristics of the commune system*

Organisation of the commune	*Corresponding settlement pattern*	*Equivalent earlier collective institution*	*Output and method of production*
Commune	cluster of villages around a market town	amalgamation of advanced co-operatives	factories; large-scale rural construction projects
Production brigade	large village or cluster of small villages	advanced co-operative	workshops and small factories
Production team	small village or neighbourhood of a large village	elementary co-operative	staple crops, possibly mechanised
Work group	group of neighbours; kinship group	mutual aid team	staple crops
Household			sideline activities; pig rearing and poultry; private plots; cultivation of collective land under contract

Below the commune is the production brigade, corresponding to the older advanced co-operative. The brigade, however, can best be visualised as a large village or in some cases as a grouping of several small villages. On average there are twelve or more brigades per commune. Next in descending order is the production team, equivalent to the earlier elementary co-operative. Each brigade would contain a number of teams, usually eight to ten or more, and it was at the level of the team that until recently most agricultural activity occurred. This, however, is now changing as the new reforms seek to shift responsibility for cultivation from the level of the team to smaller units, namely, work groups or households.

Even so, the production team remains the most important collective institution in rural China. In most communes the team is the level of account, the source of work points, the owner of the land and of draught animal power. The team corresponds essentially to the neighbourhood of a village or in the case of a small settlement, to an entire village. The members of a team inevitably are neighbours, friends and kinsmen. They are held together not only by economic interests but also by bonds of comradeship and consanguinity. Hence the team is simultaneously a production, residential and social unit and it is this which gives it its strength.

At the base of the commune, as the fourth tier, is the household and its economy. This household economy is an integral part of the commune system and should not be regarded as separate from it. Formerly the household economy consisted solely of private sector activities narrowly defined, but the new reforms have enlarged the fourth tier by encouraging teams to give collective land under contract to individual households for cultivation.

There is an economic logic behind the organisation of the commune system. The system is rational in the sense that it is at least intended that production occurs at that level at which economies of scale are exhausted. Contrary to the practice in the Soviet Union and Eastern Europe, where agriculture has been based on a false premise of unlimited economies of scale,[8] Chinese practice assumes that the economies of scale in agriculture are rather limited but that there are decreasing costs in industry. Thus at the commune level one would normally encounter fairly large-scale manufacturing and processing facilities. The commune itself would not engage in routine agricultural production or livestock operations but would leave these activities for lower-level units. In Mi Mu People's Commune in Sichuan province, for instance, there were sixteen enterprises at commune level including a brick-making plant, a leather shoe factory, a printing press, quarry, rape-seed processing plant and an agricultural machinery repair shop.

In a few cases where economies of scale cannot be fully exploited by a single commune, two or more communes will get together and establish joint enterprises. For example, Wu Gong Commune in Hebei province participated with four other communes in operating a brick kiln, a truck transportation team, a heat insulating materials factory, a power generation plant and a large repair workshop. Joint enterprises such as these are still rather unusual, however. Normally, if an activity is too large to be undertaken at commune level it would become the responsibility of the state sector and production would be located in county level factories or, if necessary, at the provincial level.

The production brigade often is responsible for running a large range of relatively small workshops and simple repair and assembly facilities. A fairly typical example of a prosperous brigade would be Sun Jin Brigade, Chun He Commune in Yunnan province. The brigade has a husking mill, shoemaking shop, a sewing group which makes clothes for the commune, a workshop that makes screws, a transportation group, a construction gang and a team of porters.

The production team is responsible primarily for organising the production of staple crops and normally has relatively few non-agricultural sideline activities. Production can be undertaken either by the team itself (the most common practice in the past) or by smaller work groups within the team or by individual households. An example of a team that combines all three methods of production is Team No. 1, Gao Chang Brigade, Gao Chang Commune, Yunnan. The team has a collective piggery,[9] a workshop to make noodles, a transport group and a construction gang; it also engages in forestry. The main cash crop, tobacco, is produced by small work groups whereas wheat, beans and rape-seed are grown under contract by individual households, the land being allocated in accordance with the labour force in each household. Rice cultivation, however, is organised differently: transplanting is done collectively, then households enter into contract with the team to weed and manage the fields until the harvest, but the harvest itself then is done collectively.

The private sector typically engages in those activities which can be done efficiently on a small scale, i.e. which do not require large amounts of capital or a large volume of production for efficient operation but which can make good use of household labour, including labour available on a part-time basis. For most of the post-liberation period the household economy has tended to concentrate on pig raising, poultry (ducks, geese, chickens), small-scale handicrafts and the cultivation of vegetables, fruits, condiments and fodder on the private plot. The household economy had almost no responsibility for food grain production but limited itself to sideline activities such as the above. However, as we have seen, this is no longer the case: the recent reforms have shifted the locus of production of grains and cash crops from the level of the team to (in most instances) the household, where it is believed these crops can be grown most efficiently. That is, the effect of the reforms has been to move most agricultural activity from one place in the institutional hierarchy to another.

It is not possible to give accurate figures on the division of income among the four tiers of the commune system. Moreover, variations from one commune to another can be very great, so that a national average has only a limited meaning. Nevertheless, it may be helpful to provide some indication of orders of magnitude even if the numbers contain a rather large margin for error. Broadly speaking, over one quarter of rural income originates in household sideline activities and the remaining three-quarters or less in the collective sector, including output produced by households on collective land under contract. Perhaps 8–10 per cent of income originates at commune level and 12–14 per cent at brigade level. The remaining 50 per cent represents agricultural products cultivated under the authority of the team by households under contract, work groups and the team itself.

THE NEW REFORMS AND THE RESPONSIBILITY SYSTEM

The reforms introduced since 1978 cover several areas. First, the team has been designated as the basic accounting unit and attempts to raise the level of account to the brigade or commune are to be resisted. By the end of 1981 only thirty-one out of some 54000 communes kept the commune as the basic accounting unit, a decline of a half in three years. Similarly, of the 720000 brigades, only 36000 were basic accounting units. This, too, represented a fall of 50 per cent in three years. Conversely, 98 per cent of the 6 million teams kept their accounts at team level. This is significant because it means that in future it will not be possible to improve the distribution of income in rural areas by raising the basic accounting unit from the team to the brigade or commune. Other methods will have to be found.

Secondly, almost all restrictions have been removed from household sideline activities. Teams are free to increase the size of private plots to

15 per cent of the cultivated land. Households are free to engage in any activity of their choice, provided the activity does not damage the nation's resources or conflict with collective production or constitute speculation and hoarding. Households also are free to acquire machinery and draught animals and thus to accumulate capital. It remains to be decided, however, whether households are free to employ as much labour as they like. Banks have authority to make loans to individual peasants and the technical centres are encouraged to provide expertise and technical assistance to households wishing to establish new enterprises, for example, a dairy farm. These changes evidently create a possibility that more enterprising households, or more prosperous households with savings to invest, could achieve rapaid gains in output and income. If sustained for a long enough period of time, this could give rise to noticeably greater inequality in the distribution of income and to the emergence of social stratification within the peasantry.

Thirdly, the teams have been given the right to make decisions about the composition of output. That is, they are free to choose their own cropping pattern. The government may attempt to influence the decisions taken by teams, but the peasants now have the final say and are expected to base their decisions on the relative profitability of different crops. The effect of this reform has been to reduce the emphasis formerly placed on grain. In fact, between 1976 and 1980 the area devoted to cash crops increased by 16 per cent whereas that devoted to grains declined by 4 per cent. The output of grains, however, did not fall because there was an offsetting rise in yields.

Fourthly, and most important, a new system of incentives has been introduced, called the production responsibility system, which is designed to link the income of individual workers or households or work groups to the output arising directly from their efforts. It is widely believed in China today that for many agricultural activities the team is too large a unit for efficient production and consequently labour and land productivity could increase if the team were subdivided. The argument seems to be that high rates of collective accumulation have not been transformed into correspondingly high rates of collective output (i.e. that the incremental output–capital ratio has been excessively low), that individual effort in agriculture has been inadequate (because of a weak connection between effort and reward) and that the timing of farm operations has on occasion been sub-optimal because of the inherently rather slow and inflexible planning at team level. In fact, a great many experiments currently are underway in which a team enters into a contract with a work group or a household for a specific task, for a specific crop or for the cultivation of a specific piece of land.

There is a bewildering variety of arrangements that can be found in rural China and it would be impossible to describe them all. The production responsibility system originated in Sichuan and spread from there to the rest of the country. It is interesting, therefore, to consider the eight main forms of the system that can be identified in that province (see Table 2.2).

The most common arrangement is called *bao gan dao hu*. The contract is with an individual household and specifies that the household may enjoy the use of a piece of land in return for a promise to deliver under quota a specified quantity of produce. The household is free to use whatever method of cultivation it prefers and the quantity of output that must be turned over to the team is relatively modest, namely, the amount needed to pay taxes, meet the team's delivery quota and replenish the public welfare and accumulation funds. The arrangement is equivalent to a fixed rental tenancy system in which the length of tenure is one year, renewable by the landowner (in this case the team) and the rent is

TABLE 2.2 *The production responsibility system in Sichuan province, 1982* (percentage of teams)

1.	Team divided into work groups along specialized lines, e.g. forestry, fishponds, etc.	0.38
2.	Land distributed to individual workers on the basis of an equal amount of land per worker	7.19
3.	Land distributed to individual households; production is distributed centrally on basis of workpoints but above quota output is retained by the household (*bao chan dao hu*).	17.06
4.	Land distributed to individual households; all output retained by household after payment of taxes and contributions to public accumulation and welfare funds (*bao gan dao hu*).	64.46
5.	Part of land (60–70 %) allocated to households for self-provisioning while remaining part (30–40 %) farmed collectively (or under contract to households) to enable team to meet state quotas and add to accumulation and welfare funds.	3.35
6.	Irrigated fields farmed collectively; unirrigated fields farmed under contract by households or groups of workers.	3.97
7.	Contracts with work groups.	2.26
8.	Contracts with individual workers for specific, seasonal tasks, e.g. plowing, weeding.	1.32

specified in volume rather than value terms. Over 64 per cent of the 617 000 teams in Sichuan practise this form of the production responsibility system.

Next most common is *bao chan dao hu*. As with the previous arrangement, land is distributed to individual households, but under this system the contract is far more detailed. In many communes, for example, the contract will specify the amount of land to be cultivated, labour input, the amount of fertiliser by value to be applied, the output (in physical or value terms) to be delivered, the number of work points to be received by the household and the size of the bonus (or penalty) for production in excess of quota (usually 100 per cent). The quota under this system is much higher than under *bao gan dao hu* and is usually the average of the previous three years' output. About 17 per cent of the teams in Sichuan use this system.

Under both of the above arrangements land may be distributed to households on a per capita basis, or in proportion to the labour power available in the household, or by a combination of the two. For example, in Feng Huan Brigade, Zhan Xiang Commune, 60 per cent of the land is allocated on the basis of the size of the labour force in each household and 40 per cent on a per capita basis. Similarly, in Mi Mu Commune each household receives 0.4 mou per person and then the rest of the land is distributed in accordance with the number of workers in the household.

Cases can also be found of contracts between the team and work groups for the production of staple crops (2.26 per cent), between the team and work groups organised into specialised groups (0.38 per cent) and between the team and individual workers (7.19 per cent). There are also contracts with individual workers for specific, seasonal tasks such as plowing a field or weeding (1.32 per cent). Some teams (namely 3.97 per cent) farm their irrigated land collectively while contracting out the unirrigated land to households or work groups. Finally, some teams distinguish between land required to meet the subsistence needs of the people and that which is in excess of subsistence requirements. The former is distributed to households under contract while the latter may or may not be farmed collectively (3.35 per cent).

The position in China as a whole is broadly similar to that in Sichuan. Roughly 8 per cent of the teams still cultivate collectively, 5 per cent have contracts with work groups along specialised lines, 12–13 per cent have contracts with work groups which are not organised by speciality, 4 or 5 per cent have entered into contracts with individual workers and the remaining 70 per cent or more have distributed land to individual households. Thus as regards the organisation of cultivation, China has moved a long way towards the universal adoption of a small peasant farming system.

Incentives to work

Quite separate from the question of economies of scale is the issue of willingness to work or of the motivation of the peasantry. China, evidently, has moved away from collective to individual incentives and from moral to material incentives. The reasons for this are not transparently clear but it is possible to imagine what may have been some of the motives of the leadership.

Essentially, there are three ways to motivate people. One works either because one is told to do so, or because it is in one's personal interest to do so or because one ought to do so. To each of these ways of motivating people there corresponds a particular type of economy and method of organisation. The first is the command economy or slave economy. Reliance is placed upon penalties and punishments, upon taxes, quotas and the like. The second is *laissez-faire* capitalism. Workers are motivated by material incentives and the price mechanism. The third can be described as utopian socialism. Workers respond to a combination of moral incentives, public spiritedness and social pressure.

While every actual society contains a mixture of all three systems of motivation, some societies put greater emphasis on commands, some on material incentives and some on public spiritedness. Moreover, within a single country the system of motivation may vary from one sector to another. The workers in the army (i.e. soldiers) respond to commands, those in industry may respond largely to material incentives while the performance of, say, primary school teachers may be influenced by moral incentives. Finally, the balance of the system of motivation may change from time to time within a single country depending on political circumstances (peace, war, post-independence enthusiasm), national objectives (e.g. a high priority for rapid industrialisation) and ideological conviction.

Seen in this light, it is not surprising that there should be shifts of emphasis in China from time to time. When priority is placed on heavy industry, quota deliveries of food grains are essential. When rural capital construction and land management projects are stressed, moral incentives can be relied upon. When a more varied diet is wanted to increase consumption of pork, poultry and vegetables, the price mechanism seems more attractive. That is, when priorities change, the system of motivation may change. Furthermore, even if priorities don't change, it may be desirable to alter the mixture from time to time because of 'diminishing returns' to any one system of motivation. After a time supply curves may become inelastic with respect to a change in price; people may resist taxation and compulsory deliveries; the response to political exhortation may decline. When one of these things happens the government may have to alter its approach and place greater emphasis on one system of motivation at the expense of another.

Having said this, it remains an open question whether the swing in China to individual and material incentives may have gone too far. Material incentives no doubt have some effect on intensity of effort, particularly when there is a close connection between effort and reward. Non-material incentives, however, should not be disregarded. Especially when the social cohesion of the collective unit is strong, as it is in the case of production teams in China, effort expended by individuals can be influenced in part by the benefit expected to accrue not just to the peasant's family but to the neighbourhood or village as a whole. When there is a strong sense of community and joint endeavour, appeals to the 'public interest' can elicit a powerful response. Perhaps for the moment such appeals have run into diminishing returns because they have been made too frequently or to promote sectarian interests. The problem now is to devise the right combination of individual and collective incentives, and there is a danger that if individual, material incentives are stressed too much, the non-material, collective incentives will be weakened and the net effect on the willingness to work may be slight. In the process the viability of the commune system as an economic organisation could be subverted. We don't claim this is happening; we claim merely that it could happen.

TWO RADICAL EXPERIMENTS

The reforms that have been discussed so far do not imply the dissolution of the commune system, but merely a strengthening of the household economy at the expense of the collective economy of the team. There are, however, two radical experiments currently underway in Sichuan province which represent alternatives to the commune system rather than modifications of it. These experiments underline in a vivid way the point made earlier about the readiness of the Chinese to experiment with a variety of approaches to rural development. If the experiments prove to be successful it can be expected that they will be extended to other parts of the country and consequently they deserve careful consideration by those interested in anticipating the future course of events.

The Qionglai experiment

The Feng Huan Brigade, formerly of Zhan Xiang Commune is in Qionglai county about 70 kilometres south of Chengdu. In early 1980 the commune was effectively dissolved, the responsibility for culture and education, sport, women's affairs, family planning, etc., was transferred to the village and the brigade was renamed the Phoenix Corporation and given responsibility for all economic activities. The five production teams were merged and then reorganised into four companies with specialised functions, namely, production of cereals and oil-bearing crops, collective sideline occupations, industrial production and marketing.

The Corporation comprises 201 households with a population of 852 and a labour force of 345. The cultivated area is 1079 mou.

The rate of growth in recent years has been extraordinarily rapid. In agriculture, wheat yields increased from 299 jin per mou in 1977 to 708 jin in 1982, or by 137 per cent; yields of paddy rice rose from 629 jin per mou in 1977 to 983 jin in 1981, or by 56 per cent. Tractor horsepower available to the Corporation increased by 550 per cent during the period 1977–81. Equally important, there has been a shift away from grains to cash crops. Formerly nearly all the land was devoted to rice and wheat, whereas today 45 per cent is devoted to rape-seed, tobacco, sugar-cane and jasmine blossoms. The engine of growth, however, has been industrialisation. In 1978 about 95 per cent of the then brigade's output originated in agriculture whereas in 1981 it was only 9 per cent. Today 38 per cent of the labour force is engaged in agriculture and the remaining 62 per cent in industrial and sideline activities.

Before the experiment began Feng Huan Brigade owned a processing mill and a highly profitable distillery. In 1979 two small projects were started, a workshop for making plastic bags for fertiliser and a yeast-making shop. Then in 1980 a small workshop was established to make sausages and hams in the winter months and, much more important, a profitable chemical plant was constructed from the profits of the distillery. The following year a third very profitable project was begun, namely, a kiln for machine-made bricks, that was partly financed from the combined profits of the distillery and chemical plant. This sequence of industrialisation was assisted by the government. A county technician helped the brigade set up the distillery and later the county helped the Corporation obtain some raw materials for the chemical plant. The plant itself benefits from a contract with a state enterprise.

In the period from 1979 to the first half of 1982, total industrial

TABLE 2.3 *Industrial investment in the Phoenix Corporation, 1979–82* (yuan)

	1979	*1980*	*1981*	*1982 (first six months)*
Reinvested profits	39 800	190 000	71 000	120 000
Share capital	14 000	0	69 000	0
Other	26 200	0	0	0
Total	80 000	190 000	140 000	120 000

NOTE In 1979 the county loaned the brigade 23 000 yuan and the commune made a grant of 80 000 bricks, the value of which was approximately 3200 yuan.

investment was 530 000 yuan. Over 80 per cent of this was financed out of the retained profits of the Corporation's enterprises. The state provided a small amount of capital in the form of a loan and the commune made a grant in the form of bricks. This was important in amassing the initial 'seed corn' although the loan and grant account for less than 5 per cent of the total capital investment. The most distinctive feature of the Phoenix Corporation is its reliance on savings provided by households to finance part of the investment programme (see table 2.3).

In 1979 households invested 14 000 yuan in industry and in 1981 a further 69 000 yuan. That is, 15.7 per cent of the total investment in the period was financed by the issue of shares to the households comprising the Corporation. Each share costs 100 yuan and earns a fixed dividend rate of 20 per cent a year.[10] Most households, namely, 176 out of 201, own some shares. The smallest holding is two shares, the largest is twenty and more than sixty households own more than ten shares. Thus the development of a capital market within the Corporation has made it possible to mobilise a significant amount of private savings for industrial expansion and in the process has enabled rural households to become shareholders. Only in China, we suspect, would it be possible to find peasants who own shares in highly profitable manufacturing enterprises.

As can be seen in Table 2.4, collective distributed income per head increased dramatically after 1978. Private income rose less rapidly but still impressively, and by the end of 1981 total income per head was 3.6 times higher than it was three years earlier. The rapid growth that was achieved was due in large part to the high propensity to save collective income. In 1981, for instance, per capita collective distributed income was 502.8 yuan as compared with 623 yuan per head set aside for fixed investment, working capital and the collective welfare fund. On top of

TABLE 2.4 *Phoenix Corporation: income per head 1977–81* (yuan)

	Collective distributed income	*Private income*	*Total income*
1977	98.0	65.1	163.1
1978	106.0	80.7	186.7
1979	225.0	115.0	340.0
1980	370.5	166.6	537.1
1981	502.8	171.0	673.8

this, as we have seen, there are substantial private savings on which the Corporation can call.

In summary, the experiment in Qionglai county is notable for four reasons. First, the brigade was separated from commune level activities and relieved of all non-economic responsibilities. Secondly, the teams were merged into the brigade and virtually lost their separate identity as economic units. The brigade then became the Phoenix Corporation with four branches or companies. Thirdly, a capital market within the Corporation was established and individual households were encouraged to purchase shares in collective industrial enterprises. Fourthly, a high rate of capital accumulation was achieved by retaining a large fraction of enterprise profits. This, in turn, led to rapid growth of industrial output and household income. Thus in this experiment the teams, although they remained the basic accounting unit, became much less important, not because household level activities expanded at their expense (although *bao chan dao hu* was practised) but because brigade-level activities became by far the largest source of income. Indeed the transformation was so great that the brigade became known as the Phoenix Corporation.

The Guanghan experiment

In Guanghan county about 40 kilometres north of Chengdu, communes as such no longer exist. In September 1981 a county-wide experiment was begun to transform all the production teams in the county, of which there were 2459, into independent co-operatives. The enterprises that formerly belonged to the brigades were transferred to the villages and the commune-level enterprises were grouped under newly established industrial corporations.

The co-operatives thus became autonomous units and they are free to form joint ventures with any other unit, be it with a co-operative from another village, a village-level enterprise or with an industrial corporation. Households, too, are free to form joint enterprises, although by the summer of 1982 fewer than ten such enterprises had been established. (An example of such a household-level undertaking is a bicycle repair shop formed by four or five people.) In practice, however, the co-operatives and households within them are primarily engaged in farming and closely related activities. For instance, Co-operative No. 7 of Heping village, Dong Nan xiang consists of fifty households of 195 persons, of whom eighty-four are able-bodied workers. The co-operative owns 193 mou of land, all of which is irrigated. Its main activities are paddy cultivation followed by wheat and rape-seed; it has a wheat and rice processing mill, a co-operative pig farm with thirty-two pigs and a tile-making workshop. It also participates in a joint company at the village level which runs several small enterprises and it owns 4000 yuan of shares in the Jinan Joint Corporation, the industrial corporation at xiang level.

Co-operative No. 7 has adopted the production responsibility system and has entered into contract with work groups. There are three such work groups, each with twenty-eight workers and each farming 64 mou. The contract specifies labour input per mou, the cost of material inputs to be used, the cropping pattern and the output quota. The quota is set at the average of the yield over the three previous years. Thus in 1982 the wheat quota was 750 jin per mou whereas actual output turned out to be 816 jin per mou; similarly, the quota for rape-seed was 390 jin per mou and this was the level of production actually achieved.[11] The labour quota was forty-four days per mou for wheat and forty days for rape-seed. The cash cost quota (for seeds, fertiliser and pesticides) was 34 yuan per mou for wheat and 32 yuan for rape-seed.

The bonus for above quota output is 100 per cent. Members of a work group earn work points and in Co-operative No. 7 the work points are awarded to individual workers in accordance with an assessment of their skill. The value of a full working day is the same in all work groups, however, because the co-operative is the basic accounting unit and the total number of work points is based on the production quota. Thus collective incomes can differ from one work group to another only to the extent that bonuses differ.

Of course, not all co-operatives organise production in quite the same way. In Heping village, for example, there are fifteen co-operatives: nine of these have contracts with work groups while six have contracts with individual workers. As far as one can tell, these differences in contractual arrangements make little difference to the average level of income earned by each co-operative or to the intra-co-operative distribution of income. The co-operatives are atomistic but so far at least they appear to be very similar.

The danger is that by separating the team (or co-operative) from commune-level (or corporation) activities, the long-run rate of accumulation and growth of the co-operatives will be impaired. The way this might happen can be seen by studying the Jinan Joint Corporation. This was the first corporation to be established in Guanghan, in October 1980, when it took over the commune-level enterprises of Xi Wai Commune in what is now three xiang or townships. The twenty-eight enterprises under the management of the Jinan Corporation are as follows:

3 distilleries;
3 brick and tile kilns;
3 construction teams;
2 chemical plants;
2 farm machinery repair and manufacturing enterprises;
2 rape-seed processing plants;
2 shops;
1 cement plant;
1 cement prefabricating plant;
1 mill producing knitted nylon fibre;
1 plant producing marble slabs;
1 quarry;
1 soft drink bottling plant;
1 sausage and ham factory;
1 factory making fur coats;
1 transportation team;
1 team of porters;
1 hotel.

In 1981 the Corporation earned 2.18 million yuan of profits (after commercial and industrial taxes) on a gross output of 15.02 million yuan. Fifty per cent of these profits were distributed to the co-operatives and villages from which the twenty-eight enterprises came and 50 per cent was retained by the Corporation. Forty per cent of the profits retained by the Corporation are used to expand production in the particular units in which the profits originated and the remaining 60 per cent goes into general corporate funds for reinvestment in existing or new activities.

The Jinan Corporation is owned by its shareholders and the Corporation issues two different kinds of shares. First, there are shares equivalent to the value of the fixed assets of the enterprises transferred from the original Xi Wai Commune. Half of these shares are divided among the teams (now co-operatives) of the commune in proportion to their population and half in proportion to the land area of each co-operative. These shares can be transferred to other shareholders but cannot be encashed. Secondly, the Corporation can issue new shares to finance investment. So far, shares to the value of 275 000 yuan have been issued. These shares can be bought and sold by anyone in units of 100 yuan and carry a fixed dividend rate of 12 per cent. In practice, most of the shares have been bought by co-operatives and villages, the largest purchase being 20 000 yuan of shares. Private shareholders account for about 1 per cent only of the shares and the Corporation does not encourage private investors.

Given that the return on industrial investment is higher than the return on farming, those co-operatives which are more prosperous than the average, and have some money to spare, could improve their position both absolutely and relatively by purchasing new issues of Jinan Corporation shares. The poorer co-operatives, on the other hand, would no longer receive direct assistance from their brigade or commune (since these have ceased to exist) but would receive instead the dividends on their portion of the initial allocation of shares (assuming they had not transferred them to another shareholder). Thus gradually over time inequality among co-operatives would increase, the ownership of what were formerly commune-level enterprises would become more uneven and the mechanisms for helping teams in difficulty would vanish. These tendencies, if they exist, are likely to be accentuated if the Jinan Corporation continues its present policy of recruiting new workers not from the co-operatives from which it was formed but from the unemployed youths of the city.

THE GROWTH OF OUTPUT

In assessing the various reforms that have been introduced in recent years, it is useful to bear in mind the long-run trends in rates of growth. One cannot give exact figures because different sources contain conflicting estimates, but it is clear that China's performance in the three decades after 1949 has not been bad. National income increased about 7 per cent a year; the annual population growth was slightly more than 2 per cent, with the rate falling over time to 1.4 per cent today; and consequently income per head rose between 4.5 and 5.5 per cent a year. This is a very good aggregate growth performance compared with other low-income countries.

Somewhat more worrying is food grain production. The data in Table 2.5 indicate that the output of grains increased faster than the population over the period as a whole. Between 1957 and 1965, however, production was stagnant and hence fell markedly in per capita terms. Of course, per capita consumption of grain in China already is exceptionally high and there may be little need for the direct consumption of grains to rise further, but as average incomes in the country continue to increase, the demand for meat can be expected to rise sharply and this will increase the indirect demand for grain. The authorities clearly are right, therefore, to continue to attach importance to increasing grain production.

The output of all food items, and especially meat, increased faster than grains alone and non-food agricultural production, notably cotton, expanded more rapidly than the output of food. A reasonable estimate is that during the period 1952–79 the gross value of total agricultural output grew about 3 per cent and the net value about 2.7 per cent a year. This implies that agricultural output per head during this period probably increased about 1 per cent per annum, with the growth

TABLE 2.5 *Aggregate rates of growth*
(per cent per annum)

	Period	*Growth rate*
National income	1949–79	7.0
Gross value of industrial output	1949–79	13.3
heavy industry	1950–79	16.5
bicycles	1950–79	24.5
cloth	1949–80	6.5
Gross value of agricultural output	1949–80	5.4
food grains	1949–80	3.4
sugar	1949–80	8.6
edible oils	1949–80	3.6
cotton	1949–80	6.0
pork, beef and mutton	1952–80	4.6

SOURCE *Economic Readjustment and Reform*, Beijing Review, 1982, Appendix Tables, pp. 208–18 and other official sources.

rates being faster both before 1952 and after 1979. Once again, this is a noticeably better performance than that achieved by most other low-income countries.

Furthermore, if one focuses not on agricultural output but on rural incomes, one should take into account the income generated by industrial and sideline activities within the commune. Indeed, one of the great virtues of the commune system, as we have seen, is that it provides a framework in which to industrialise the countryside. Unfortunately, it is not possible to provide accurate estimates of long-run rates of growth of commune and brigade-level industries but the correct figure is likely to be between 10 and 15 per cent a year. Whatever the precise figure, it is evident that the size of the rural industrial sector and its rate of growth are sufficiently large to lift the rate of growth of total income in rural areas to well above 5 per cent a year.

In recent years, in fact, the growth of rural incomes has been extraordinarily rapid. For example, between 1978 and 1981 collective distributed income per head in China as a whole increased 12 per cent a year. In the two counties where much of our field-work was concentrated the rates of growth were even faster, namely, 17.2 per cent in Yu Xi county, Yunnan (1978–81) and 21.3 per cent in Guanghan county, Sichuan (1976–81). There are a variety of reasons for this rapid short-term growth in incomes: generally good weather (despite the floods of 1981), a substantial but unquantifiable improvement in agriculture's terms of trade, an expansion of the area under shifting cultivation farmed by households (as a combined result of better terms of trade and the introduction of the responsibility system), and possibly some effect of the new incentive system on yields. There may also have been a slight tendency for a lower proportion of collective income to be set aside for accumulation and consequently a higher proportion to be available for distribution.

THE DISTRIBUTION OF COLLECTIVE INCOME

Let us turn now to the distribution of collective income. We shall begin by considering the distribution of income among households of a team. In Table 2.6 we summarise the results of our field research in Sichuan and Yunnan in the summer of 1982 and append at the end seven tables containing the raw data and a few explanatory notes. As can be seen, we have included data from five teams – four in Yunnan and one in Sichuan – and have a total of eight annual observations. The size of team varies considerably from a low of fourteen households to a high of 159 households. Similarly, the average income varies from 71.99 yuan in Team No. 2 of the Phoenix Corporation in 1977 to 496.69 yuan in the same team in 1981.

Although average income of all five teams was above the national average in 1981, the teams are rather different from one another in most other respects. The Phoenix Corporation, as we have seen, is the product of a radical reform in Qionglai county, Sichuan and hence is truly exceptional. Team No. 1 of Gao Chang Brigade, Gao Chang Commune is a good example of a rich team located in a fertile valley enjoying excellent irrigation facilities. It is in Yu Xi county, Yunnan and is in fact the richest team in the county. Team No. 7 of Xiang Sui Brigade, Xiao She Qiao Commune (also in Yu Xi county) was a rather poor team in 1979 that has since prospered. It is in the hills about 2100 metres above sea level and specialises in maize, wheat and pear orchards. Team No. 1 has contracts with small work groups and individual workers while Team No. 7 practises *bao gan dan hu.*

Gao Chio Team of Pu Chao Brigade, Ala Commune is near the city of Kunming in Yunnan province. It is distinctive because its members are Samei, a branch of the Yi nationality and thus are representative of China's minority nationalities. The team enters into contracts with households but practises the 'lesser' *bao gan dao hu* in which it maintains a few collective activities, for example, a kiln, a mill and an orchard. More important is the fact that some of the team's assets are being sold to individual households, notably the buffaloes which provide draught animal power. There are no brigade-level activities. Evidently, the commune system here is disintegrating rapidly and social differentiation among the peasantry is appearing.

Team No. 3 of Fu Bao Brigade, Liu Jia Commune also is near Kunming. Contracts are with work groups, but the most important feature of the brigade is that 75.1 per cent of total output originates in the industrial sector.

Several points are suggested by the data in Table 2.6. First, in general the degree of inequality appears to be low as measured either by the Gini coefficient or the coefficient of variation or by the ratio of highest to lowest income. For instance, in none of the five teams in 1981 was the coefficient of variation greater than 0.36. Second, in Gao Chio Team where the ratio of incomes is high, this may reflect the consequences of the disintegration of the commune that is occurring and the resulting social stratification. Third, the high ratio of incomes in Team No. 3 of Fu Bao Brigade probably is the consequence of a high wage differential

Table 2.6 *Summary results: distributed collective income per capita among households*

Unit	*Year*	*Number of households*	*Average income (yuan)*	*Ratio of highest to lowest income*	*Coefficient of variation*	*Gini coefficient*
1. Team No. 2, Phoenix Corporation, Sichuan	1977	29	71.98	5.04	0.32	0.18
	1981	30	496.69	2.39	0.22	0.11
2. Team No. 1, Gao Chang Brigade, Gao Chang Commune, Yunnan	1981	86	403.06	6.54	0.31	0.18
3. Team No. 7, Xiang Sui Brigade, Xiao She Qiao Commune, Yunnan	1979	14	43.13	3.73	0.45	0.23
	1980	14	163.27	2.83	0.27	0.14
	1981	14	211.59	3.33	0.36	0.20
4. Gao Chio Team, Pu Chao Brigade, Ala Commune, Yunnan	1981	52	128.43	10.90	0.36	0.20
5. Team No. 3, Fu Bao Brigade,	1981	159	361.02	10.79	0.31	0.17

Note Average income, the Gini coefficient and the coefficient of variation are weighted by size of household.

between industry and agriculture. Each industrial worker in the brigade receives an extra payment of 2.42 yuan for every 100 yuan of gross output, but until recently there was nothing comparable for those engaged in agriculture. Since the autumn harvest of 1981, however, agricultural workers have received 0.94 yuan for every 100 jin of output and this additional payment can be expected to narrow income inequalities considerably.

Fourth, there is no evidence from the table that the introduction of the production responsibility system has led to an increase in inequality. True, there are only two cases where we have observations for more than one year, namely, Team No. 2 of the Phoenix Corporation and Team No. 7 of Xiang Sui Brigade, and in both the period covered is very brief, but in both cases the increase in per capita income was substantial. Hence if the new incentives for growth are likely to be accompanied by greater inequality, some signs of this might have been expected to appear in our data. Instead we find that in Team No. 2 the ratio of highest to lowest income, the Gini coefficient and the coefficient of variation declined markedly between 1977 and 1981, indicating less inequality, not more. Similarly, in Team No. 7 there is no evidence of increasing inequality; if anything, the data indicate the reverse. These conclusions are of course only suggestive and must be regarded as highly tentative, but our field data are not consistent with the widely held proposition that the reforms introduced in China after 1978 are bound to result in greater inequality in the distribution of income among households. We regard this as an encouraging finding.

Let us consider next the distribution of collective income among teams of a brigade. The results of our field investigations are summarised in Table 2.7 and the original data are presented in Appendix Tables 2.8–2.11. Four cases are examined. The first is the fifteen co-operatives or ex-teams of Heping village in Guanghan county, Sichuan. This is a product of the radical experiment in the province of dissolving the commune and establishing the teams or co-operatives as independent units. As can be seen in the table, the dissolution seems not to have affected the distribution of collective income at the level of the co-operative, at least not by 1981. The coefficient of variation and the Gini coefficient are remarkably low and the richest co-operative is only 45 per cent better off than the poorest.

Our second case is Chao Tan Brigade located in Yuan Men Ko Commune just outside Chengdu, the capital of Sichuan. The brigade specialises in growing vegetables and in a number of industrial activities, notably, a prefabricated cement plant, a potassium nitrate plant, an agricultural machinery shop and a printing shop. The teams also have several small collective enterprises, including a piggery. In general, however, the brigade is expanding very rapidly while incomes generated at the team level actually are falling. The distribution of collective income among the five teams of the brigade is very equal, the most prosperous being only 57 per cent richer than the least prosperous. The Gini coefficient also is very small.

Third is Sun Jin Brigade of Chun He Commune in Yu Xi county, Yunnan. The brigade includes eight teams in seven hamlets. It contains 607 households with a total population of 2563 of which 1140 persons work either full time or part time. It cultivates 1983 mou of mostly irrigated land, or 0.77 mou per head. Two harvests a year are obtained, namely, paddy rice in the autumn and wheat, beans and rape-seed in the summer; tobacco also is grown and is an important cash crop. The responsibility system used is *bao chan dao lao*, that is, contracts between the teams and individual workers on a basis similar to *bao chan dao hu*. Thus work points are retained and the output quota is relatively high. The teams in the brigade do not wish to switch to *bao gan dao lao* or *bao gan dao hu* because they have a large number of brigade-level enterprises which they wish to maintain intact, they have a substantial collective accumulation fund and because they believe they can advance more rapidly to scientific farming if the commune system is not weakened by dividing team and brigade assets such as draught animals and walking tractors among individual households.

As can be seen in Table 2.7, the ratio of incomes, the Gini coefficient and the coefficient of variation indicate that there is a high degree of equality among the teams of the brigade. Moreover, the growth in average income of 59.75 per cent betwen 1978 and 1981 clearly was not accompanied by increased inequality. Thus once again the initial indications are that the introduction of the responsibility system has not led to wider income differentials at the local level. The evidence from our fourth case, Fu Bao Brigade, is consistent with this finding. The spread of average team incomes over the four teams is fairly modest and the differences seem to have declined between 1978 and 1981. Hence all the data from the four brigades point in the same direction, namely, a low initial degree of inequality and no observable tendency for inequality to increase with growth over time.

If one looks at the distribution of collective income among the brigades of a commune, one finds much the same thing. Consider, for example, Mi Mu People's Commune in Xindu county, Sichuan. This is a commune of 6371 households with a population of 25 953. There are

TABLE 2.7 *Summary results: distributed collective income per capita among teams*

Unit	*Year*	*Number of teams*	*Average income (yuan)*	*Ratio of highest to lowest income*	*Coefficient of variation*	*Gini coefficient*
1. Heping village, Dong Nan Xiang, Guanghan county, Sichuan	1981	15	252.13	1.45	0.11	0.06
2. Chao Tan Brigade, Yuan Men Ko Commune, Sichuan	1980	5	269.28	1.57		0.05
3. Sun Jin Brigade, Chun He Commune, Yu Xi county, Yunnan	1978	8	162.75	1.44	0.12	0.06
	1979	8	180.88	1.33	0.10	0.05
	1980	8	212.75	1.44	0.12	0.05
	1981	8	260.00	1.36	0.10	0.05
4. Fu Bao Brigade, Liu Jia Commune, Yunnan	1978	4	252.00	1.77		0.12
	1981	4	320.00	1.50		0.08

twelve brigades divided into 107 teams. The cultivated area is 18 396 mou of which all but 196 mou are irrigated. In addition, there are 2486 mou of private plots or 11.9 per cent of the total cultivated area. The labour force is 12 658 of which 2935 workers are employed on commune- and brigade-level enterprises. The main agricultural crops are wheat and rape-seed harvested in the summer and paddy and tobacco in the autumn.

In Table 2.8 we present the per capita distributed collective income for the twelve brigades of the commune for 1980. We chose 1980 because in July 1981 the commune was affected by floods and hence the income figures for that year might not be representative of a normal or typical year.[12] The responsibility system evolved rapidly after the initial experiments in late 1979. Thus in 1980 just over half the teams had contracts with individual households or workers. By 1982 all but ten of the teams had switched to contracts with individual workers or households of the *bao chan dao hu* type, i.e. with production quotas equal to the average of the previous three years.

It is clear from the table that income differentials among brigades of a commune are modest. The most prosperous brigade is only 61 per cent richer than the least prosperous and the low coefficient of variation indicates that the overall degree of inequality is small.

TABLE 2.8 *Distributed collective income per capita in 12 brigades of Mi Mu People's Commune, Xindu county, Sichuan, 1980*

	Brigade Number	*Distributed collective income* (yuan)
	1	160.03
	2	116.00
	3	183.90
	4	165.40
	5	180.81
	6	169.00
	7	186.85
	8	134.20
	9	139.80
	10	137.09
	11	170.40
	12	181.51
Average		160.42
Ratio of highest to lowest income		1.61
Coefficient of variation		0.14
Gini coefficient		0.08

Income distribution within a county

It is not surprising perhaps that the distribution of income within a collective institution would be relatively egalitarian. One of the purposes of collective institutions, after all, is to pool resources and to provide equal opportunities to all members to obtain employment and enjoy equal access to land, irrigation facilities, animal power and mechanical equipment. It can be argued, in fact, that there are various mechanisms within a team, brigade or commune which ensure that equality is achieved more or less automatically.[13] There are no such automatic mechanisms, however, that ensure that equality is achieved between communes as compared to within communes. It is easy to imagine that richer communes (or regions or provinces) would grow faster than poorer communes (or regions or provinces) and thus that inter-commune inequality would tend to increase over time.

Unfortunately, the data do not exist to test this hypothesis properly. We can, however, shed a little light on the topic by examining the ten communes of Yu Xi county, Yunnan during the period 1978 to 1981. There are in Yunnan 131 counties or regions of equivalent size: in eighteen of these counties, 99 per cent of the land is mountainous; in ninety-three counties, 90 per cent of the land is mountainous and only twenty counties are located in flat land along a railway line. Yu Xi county is in the last category and is three and a half hours south of Kunming by road. By the standards of the province it is a prosperous region.

The three communes that we visited are named in Table 2.9. It can be seen that the communes we visited were in 1981 the poorest (Xiao She Qiao), one close to the average (Chun He) and the third richest (Gao Chang). The ratio of highest to lowest income of the ten communes, however, is only 2.02, indicating that the richest commune is only twice as rich as the poorest. The coefficient of variation is correspondingly low at 0.20. Nonetheless, there is a suggestion in the data that during 1978–81, when average income grew 16.6 per cent a year, there was a tendency for the distribution of income to become less equal, since the ratio of incomes, the Gini coefficient and the coefficient of variation all increased. This is a question we shall want to probe more deeply below.

There are, however, a number of policy measures adopted by the county to ensure that the degree of inequality does not become unacceptably large. These measures are directed towards assisting weak teams rather than entire communes, and of the 756 teams in the county, eighty are considered to be weak and in need of assistance.[14] Of the

TABLE 2.9 *Distributed collective income per capita among the ten Communes of Yu Xi county, Yunnan, 1978–81*
(yuan)

Commune	*1978*	*1979*	*1980*	*1981*
1.	135	163	206	240
2. Gao Chang	114	149	181	221
3.	129	162	193	224
4.	128	138	152	163
5. Xiao She Qiao	78	86	107	119
6.	118	147	167	185
7.	140	158	185	209
8.	110	127	144	158
9.	114	132	142	171
10. Chun He	133	157	187	213
Average	119.90	141.90	166.40	190.30
Ratio of highest to lowest income	1.80	1.90	1.93	2.02
Coefficient of variation	0.15	0.16	0.18	0.20
Gini coefficient	0.07	0.08	0.09	0.10

latter, seventy-six are teams composed of minority nationalities or are mixtures of minority nationalities and Han. In the county as a whole 110 teams are composed of minorities or of minorities plus Han.

The first measure that is used to help weak teams is to exempt them in whole or in part from the compulsory grain quota. In 1981, all eighty teams were exempt. Next, the county can pay weak teams the 'discussion price' for any surplus grain sold. This price is about double the price paid for grain delivered under quota. Third, loans at preferential terms are made to weak teams. These loans are interest free or carry a very low rate of interest. They usually are for one year but can be renewed. Then, fourth, the prefecture can make capital grants to poor teams for water projects, schools and directly productive activities. In 1981 there were capital grants of 200 000 yuan of this type and priority was given to the eighty teams in need of assistance. Fifth, the county allocates more than 10 per cent of its budget to grants to poor teams. Since 1978 the county has spent between 500 000 and 700 000 yuan a year on assistance to weak teams. This is in addition to grants from the prefecture. In 1980, for instance, thirty-five out of the eighty teams were helped to install piped water in their village.

The county, sixth, also provides technical assistance. Priority is given to minority nationalities and at present effort is concentrated on helping them select the right varieties for cash crop production. Seventh, the county organises training seminars for team leaders, accountants and those in charge of scientific farming. These seminars are open to all teams but special assistance is given to 100 teams in mountainous areas. In addition, poor teams located in the mountains receive free of charge from the county 30 jin per mou of phosphate fertiliser equivalent in value to 1.80 yuan per mou. Finally, county trucks are used to transport chemical fertilisers to teams in hilly or mountainous regions free of charge when they are on logging expeditions and have to be in the region in any case.

These measures clearly lean in the right direction and temper any tendency there may be for inequality to increase over time. The county's industrial policy may also help to alleviate rural poverty and inequality by providing a large number of jobs in county run enterprises. The number of such enterprises is large and includes a chemical plant, a fertiliser plant, a machine tools factory, an agricultural machinery factory, a paper mill, printing press, food processing plant, etc. It is uncertain whether labour recruitment practices explicitly favour workers from poorer teams in Yu Xi county, but such policies are not uncommon in other parts of the country. Whatever the specific practices here as regards industry, it is evident that county officials are sensitive to the need to maintain a high degree of equality and have taken steps to do so.

CHANGES OVER TIME IN THE DEGREE OF EQUALITY

It is possible to examine a bit more systematically some of the data to see whether there have been changes over time in the degree of equality. It is widely feared that the reforms recently introduced in rural China have led, or eventually will lead, to greater inequality in the distribution of income and consequently it is well worth while considering such information as exists. Unfortunately, the data are sparse and our findings must be treated with caution, but they do shed some light on this important topic.

We are interested in two questions. First, is the structure of inequality unchanging in the sense that rich households or teams or communes tend to remain relatively rich while poor households, teams and communes remain relatively poor, regardless of what happens to the average level of income? To answer this question we have compared the ranking of incomes of, say, households within a team at some initial year with the ranking at a terminal year. A rank correlation coefficient (*RY*) that is positive and statistically significant indicates that the structure of inequality is unchanging, while a coefficient that is not significant (or negative) indicates that there is no tendency for the rich to remain rich and the poor to remain relatively poor. That is, *RY* indicates whether or not there is mobility within a given ordering of incomes.

The second question that interests us is whether there is any tendency for rich households, teams or communes to grow faster than poor households, teams or communes. To answer this second question we compare the rank of the level of income in the initial period with the rank of the percentage rate of increase in income over the entire period. A rank correlation coefficient (*RgY*) that is positive and statistically significant indicates that there is a systematic tendency for those households, etc. that were relatively prosperous in the beginning to increase their advantage subsequently as a result of relatively faster rates of growth. In this case, inequality clearly would tend to increase over time. Conversely, a negative and statistically significant *RgY* indicates that the poor tend to grow faster than the rich and hence that inequality in the distribution of income tends to diminish over time.

Let us consider three cases, all from Yunnan and all covering the early years after the introduction of the institutional reforms. The first refers to the fourteen households of Team No. 7, Xiang Sui Brigade during the period 1979–81 when *bao gan dao hu* was practised, i.e. the form of the responsibility system widely thought as most likely to lead to increased inequality. The analysis summarised in Table 2.10, however, is not consistent with the hypothesis of rising inequality. It is true that the correlation coefficient is positive (*RY* = 0.44) when the level of household income per capita in 1979 is compared with the level in 1981, but the

TABLE 2.10 *Rank correlation analysis*

Unit	*Number of observations*	*Period*	*RY*	*RgY*
1. Team No. 7, Xiang Sui Brigade, Xiao She Qiao Commune, Yunnan	14 households	1979–81	0.44	−0.63*
2. Sun Jin Brigade, Chun He Commune, Yunnan	8 teams	1978–81	0.43	−0.76*
3. Yu Xi county, Yunnan.	10 communes	1978–81	0.69*	0.18

NOTE An asterisk indicates the correlation coefficient is significant at the five per cent level.

coefficient is not statistically significant and thus it cannot be claimed that the relative position of households is unchanging and the structure of inequality is fixed. Moreover, there is clear evidence that over the period 1979–81 the poorer households tended to grow more rapidly than the rich, and consequently the overall distribution of income tended to become more equal, not less ($RgY = -0.63$ and statistically significant.)

The next case covers the eight teams of Sun Jin Brigade, Chun He Commune during the period 1978–81. This brigade practised *bao chan dao lao*, entering into contract with individual workers and specifying large output quotas. Despite these differences in the production responsibility system adopted, the results are identical to those of the previous case. RY is positive but not significant, indicating there is no absence of mobility of relative position among teams, and RgY is significantly negative, indicating a tendency for inequality in the distribution of income to diminish.

Finally, there are the ten communes of Yu Xi county. When examining the data in Table 2.9 we noted that there was a hint of increasing inequality over time. Further analysis, however, does not confirm that suggestion. What the analysis does show is that the relative position of the ten communes tended to remain stable during 1978–81 ($RY = 0.69$ and statistically significant), but that there is no observable tendency for richer communes to grow faster than poorer ones ($RgY = 0.18$ but not statistically significant) and hence no evidence that inequality is increasing systematically. Thus the results of our three case studies, although far from conclusive, are encouraging: in two cases inequality was tending to diminish and in the other case there was no evidence it was increasing. These findings are similar to those of an earlier study of the immediate pre-reform period.[15] Assuming our findings are confirmed by other investigators covering other regions, longer periods of time and a larger number of units, they suggest that the recent institutional changes are unlikely to have adverse consequences for the distribution of income, at least at the local level.

Indeed, one could go further. Under the old work point system that existed until around 1978, differences in per capita distributed collective income among households of, say, a team arose in large part because of differences in dependency ratios. That is, households with a high proportion of able-bodied workers tended to be more prosperous than households with a high proportion of infants and old people. Under the present 'responsibility system', however, most collectively owned land is farmed by households. The per capita collective income of these households depends to a considerable degree on the amount of collectively owned land farmed by each household. In practice, land usually is distributed either wholly or at least in large part on a per capita (not a per worker) basis, and hence one should expect that collective income would be more evenly distributed today than in the 1970s. Moreover, provided teams periodically reallocate land under contract over the life-cycle of households, there is no reason to fear that pronounced inequalities will emerge in future.

THE HOUSEHOLD ECONOMY

Everything we have said so far about income distribution refers to the distribution of collective income. There are reasons to believe, however, that the distribution among households of income arising from the collective sector of the commune is more unequal than the distribution of total income. Three points in particular are worth considering.

First, households with low collective incomes from commune sources may attempt to secure employment for one or more of their members in nearby state factories, for instance, those located in the county in which the commune is situated. Household income from employment in county factories is not recorded in the commune's accounts and hence collective income tends to understate total household income. Earnings in state factories normally are higher than earnings in communes and consequently the distribution of factory jobs among households could have a significant impact on the overall distribution of income. As mentioned earlier, it is known that in at least some counties recruitment of labour for employment in state enterprises is biased in favour of relatively poor households and teams and in this way the county contributes directly to greater equality. Even where this does not occur, however, county-level employment may be equalising. That is, provided only that employment in county factories is not biased in favour of households with high collective incomes, such employment will tend to reduce overall inequality in the locality.

Second, households with relatively low collective incomes could attempt to send one or more of their members to distant cities to obtain employment in major state enterprises. Such emigrants would cease to be members of the rural household and would live elsewhere, presumably near their source of employment. Remittances sent back to the rural areas, however, would be an important source of unrecorded income. Again, provided only that employment of rural migrants in state enterprises is not biased in favour of households with relatively high collective incomes, emigrants' remittances would help to reduce inequality.

The importance and complexity of intra-family transfers can be seen by examining the household accounts of one family interviewed by the authors on a commune not far from Chengdu, Sichuan. The net income of the household originated from six separate sources and came to a total of 1849 yuan as follows:

1. income from pig raising (3 per year)	363
2. output of the private plot	40
3. husband's earnings from factory employment in Chengdu	900
4. remittances from two sons	240
5. gift from a son living in a separate household in the same commune	102
6. compensation paid by the brigade for the absence of one son in the army	204

Clearly the couple who comprised this household were fortunate in having four sons, all of whom contributed to their parents either directly through remittances and gifts or indirectly through compensation paid by the brigade. Most important of all, however, was the income earned by the husband from his job in a factory in Chengdu. Curiously, in the case of this household, collective distributed income was nil, but the couple were far from poor.

Third, households with relatively low collective incomes could attempt to exploit relatively more intensively the opportunities that exist in the private sector. That is, they could devote their energies to pig raising, poultry, cultivating the private plot (which can be as much as 15 per cent of the total area) and handicraft production. These activities are distinct from collective agriculture although the distinction is rather blurred when households farm collective land under contract and receive no work points, for example, as under *bao gan dao hu*.

Even so, farming under contract is not quite the same as cultivating one's private plot. This is because the contract specifies the cropping pattern, obliges the producer to deliver a specified volume of output at an agreed (low) price and imposes a deduction of part of the output produced under contract as a contribution to the collective welfare and accumulation funds. No such constraints and deductions apply to the private plot or to other private sector activities. Moreover, under many contractual arrangements work points continue to be an important source of household income. Under *bao gan dao hu*, however, work points disappear; the team remains the 'basic accounting unit' but it no longer is true that within the team equal effort in the collective sector is rewarded by equal income. Despite these qualifications it probably is useful to maintain the distinction between the private and collective sectors. The flexibility and small scale of the private sector set it apart even from the collective contract farming in the household economy.

It can be argued that the private sector helps to reduce inequality below what it otherwise would have been. The argument is that within a particular commune

> opportunities in the private sector are exploited most intensively by two types of households, namely, those with an above average number of elderly persons and those with an above average number of infants. In the case of the former, the private sector enables the old to generate an income and contribute to the household despite the fact that they are too infirm to engage in collective agricultural labour. In the case of the latter, private sector activities enable mothers with young children to continue earning an income despite the fact that their maternal responsibilities deprive them of an opportunity to engage in full-time collective activities. The children can also make useful contributions of labour. Thus the importance of the private sector varies over the life cycle and, in effect, the private sector allows households with an unfavourable dependency ratio to compensate for this.[16]

Data to test this hypothesis are scarce but the results of a survey of twenty-three households of a production team in Shujing Commune, Shanghai municipality indicate clearly that collective income per head is higher the lower is the dependency ratio, i.e. the size of household divided by the number of wage earners (see Table 2.11). Households in which three-quarters or more of the members are earners (and hence have a dependency ratio of 1.33 or less) enjoy a higher than average per capita collective income whereas households in which only half the members are wage earners (and hence have a dependency ratio of 2.0) fall below the median collective income. This is not very surprising.

It is sometimes argued both in China and by outside observers that there is a conflict between the production responsibility system and policies to reduce the rate of growth of the population. This conflict is thought to arise because in strengthening the household economy the production responsibility system also increases the incentive of couples to have a bigger family. That is, it is believed that in the rural areas a large family is an economic advantage in the sense that relatively big households tend to enjoy a per capita income above the average.

The available data, however, lend no support to this view. If large

TABLE 2.11 *Twenty-three households from a production team of Shujing Commune, Shanghai municipality, 1980*

Household number	*Household size*	*Dependency ratio*	*Collective income per head (yuan)*	*Private income as a percentage of collective income*
20	4	1.00	745.7	17.0
22	2	1.00	662.5	0.0
23	4	1.33	468.0	19.2
3	6	1.20	465.0	22.9
6	3	1.50	460.0	0.0
7	5	1.22	452.2	19.7
11	4	1.33	421.0	24.0
16	3	1.50	412.6	20.2
13	3	1.50	403.0	19.3
10	5	1.25	378.8	22.1
2	3	1.00	376.7	12.1
8	4	1.33	372.0	30.2
17	4	2.00	351.0	35.8
1	4	1.33	341.0	20.5
14	5	1.67	323.0	38.3
18	4	2.00	322.0	15.5
4	4	2.00	319.0	11.6
19	5	1.67	313.0	22.1
12	3	1.50	311.0	8.2
5	4	2.00	310.0	8.1
21	3	1.50	300.0	13.9
15	4	2.00	275.0	33.9
9	6	2.00	272.0	17.5

SOURCE Elizabeth J. Croll, *The Chinese Household and Its Economy: Urban and Rural Survey Data*, Queen Elizabeth House, Contemporary China Centre, Resource Paper, Oxford, 1982, tables 20 and 49.

families are an asset one would expect to find a close positive correlation between size of household and distributed collective income per head. In fact, a rank correlation analysis of households in eight different collective units in Yunnan, Sichuan, Jiangsu, the Shanghai municipality and the Beijing municipality failed to produce a single positive coefficient. All eight of the coefficients were negative and of these, three were significant. The results are summarised in Table 2.12. Our results, thus, tend to support the conventional view that a high dependency ratio is economically disadvantageous and a large family does not *per se* confer economic benefits.

In two instances we were able to see whether the addition of private income to distributed collective income altered the conclusion. In the case of the twenty-three households of the production team of Shujing Commune the rank correlation between size of household and total collective plus private income per head was −0.11, indicating that if anything the relationship was inverse (although the coefficient was not statistically significant). In the case of ninety-two households of Zhang Qing Commune, for which we have reliable data, discussed further below, the correlation coefficient also was negative, namely, −0.23. Thus, once again, there appears to be no support for the view that large families are a means to prosperity in rural China. They may, however, be a means for reducing economic risk (since the larger the number of workers per household, the greater the possibility for diversifying sources of income), and they may also constitute a form of old age

TABLE 2.12 *Rank correlation between family size and distributed collective income per head*

Unit	*Number of observations*	*Year*	*Rank correlation coefficient*
1. Team No. 7, Xiang Sui Brigade, Xiao She Qiao Commune, Yunnan	14	1980	−0.51*
2. Gao Chio Team, Pu Chao Brigade, Ala Commune, Yunnan	52	1981	−0.08
3. Team No. 3, Fu Bao Brigade, Liu Jia Commune, Yunnan	159	1981	−0.20*
4. Team No. 2, Phoenix Corporation, Sichuan	29	1977	−0.29
5. Team No. 2, Phoenix Corporation, Sichuan	30	1981	−0.52*
6. Anonymous Team, Shujing Commune, Shanghai municipality	23	1980	−0.22
7. Anonymous Team, Sanjiao Commune, Beijing municipality	17	1980	−0.17
8. Zhang Qing Commune, near Suzhou, Jiangsu	96	1979	−0.18

NOTE An asterisk indicates the rank correlation coefficient is significant at the five per cent level.

SOURCES Units 1–5, our own field data; units 6 and 7, Elizabeth J. Croll, *The Chinese Household and Its Economy: Urban and Rural Survey Data*, Queen Elizabeth House, Contemporary China Centre, Resource Paper, Oxford, 1982; unit 8, field data kindly supplied by Roger Hay, Director of the Food Supply Analysis Group, Queen Elizabeth House, Oxford.

insurance in the vast majority of communes which are not yet able to provide pensions to the elderly. Moreover, to the extent that the 'five guarantees' and other forms of public welfare are allowed to decline in importance as the 'responsibility system' takes root, a large household may become more attractive to peasants as a source of security. Hence it would be mistaken to deny that potentially a limited conflict between the economic reforms and population policy could exist, but this conflict is not inherent in the type of reforms introduced.

Returning to the Shujing Commune, it is noteworthy that households with a high dependency ratio tend to obtain a higher proportion of their income from the private sector. Compare, for example, the six households with a dependency ratio of 2.0 with the six households with a dependency ratio of 1.25 or less. In the former, private sector income is 20.4 per cent as large as collective income, while for the latter it is noticeably lower at 15.6 per cent. Finally, there is a suggestion in the data from Shujing Commune of an inverse relationship between collective income per capita and the ratio of private to collective income. Correlation analysis, however, showed that while the regression coefficient was negative it was not statistically significant. Hence the equalising effects of the private sector, if any, would appear to be rather weak, but there certainly is no support from this sample for the contrary view that the presence of a private sector tends to accentuate inequality arising from differences in dependency ratios.

So far we have considered evidence from only one team and that from a commune in the richest agricultural area in the whole of China. Let us turn now to another commune in a different region of the country, namely, a commune near the city of Suzhou in Jiangsu province. This, too, is a prosperous region thanks to the presence of an important city, but the degree of prosperity in the rural areas is not as great as in the Shanghai municipality. A fairly large survey was conducted in Zhang Qing Commune, near Suzhou and the results of this survey shed more light on the role of the private sector in the Chinese countryside.[17] Eleven of the 163 teams in the commune were sampled, as well as ninety-six households from the sampled teams. It was possible to obtain from the survey information on collective income and on private income from crop and livestock production (but unfortunately not private income from handicrafts, etc.). (See Table 2.13.)

Analysis at the team level indicates that when private income is added to collective income, inequality diminishes. For instance, the Gini coefficient of collective income is 0.12, whereas the coefficient of collective plus private income is 0.11. Similarly, the coefficient of variation

TABLE 2.13 *Collective and private income in Zhang Qing Commune, Jiangsu, 1979*

Team	*Mean collective income per capita*	*Mean private income per capita*	*Private income as a percentage of collective income*
i.	337.4	55.1	16.3
ii.	283.5	53.2	18.8
iii.	255.1	26.2	10.3
iv.	248.1	35.4	14.3
v.	223.5	28.4	12.7
vi.	221.9	45.3	20.4
vii.	216.0	16.5	7.6
viii.	207.2	35.8	17.3
ix.	205.3	61.7	30.1
x.	166.6	53.6	32.2
xi.	148.1	25.6	17.3

SOURCE Alison Ansell, Roger W. Hay and Keith Griffin, 'Private Production and Income Distribution in a Chinese Commune', *Food Policy*, February 1982.

declines from 0.22 to 0.20 when private income is combined with collective income. These are not dramatic changes perhaps, but they point in the expected direction.

Further support is provided by an analysis at the household level of the ninety-two households from which reliable data were obtained. (Three households were excluded because of allegedly negative private income and one because the information was incomplete.) The test consisted of a regression equation in which private income as a percentage of collective income (PY/CY) was regressed on collective income per head (CY/N). The regression coefficient turned out to be negative, as anticipated, indicating that the lower is the level of collective income per head the greater is the relative importance of the private sector.[18]

The operation of this tendency within one team can be seen unusually clearly in Figure 2.1. The data from a sample of ten households from Production Team No. 10 of Ming Zhu Brigade, Zhang Qing Commune indicate there is a strong inverse relationship between the level of collective income per capita and the relative importance of private sector income. This is reflected in the highly significant coefficients in the regression equation fitted to the data:

$$PY/CY = 38.61 - \underset{(4.78)}{0.09}\,(CY/N);\quad R^2 = 0.74,\quad N = 10$$

where the figure in brackets is the t-statistic.

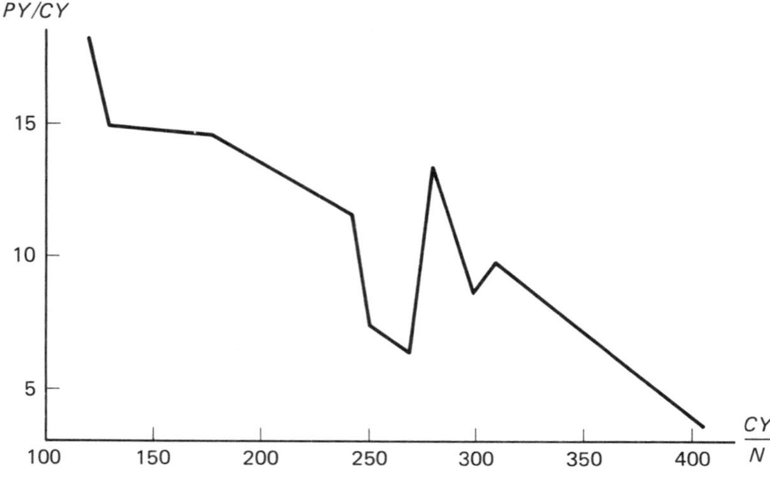

FIGURE 2.1 *The relationship between private and collective income*

In 1979 private income in Production Team No. 10 accounted for 13.5 per cent of total household income, i.e. private plus collective income. In Zhang Qing Commune as a whole the figure was 17.9 per cent. According to official statistics, the national average in that year was much higher, namely, 27.5 per cent and rising. We know, however, that communes in the area around Suzhou are considerably more prosperous than the average, and hence if the equalising tendency we have identified at the local level also applies across regions, we should expect the private sector in this part of China to be much smaller than average.

This, of course, is a rather bold hypothesis. Unfortunately, there are not enough data to test the proposition that the private sector helps to reduce regional inequality, but the topic will be worth investigating when information becomes more readily available. Meanwhile, there is a hint that the relative importance of the private sector varies inversely with regional per capita income in Table 2.14. In that table we have data for five provinces in 1980, based on official surveys of several hundred households in each region, and it is clear from inspection that at least in those provinces inter-regional inequality is diminished by the presence of private sector activities. If these inconclusive speculations and fragments of data turn out to be valid throughout China, they imply that the private sector has been inserted into the socialist economy in the

TABLE 2.14 *The private sector in five provinces, 1980*

Province	*Income per head (yuan)*	*Private sector income as a percentage of total income*
Yunnan	147.1	47
Guizhou	189.5	47
Inner Mongolia	217.3	40
Jilin	244.8	42
Liaoning	273.0	31

SOURCE SWB FE/W1134/A/pp. 2–5; 20 May 1981.

rural areas in such a way that it actually reduces inequality in the distribution of income both within a given locality and inter-regionally. This, too, if true would be a remarkable achievement of the commune system.

SUMMARY

Our conclusions can best be summarised in a series of simple propositions:

1. The commune system should be seen in historical perspective as a product of evolutionary adaptation and not as an immutable institution created during a heroic period of socialist construction.

2. Experimentation with alternative institutional arrangements has always been part of the Chinese style of rural development and thus the recent innovations and experiments are consistent with past approaches to development problems.

3. There is an economic logic to the commune system that can best be understood when the household economy is regarded as the base of the system and the fourth tier of a four-tiered institutional hierarchy.

4. The essence of the new reforms is a shift of responsibility for crop cultivation from the production team to the household economy. This shift does not imply the imminent disbandment of the commune system although in some circumstances the commune system could be severely weakened and even destroyed.

5. Some aspects of the new reforms, if not corrected, could lead to greater inequality, lower levels of capital accumulation and slower long-run rates of growth of output, but these consequences are not inherent in the reforms.

6. Such evidence as exists indicates that the distribution of collective income in rural areas continues to be relatively egalitarian.

7. Moreover, in the few cases where comparisons over time are possible, there is no evidence that the reforms have been associated with an increase in the degree of inequality at the local level. As long as collectively owned land within a team is allocated at least partly on a per capita rather than a per worker basis, and as long as land is periodically reallocated to take into account changes in the size of households, a high degree of equality is likely to persist indefinitely.

8. Contrary to what many believe, private sector activities have not resulted in greater inequality in the distribution of total household income and may well have helped to reduce inequality. Moreover, the 'pure' private sector is significantly larger today than it was in the late 1970s. The size of the private plot, for example, has been increased from 5–7 per cent of the cultivated area to up to 15 per cent. If our view is correct, and if the relationship between private and collective income still holds in the weak form that the present distribution of 'pure' private income is more equal than, say, the pre-1978 distribution of collective income, then total income today (collective plus private) should be more equally distributed than it was in the 1970s.

Appendix Table 2.1 *The distribution of per capita distributed collective income among households, Team No. 2, Phoenix Corporation, Sichuan, 1977*

Household number	*Family size*	*Distributed collective income per capita*
1	5	72.96
2	4	39.24
3	3	76.96
4	1	76.80
5	1	2.88
6	5	90.24
7	4	84.24
8	2	138.00
9	7	66.86
10	5	66.43
11	5	31.01
12	2	84.48
13	6	83.52
14	6	78.24
15	3	116.16
16	5	55.78
17	6	55.28
18	2	89.76
19	5	97.63
20	8	27.36
21	1	65.84
22	4	42.00
23	3	93.76
24	9	91.52
25	4	94.68
26	6	78.48
27	5	53.95
28	2	71.76
29	8	73.44
30	1	119.04
31	1	163.68
32	1	45.60
Average (weighted)		71.98
Ratio of highest to lowest income		5.04
Coefficient of variation (weighted)		0.32
Gini coefficient (weighted)		0.18

Note When calculating the average, ratio, Gini coefficient and coefficient of variation household numbers 5, 31 and 32 were excluded. Households 31 and 32 were unemployed educated youth and household 5 almost certainly was living off welfare under the 'five guarantees' scheme.

Appendix Table 2.2 *The distribution of per capita distributed collective income among households, Team No. 2, Phoenix Corporation, Sichuan, 1981.*

Household number	*Family size*	*Distributed collective income per capita*
1	3	796.00
2	3	634.00
3	5	507.80
4	4	411.75
5	5	496.40
6	4	467.75
7	2	889.00
8	5	437.20
9	7	446.00
10	6	452.50
11	5	409.40
12	2	491.50
13	2	409.50
14	7	462.57
15	5	377.00
16	6	371.83
17	2	468.00
18	5	520.40
19	8	509.88
20	3	621.67
21	3	434.00
22	3	542.67
23	5	409.20
24	3	666.30
25	3	817.67
26	1	806.00
27	4	562.25
28	5	512.60
29	6	458.50
30	9	439.33
31	1	0.00
Average (weighted)		496.69
Ratio of highest to lowest income		2.39
Coefficient of variation (weighted)		0.22
Gini coefficient (weighted)		0.11

Note 1 When calculating the average, ratio, Gini coefficient and coefficient of variation household number 31 was excluded because that person was a recipient of income under the 'five guarantees' scheme.

Note 2 Distributed collective income in 1981 includes the agricultural bonus and a rough adjustment for the industrial bonus. The average annual bonus for industrial workers was 164 yuan. This amount, multiplied by the number of industrial workers in each family, was added to household income.

Appendix Table 2.3 *The distribution of distributed collective income per capita among households, Team No. 1, Gao Chang Brigade, Gao Chang Commune, Yunnan, 1981*

Household number	*Family size*	*Distributed collective income per capita*
1	6	387.55
2	5	389.16
3	1	115.00
4	1	407.10
5	4	250.00
6	6	496.42
7	5	404.88
8	7	496.14
9	3	483.00
10	2	471.50
11	5	362.48
12	6	527.85
13	5	272.78
14	3	463.07
15	5	428.72
16	4	456.55
17	6	414.77
18	6	541.27
19	4	128.80
20	3	575.77
21	1	255.30
22	4	280.60
23	6	293.63
24	5	401.58
25	9	401.99
26	3	532.07
27	2	644.00
28	5	232.76
29	6	391.00
30	5	751.64
31	5	264.50
32	2	624.45
33	7	358.80
34	2	575.00
35	4	618.13
36	1	103.34
37	6	142.60
38	1	485.30
39	2	547.40
40	5	528.08
41	5	360.18
42	2	435.85
43	4	657.23

Appendix Table 2.3 (*Contd.*)

Household number	Family size	Distributed collective income Per capita
44	4	339.83
45	3	554.30
46	2	626.75
47	1	115.00
48	3	227.70
49	6	428.18
50	3	545.87
51	5	319.70
52	4	220.80
53	5	575.46
54	6	330.82
55	9	377.20
56	5	721.74
57	1	115.00
58	2	422.05
59	5	299.00
60	7	278.63
61	5	514.94
62	3	492.97
63	6	398.82
64	5	419.06
65	3	315.56
66	5	377.66
67	5	392.84
68	4	266.80
69	2	560.05
70	5	326.14
71	6	389.08
72	2	371.45
73	4	235.18
74	5	484.84
75	4	377.20
76	5	450.80
77	6	294.02
78	5	420.44
79	1	170.20
80	5	409.86
81	1	276.00
82	3	425.50
83	4	185.15
84	5	532.22
85	6	314.33
86	4	131.43
87	5	412.16
88	4	484.73

Appendix Table 2.3 (*Contd.*)

Household number	Family size	Distributed collective income per capita
89	3	412.47
90	3	322.00
Average (weighted)		403.06
Ratio of highest to lowest income		6.54
Coefficient of variation (weighted)		0.31
Gini coefficient (weighted)		0.18

Note When calculating the average, ratio, Gini coefficient and coefficient of variation household numbers, 3, 36, 57 and 79 were excluded. All four were living on payments received under the 'five guarantees' scheme. Household No. 3 was a mentally retarded person, No. 57 was disabled and No. 79 was an elderly lady who died in 1982.

Appendix Table 2.4 *The distribution of per capita distributed collective income among households, Team No. 7, Xiang Sui Brigade, Xiao She Qiao Commune, Yunnan 1979*

Household number	Family size	Distributed collective income per capita
1	5	34.40
2	4	59.00
3	4	46.00
4	4	75.00
5	5	41.00
6	9	27.00
7	7	46.00
8	8	27.00
9	2	97.00
10	7	35.00
11	4	68.00
12	4	88.00
13	7	33.00
14	7	26.00
15	1	—
Average (weighted)		43.13
Ratio of highest to lowest income		3.73
Coefficient of variation (weighted)		0.45
Gini coefficient (weighted)		0.23

Note Household No. 15 was excluded when calculating the average, ratio, Gini coefficient and coefficient of variation because she is an elderly lady living on the 'five guarantees'.

Appendix Table 2.5 *The distribution of per capita distributed collective income among households, Team No. 7, Xiang Sui Brigade, Xiao She Chiao Commune, Yunnan 1980 and 1981.*

Household number	*Family size*	*Distributed collective income per capita* 1980	1981
1	5	129.00	109.00
2	4	178.00	277.00
3	4	174.00	210.00
4	4	259.00	281.25
5	5	138.00	182.00
6	9	157.00	173.89
7	7	157.00	296.71
8	8	167.00	222.50
9	2	295.00	335.00
10	7	221.00	327.86
11	4	191.50	297.50
12	7	129.30	100.71
13	7	127.90	180.00
14	7	104.40	123.57
15	1	204.00	204.00
Average (weighted)		163.27	211.59
Ratio of highest to lowest income		2.83	3.33
Coefficient of variation (weighted)		0.27	0.36
Gini coefficient (weighted)		0.14	0.20

Note 1 Household No. 15 was excluded when calculating the average, ratio, Gini coefficient and coefficient of variation because she is an 80 year old woman living on the 'five guarantees'.

Note 2 The income figures, following the introduction of the production responsibility system, refer to total gross cash income, both collective and private, obtained from a survey of each household.

Appendix Table 2.6 *The distribution of per capita distributed collective income among households, Gao Chio Team, Pu Chao Brigade, Ala Commune, Yunnan 1981*

Household number	*Family size*	*Distributed collective income per capita*
1	6	124.32
2	5	113.37
3	4	61.56
4	6	110.86
5	5	70.34
6	6	150.31
7	5	190.67

Appendix Table 2.6 (*Contd.*)

Household number	*Family size*	*Distributed collective income per capita*
8	2	24.65
9	1	2.13
10	4	103.48
11	10	138.28
12	3	180.86
13	8	169.93
14	3	142.00
15	6	102.00
16	2	260.82
17	4	50.47
18	5	137.38
19	8	108.50
20	3	250.92
21	7	203.35
22	6	97.66
23	3	232.11
24	1	30.49
25	1	268.77
26	4	101.69
27	4	119.60
28	5	158.47
29	7	66.73
30	6	182.84
31	5	175.42
32	8	97.37
33	5	125.15
34	7	178.35
35	7	76.13
36	4	158.11
37	6	155.19
38	5	123.66
39	4	85.07
40	4	124.43
41	7	59.74
42	6	136.31
43	4	192.82
44	5	131.63
45	9	81.14
46	7	132.16
47	7	90.35
48	6	107.70
49	8	131.64
50	10	152.11
51	5	59.25

Appendix Table 2.6 (*Contd.*)

Household number	*Family size*	*Distributed collective income per capita*
52	7	218.35
53	7	114.95
54	5	76.09
Average (weighted)		128.43
Ratio of highest to lowest income		10.90
Coefficient of variation (weighted)		0.36
Gini coefficient (weighted)		0.20

Note When calculating the average, ratio, Gini coefficient and coefficient of variation household numbers 9 and 24 were excluded because both were one person households consisting of elderly persons no longer in the labour force and living on the 'five guarantees'.

Appendix Table 2.7 *The distribution of per capita distributed collective income among households, Team No. 3, Fu Bao Brigade, Liu Jia Commune, Yunnan, 1981*

Household number	*Family size*	*Distributed collective income per capita*
1	6	282.67
2	3	508.67
3	3	261.00
4	4	353.25
5	8	379.88
6	6	376.33
7	7	322.43
8	1	281.00
9	3	160.67
10	5	357.80
11	5	382.00
12	1	0.00
13	7	399.57
14	2	777.00
15	6	427.83
16	6	278.83
17	7	526.00
18	1	176.00
19	3	103.33
20	4	587.50
21	6	403.50

Appendix Table 2.7 (*Contd.*)

Household number	*Family size*	*Distributed collective income per capita*
22	6	367.00
23	6	431.00
24	5	437.80
25	1	256.00
26	4	418.50
27	5	310.40
28	3	449.00
29	7	374.14
30	5	86.60
31	6	321.17
32	4	424.25
33	6	282.50
34	6	260.83
35	5	357.80
36	6	316.33
37	5	353.60
38	5	376.40
39	6	324.00
40	4	501.50
41	4	459.50
42	5	346.40
43	3	672.33
44	5	579.20
45	6	398.83
46	5	416.60
47	2	237.50
48	4	418.00
49	6	544.17
50	7	260.86
51	3	518.00
52	4	382.50
53	4	130.50
54	8	305.13
55	3	108.00
56	5	292.40
57	5	355.40
58	6	397.00
59	6	208.67
60	5	372.60
61	6	269.00
62	6	239.33
63	8	197.88
64	5	593.00

Appendix Table 2.7 (*Contd.*)

Household number	*Family size*	*Distributed collective income per capita*
65	5	434.40
66	3	534.00
67	4	697.00
68	6	382.17
69	3	814.00
70	5	385.40
71	5	443.40
72	3	528.33
73	4	356.50
74	7	253.43
75	5	345.40
76	7	447.57
77	4	484.25
78	2	601.50
79	5	224.00
80	5	454.20
81	2	453.50
82	7	245.86
83	3	291.67
84	5	358.80
85	5	578.40
86	6	418.17
87	8	325.50
88	5	320.60
89	3	461.67
90	7	251.00
91	6	151.33
92	5	424.80
93	5	502.20
94	7	348.57
95	6	454.00
96	6	271.00
97	5	304.40
98	4	302.00
99	2	587.00
100	6	558.33
101	3	185.33
102	7	475.14
103	3	357.67
104	7	473.29
105	5	297.40
106	3	447.33

Appendix Table 2.7 (*Contd.*)

Household number	*Family size*	*Distributed collective income per capita*
107	4	381.25
108	5	332.80
109	4	393.75
110	4	389.75
111	4	367.50
112	5	282.60
113	3	490.00
114	4	279.00
115	3	565.67
116	1	397.00
117	6	347.00
118	4	327.50
119	5	281.20
120	6	251.00
121	6	252.00
122	5	334.40
123	4	291.50
124	5	349.80
125	1	192.00
126	5	399.20
127	6	235.33
128	4	373.00
129	5	240.80
130	4	321.25
131	4	392.25
132	5	249.60
133	4	451.75
134	1	934.00
135	4	143.00
136	4	377.75
137	7	238.29
138	5	325.40
139	4	312.50
140	4	369.75
141	4	395.75
142	4	377.50
143	5	295.20
144	4	351.00
145	5	338.00
146	5	307.40
147	1	269.00
148	4	356.25

Appendix Table 2.7 (*Contd.*)

Household number	Family size	Distributed collective income per capita
149	4	376.25
150	4	298.00
151	4	284.25
152	4	381.25
153	4	367.75
154	4	329.75
155	3	337.67
156	3	357.67
157	4	275.25
158	3	355.67
159	3	458.00
160	3	362.67
Average (weighted)		361.02
Ratio of highest to lowest income		10.79
Coefficient of variation (weighted)		0.31
Gini coefficient (weighted)		0.17

Note When calculating the average, ratio, Gini coefficient and coefficient of variation household number 12 was excluded because it consisted of a single old man living on the 'five guarantees'.

Appendix Table 2.8 *Distributed collective income per capita among fifteen co-operatives, Heping village, Dong Nan Xiang, Guanghan county, Sichuan, 1981*

Team number	Distributed collective income per capita
1	235.30
2	264.12
3	241.14
4	280.56
5	287.53
6	221.49
7	286.80
8	238.63
9	238.24
10	253.24
11	303.00
12	214.99
13	209.46

Appendix Table 2.8 (*Contd.*)

Team number	Distributed collective income per capita
14	238.90
15	268.59
Average	252.13
Ratio of highest to lowest income	1.45
Coefficient of variation	0.11
Gini coefficient	0.06

Appendix Table 2.9 *Distributed collective income per capita among five teams, Chao Tan Brigade, Yuan Men Ko Commune, Sichuan, 1980*

Team number	Population	Income (yuan)
1	602	287.84
2	178	327.09
3	174	273.03
4	334	283.86
5	442	208.21
Weighted average		269.28
Ratio of highest to lowest income		1.57
Gini coefficient		0.05

Appendix Table 2.10 *Distributed collective income per capita among eight teams, Sun Jin Brigade, Chun He Commune, Yunnan, 1978–81*

Team number	Distributed collective income per capita			
	1978	1979	1980	1981
1	176	187	205	267
2	177	192	228	281
3	146	171	201	254
4	138	172	188	268
5	154	165	204	234
6	153	176	201	255
7	159	165	205	221
8	199	219	270	300

Appendix Table 2.10 (*Contd.*)

Team number	*Distributed collective income per capita* 1978	1979	1980	1981
Average	162.75	180.88	212.75	260.00
Ratio of highest to lowest income	1.44	1.33	1.44	1.36
Coefficient of variation	0.12	0.10	0.12	0.10
Gini coefficient	0.06	0.05	0.05	0.05

Appendix Table 2.11 *Distributed collective income per capita among four teams, Fu Bao Brigade, Liu Jia Commune, Yunnan, 1978 and 1981*

Team number	*Distributed collective income per capita* 1978	1981
1	205	288
2	239	254
3	230	382
4	362	312
Average	259	309
Ratio of highest to lowest income	1.77	1.50
Gini coefficient	0.12	0.08

NOTES AND REFERENCES

1. We are grateful to Cyril Lin of St Antony's College, Oxford and Professor Shigeru Ishikawa for observations on an earlier draft of this chapter.
2. Benedict Stavis, *The Politics of Agricultural Mechanization in China* (Cornell University Press, 1978) p. 39. Also see Vivienne Shue, *Peasant China in Transition* (University of California Press, 1980) chapter 4.
3. The story is well told in Vivienne Shue, *Peasant China in Transition*, chapter 7.
4. The classic case study is William Hinton, *Fanshen* (Monthly Review Press, 1966).
5. Mark Selden, 'Co-operation and Conflict: Co-operative and Collective Formation in China's Countryside', in Mark Selden and Victor Lippit, eds., *The Transition to Socialism in China* (M. E. Sharpe Ltd., 1982) p. 85. Also of interest is Willem F. Wertheim and Matthias Stiefel, *Production, Equality and Participation in Rural China*, UNRISD: Geneva, 1982. Selden, however,

believes that there were departures from the model of gradual, voluntary co-operation in 1956 and again in 1958.

6. Vivienne Shue, *Peasant China in Transition*, p. 328.
7. See Chapter 6.
8. See Michael Ellman, 'Agricultural Productivity Under Socialism', *World Development*, September–October, 1981.
9. This is unusual since pig raising has been de-collectivised in most communes.
10. In comparison, interest rates in banks are 5 per cent on short-term deposits and 6 per cent on long-term deposits.
11. The paddy quota was 1200 jin/mou as compared to the maximum previous yield of 1250. The land allocation by crop was 121 mou for wheat, 46 mou for rapeseed and 187 mou for paddy.
12. Per capita distributed collective income in Mi Mu Commune was 129.32 yuan in 1978; 149.26 yuan in 1979; 160.42 yuan in 1980 and 152.20 yuan in 1981.
13. See Keith Griffin and Ashwani Saith, *Growth and Equality in Rural China* (published for the ILO by Maruzen: Singapore, 1981).
14. Weak teams are defined as those where collective distributed income is less than 100 yuan and where the per capita food ration is less than 400 jin. By 1981 all teams had exceeded the food target but 28 teams still had a collective income of less than 100 yuan.
15. Keith Griffin and Ashwani Saith, *Growth and Equality in Rural China*.
16. Keith Griffin and Ashwani Saith, 'The Pattern of Income Inequality in Rural China', *Oxford Economic Papers*, March 1982, p. 173.
17. See Alison Ansell, Roger Hay and Keith Griffin, 'Private Production and Income Distribution in a Chinese Commune', *Food Policy*, February 1982.
18. The equation is the following:

$$PY/CY = 35.85 - 0.07^{*}\ (CY/N);\quad R^2 = 0.14.$$
$$N = 92$$

* = significant at 1% level.

3 The Responsibility System and Institutional Change

AZIZUR RAHMAN KHAN

Ever since their formation in 1958, the communes have experienced periodic changes in the structure of their organisation and in the overall institutional environment in which they operate. The initial experimentation with extreme egalitarianism – characterised by too high a level of the basic accounting unit and too great an emphasis on the principle of 'to each according to his need' as the criterion of distribution – soon gave way to the emergence of the three-level organisation under which the lowest level, the team, became the basic accounting unit and collective income began to be distributed according to the work points earned. This structure was basically consolidated by the early 1960s and continued to survive to the time Mao Zedong died in September 1976, although certain tendencies had started to manifest themselves during the years of the Cultural Revolution as precursors of future changes envisaged by the dominant groups in the Chinese leadership of the time. In tracing the steps in the transformation initiated in the post-Mao period, it is useful to begin with a description of the basic structure of the system and the various tendencies that had begun to appear prior to Mao's death.

CHANGES IN THE POST-MAO PERIOD

The commune was the highest of the three-level organisational structure. It was both an economic organisation and a unit of local government. Its economic functions consisted of operating workshops and enterprises and organising capital construction that transcended the jurisdiction of individual brigades. In its capacity as the lowest unit of local government it maintained hospitals, educational institutions, other infrastructural facilities and local militia.

An average commune had 13.5 production brigades.[1] The brigades managed smaller workshops and enterprises, all heavy machines and equipment and irrigation facilities for agriculture. They also organised capital construction within their realm (transcending the individual teams) and managed schools, kindergartens and nurseries.

An average brigade had 7.4 production teams each having an average of twenty-six households.[1] The team 'owned' all cultivated land, livestock (except those permitted to be held by the households), smaller machines and agricultural tools. In general the team was the basic accounting unit in the sense that within it the payment for a given amount of work (measured by a work point or a workday) was the same for all workers.

During the Cultural Revolution the dominant group in China began to argue that the level of the basic accounting unit should gradually be raised in order to curb 'bourgeois right' in the realm of ownership. By raising the level of accounting from the team to the brigade, one source of income inequality, namely, the difference between the teams with respect to land and other resource endowment, is eliminated. A move had begun, therefore, to raise the accounting level to that of the brigade and ultimately to that of the commune. By the end of the Cultural Revolution, 10 per cent of the brigades had become the basic accounting units and in about sixty cases the level of accounting had been raised to that of the commune.[2]

Within the basic accounting unit income was distributed in proportion to work points earned. Another tendency of the dominant group during the Cultural Revolution was to argue that making work points proportional to one's contribution to production according to the dictate of the socialist principle of distribution, that is, 'to each according to his work', would amount to the preservation of a bourgeois right. Such a principle of distribution would perpetrate inequality in so far as individuals differ in terms of capacity to work and families differ in terms of labour endowment. It was, therefore, argued that the principle of payment according to need should be gradually introduced.

This was to be done, first, by changing the method of calculation of work points. Piece rates were to be abolished. Instead of calculating work points daily, assessments were to be made in advance for considerable periods of time to bring the system closer to that of fixed wage rates. A 'correct attitude to work' and a 'devotion to the cause of serving the people' should become important criteria for assessing work points. Physical strength and skill should be correspondingly de-emphasised.

Another policy that was gradually being implemented to curb the 'bourgeois right' inherent in the socialist principle of distribution was the distribution of a part of collective income according to need (i.e. equal amounts per 'adult-unit') irrespective of work points earned. In some collective units income distributed on the basis of need had come to be well over 10 per cent of collective income.[3]

Individual households had private plots which had a nearly perfectly equal per capita distribution, especially within a given collective unit. Together private plots were restricted to 5 to 7 per cent of cultivated land.[4] Individual households were allowed to engage in some private sideline activities, for example, raising of poultry and pigs. There were rural fairs at which private produce could be sold. The private activities were, however, severely circumscribed by the requirement imposed upon each member to engage in a certain minimum number of days of collective work.

During the Cultural Revolution private plots, sideline activities and private commerce at village fairs came under strong attack as capitalist practices. In many areas the tendency to abolish private plots or cultivate them jointly became strong. Similarly, private sidelines and village fairs came under increasing restriction.

Collective units were subject to a small rate of direct agricultural tax and a concealed tax in the form of compulsory procurement.[5] The system of procurement was based on a basic quota for which a low price was paid. For sales to the state above the basic quota a premium – usually 50 per cent – was paid over the procurement price. Over the years the average price paid for agricultural procurement and the terms of trade for agriculture improved steadily.[6] The improvement in agriculture's terms of trade was particularly rapid during the earlier years and decelerated during the later years: the annual rate of increase in the index of terms of trade[7] was 3.3 per cent between 1952 and 1957, 2.5 per cent between 1957 and 1965 and 1.8 per cent between 1965 and 1975. By the latter date state trading in agricultural goods had resulted in a fairly large deficit. Such an outcome was due to the rising agricultural purchase prices over the years with unchanged retail prices for the distribution of farm goods.

Changes since 1976

On 6 October – within less than a month of Mao's death – the leadership of the dominant group during the Cultural Revolution was overthrown and put under arrest. However, there was little immediate change in the policies towards the rural sector. Indeed, the holding of the Second Conference on Learning from Dazhai in December 1976 seemed to indicate that the policies would remain unchanged. Both Hua Guofeng and Chen Yonggui, the Agricultural Minister and the former leader of the Dazhai brigade, extolled the virtue of learning from Dazhai as the key to quickening the pace of agricultural development. As is well known, Dazhai stood for much of the left wing tendencies that were manifested during the Cultural Revolution.[8] Indeed, the doctrine of learning from Dazhai continued to be publicly proclaimed until the middle of 1978.[9]

A new Constitution of the People's Republic of China, adopted on 5 March 1978 by the Fifth National People's Congress, also upheld the principle of gradually making the brigades the basic accounting units. It also permitted personal plots and sideline activities only to the extent that they were strictly consistent with the dominant role of the collective economy.[10]

The year 1978 was, however, marked by the consolidation of power of a new leadership which was strongly opposed to the tendencies that had become pronounced during the Cultural Revolution. This force stood for a basic reversal in the evolution of the communes and rural institutions by relating payments more directly to work; opposing the trend towards a higher level of collectivisation (i.e. gradual transition towards the brigades as basic accounting units) and indeed reversing it; and promoting private plots, sideline activities and private markets.[11] By the end of 1978, at the Third Plenum of the 11th Central Committee of the Chinese Communist Party in December, this force achieved decisive victory in their struggle to chart a new course for China's rural institutions. Many of the trends discussed below were given a decisive stamp of legitimacy at the Third Plenum of the 11th Central Committee of the Chinese Communist Party.

The system of payment

The *Renmin Ribao* of 5 May 1978 began the campaign for the restoration of the socialist principle of distribution 'to each according to his work', a principle that had recently been enshrined in Article 10 of Chapter 1 of the 1978 Constitution. It was argued that the past system of workpoint allocation resulted in so great a divorce between reward and work that it had become a major obstacle to incentives to work. Payment of a part of collective output on the basis of need, it was argued, had the same effect. These past systems came to be ridiculed as the doctrine of 'eating from one big public pot'. It was emphasised that 'there is a fundamental difference between enthusiasm for socialism and the inherent demand for egalitarianism of the small proprietors . . . Experience proves that egalitarianism is a disaster to the socialist cause, a throttle on enthusiasm for labour and a corrosive agent to the social productive forces.'[12]

In the wake of changes that were ushered in, the amount of work done has emerged as the sole criterion of distribution of collective output. In the calculation of work points output actually produced is the guide wherever possible. Elsewhere work points are tied to specific pieces of work. As we shall see later, certain widespread forms of contracting with individual households or workers have done away with the need to calculate work points in the teams which have adopted these practices. It will be shown later that in these cases difference in income receipt is usually far greater than the difference in performance at the margin.

Need based payments, except for the old, weak and disabled, have been abolished. In some cases, even the system of 'five guarantees' (food, clothing, housing, medical care and burial expenses) to the old, weak and disabled appears to have faced erosion and partial dismantlement.[13]

The basic accounting unit

One of the earliest measures of the current phase of reform was to stop any further transition of the basic accounting units from the team to the higher levels. Indeed, the level of collectivisation was brought down by gradually lowering the basic accounting units from the higher levels to the team. By 1978 about 10 per cent of the brigades had become basic accounting units. By 1981 in about half of them the level of accounting had reverted to that of the team. It is claimed that by the end of 1981, thirty-one communes and 36 000 brigades were still serving as basic accounting units. On closer examination it becomes clear, however, that even this is a gross exaggeration. It is quite common nowadays, for example, to claim that the brigade is the basic accounting unit in a collective which has completely gone over to a system of contracting with individual households. This can only mean that the connotation of the term 'basic accounting unit' has undergone fundamental change. As we have seen above, the principal characteristic that makes a collective unit a basic accounting unit is that all work points earned in it have the same value. Once contracting with individual households is practised no collective unit – not even the team – can claim to satisfy this criterion. Indeed, under the most widespread type of contracting the calculation of work points is no longer necessary. Thus, in current usage the term 'basic accounting unit' appears to have come to mean something quite different from what it used to in the past. It is perhaps nothing more than what is known as the organ of 'unified management', the unit that enters into and administers contracts with individual households and groups.

The process of going below the team as the basic accounting unit was under way by the end of 1978. The earliest case is probably that of Sichuan where Zhao Ziyang recommended the divison of the teams into smaller groups and is reported to have used the term 'basic accounting units' to describe the role of these smaller units.[14] Since then contracting with individual households and labourers has become so widespread that in an overwhelmingly large part of rural China it makes little sense to talk in terms of a basic accounting unit above the level of the households. This aspect of the change will be discussed in detail.

Private plots, sidelines and private markets

Reference has already been made to the facts that during the Cultural Revolution private plots averaged 6.4 per cent of arable land, that in some areas they had been abolished and that the Constitution of 1978 restored the right to private plots and sidelines under the strict qualification that their operation would be within the framework of the 'absolute predominance of the collective economy'. By the end of 1978 private plots were restored where they had been abolished. Simultaneously a move was on to expand the size of the private plots. Once again the lead was taken by Zhao Ziyang in Sichuan where in early 1979 the share of such plots was increased to 10 to 12 per cent of arable land. The ceiling was raised further to 15 per cent in Sichuan in late 1979 and this was followed by a similar move in certain other provinces. In March 1981 the Central Committee of the Chinese Communist Party and the State Council decided that in those rural areas in which the system of fixing farm output quotas on a household basis had not been carried out, private plots may be expanded to the limit of 15 per cent of the total cultivated area of a production team.

Restrictions on what could be produced on private plots and sideline activities were substantially eased. Previously only one pig *per family* per year was the usual limit. In early 1979 the principle of permitting the raising of one pig per year *per person* was adopted. By early 1980 in most provinces all restrictions on the raising of pigs were abolished. Private raising of sheep and some cattle was permitted in Xinjiang and Jansu from 1980.

A logical corollary of the expansion of private plots and sideline activities was the expansion of marketing opportunities for their products. The legitimacy and the inviolability of the rural private markets (somewhat misleadingly called rural fairs) were assured by the Third Plenum of the 11th Central Committee of the Chinese Communist Party in December 1978. A more important development was the legitimisation of private markets for agricultural goods in urban areas since early 1979. Prices in these markets are allowed to be determined by the interaction of supply and demand.[15] Almost any produce of private plot and sideline activity can be sold in these markets. The only restriction seems to apply to grain which can enter these markets only after the passage of a certain period of time after harvest. 'A man cannot buy at the fair and resell in the country without the written approval of his team and the city commercial department'[16]; however, it is not known to what extent such restrictions are effective.

Another concomitant of the spread of private activities is the lowering of the requirement to undertake collective labour. While the requirement has generally been relaxed, 'a small number of commune members may devote themselves to household sideline occupations or work on their private plots instead of taking part in collective production.'[17]

In those areas in which all round contracting with individual households has been adopted, the output and labour on contracted out land continue to be classified as collective output and collective labour. Such land is also considered to be collective land. The distinction between this so-called collective land and private plot is due to the following factors: (a) the output of the former is subject to a deduction for collective reserves, welfare tax, and accumulation; (b) it is subject to a quota of compulsory sale to the state which amounts to a concealed tax since the procurement price is lower than what the peasants could get in the private market; and (c) the compulsory sale quota and other practices concerning 'unified planning' impose restriction on the cropping pattern on the former type of land. Private plots are free of any of these deductions and restrictions.

Abolition of administrative powers and functions

As we have seen, the rural people's communes combined local government administration with the management of economic activities. The new Constitution of the People's Republic presented in draft form at the National People's Congress in April 1982 and finally adopted in December 1982 has made provision for the separation of the administrative functions from the economic ones. 'In order to strengthen the grass-roots state power organs in the countryside and to perfect the rural collective economic organisations, the draft provides for establishing organs of township state power according to the principle of separating government administration from commune management, while retaining the people's communes as collective economic organisations.'[18]

Long before the legitimisation provided by the draft Constitution of 1982 experimental separation of functions had been in trial operation in three counties in Sichuan.[19] By the middle of 1982 these experiments were being described as success stories clearly pointing to the strong possibility of their nationwide replication.[20]

In a later section of this chapter an exposition of this change will be provided. All that is necessary to note at this stage is that the change is much more far reaching than merely taking away from the top level of the three-level commune organisation the administrative functions and giving them to the newly created local government body. The measures have effectively resulted in the substantial delinking of the three levels of the commune organisation.

Summary

In the year or two after Mao's death, policy-making for rural China was very much in the hands of people like Hua Guofeng and Chen Yonggui, those who had been a part of the leadership during the Cultural Revolution. Changes during this period gave the appearance of nothing more than fine tuning of the system to overcome the aberrations resulting from the 'misdeeds of the gang of four'. After the rehabilitation of Deng Xiaoping the movement for the reversal of past policies gained momentum. The year 1978 was of crucial importance. At the end of that year a decisive victory for those who wanted change was won at the Third Plenary Session of the 11th Central Committee of the Chinese Communist Party (18–22 December). Since then both the structure of communes and rural policies in China have been changing at a breathtaking pace. The level of collectivisation was brought down, first, to the level of teams and then to smaller groups. This was soon replaced by a system of widespread contracting with individual households and workers. Private plots, sideline activities and private markets were vastly expanded and guaranteed as inviolate. Egalitarianism was identified as the outstanding obstacle to progress and need was eliminated as a basis for distribution. The stripping of the communes of their administrative functions was combined with the experimental delinking of the three levels of organisation. Dazhai was rejected as the model to emulate.[21]

There is no reason to think that the changes have or are about to come to an end. If anything, one gets the impression of acceleration in their pace. In the past the actual organisation of China's rural economy and society appeared to lag behind the rhetorical position of the dominant group in the leadership. Now the reverse seems closer to the truth. Vast changes precede official announcement and, sometimes, legitimisation. Further dramatic changes along the path traversed since 1978 are more than a possibility. The present study is, therefore, no more than the current still life version of a continuously moving and changing scene.

THE RESPONSIBILITY SYSTEM

The responsibility system spread like wildfire to encompass virtually the whole of rural China within the short period between 1979 and 1982. There is such a great variety of forms of the system currently in operation that it is very difficult to attempt a precise definition or description of it.

The motivation behind the numerous experiments with different forms of the system seems to be a quest for a method or methods of farming that relate payment (or income) to production as directly as possible. In the preceding section an account was given of how the quest for greater egalitarianism during the Cultural Revolution has gradually made the system of payments – based on the distribution of work points earned – increasingly resemble a system of fixed wages. This created a serious problem of incentive. Due to the special nature of agricultural work it becomes exceedingly difficult to evaluate performance, institute a system of payments and organise management decisions and related matters as one moves out of the organisational framework of the peasant family into that of a collective.

Even piece rates are not quite the same in terms of linking reward with output in agriculture as in other activities. Whether a piece of work (e.g.

weeding on a given piece of land or transplanting on a given plot) is well done or not is rarely possible to relate directly to variation in final output which, unlike in manufacturing or other activities, not only comes with a long lag but is also subject to too many other influences. The degree of perfection with which a given piece of work is done can at best be evaluated ex-post while the piece rates are largely decided ex-ante. Finally, such perfection is usually less decisive a factor in determining final output than the overall co-ordination and management of all stages.

Thus, if the concern for an increase in the quantity of output is so desperate as to lead one to look for a more direct linkage between payment and production the only way out seems to ask an individual, a household or a small group to take responsibility for final output and bear the consequences of shortfall from or overfulfilment of a norm that appears to be a reasonable target. This must then amount to the delegation of responsibility for the application of inputs and production of output to identifiable individuals, families or groups.

It may be useful to take a look at past attempts to institute similar systems and their historical context. Yan Ling, an advocate of this system as early as the 1950s, has recently published the following account of how this system was tried out and overthrown in the past.[22]

> Peasants in more backward areas, where the basis for mutual aid and co-operation was weak, adopted a system of contracting output quotas to individual households. In 1956, this practice, commonly referred to as the household responsibility system, was spontaneously carried out by many of the poorer co-operatives in mountainous and remote areas in Shanxi. Henan, Zhejiang and Guangdong . . . However, in the 'great debate on the struggle between socialism and capitalism' in 1957, this method was criticised as 'a mistake of principle departing from the socialist road'. After the communes were set up, this system was abolished. However, some communes and production brigades, in resistance to egalitarian practices, revived the household responsibility system. Later, in the campaign to 'oppose Right deviations', the system was still more ruthlessly criticised as 'extremely backward, retrogressive and reactionary'. In the three-year period of economic difficulties in the early 1960s, many communes and production brigades again turned to the household responsibility system or other similar practices ('responsibility plots' and 'fixed production quotas on a large scale'). At the Tenth Plenary Session of the Eighth Central Committee in 1962, it was again discredited as 'whipping up the wind of going it alone' and a manifestation of the sharpening of class struggle . . . It was again criticised and prohibited in the 'four clean-ups' campaign in 1965.

Several facts emerge from the above account. The system is not an innovation in response to the problems faced by the rural institutions in China during the late 1970s. It was originally proposed by its protagonists as an alternative to the advanced co-operatives at the time the latter were first being organised (1956). The system was repeatedly subjected to criticism as being inconsistent with China's socialist path and was not endorsed even during the difficult period of readjustment after the Great Leap Forward. It is probable that the successful recovery from the disastrous period of 1959–61, within the framework of the commune system, was seen as the decisive evidence that there was no need to go back on collectivisation and that this confidence was the basis for what appeared to be the decisive rejection of the responsibility system by the mid 1960s.

The responsibility system and its various forms

The essence of the responsibility system is the contract that the team – the 'owner' of land, major capital equipment and large livestock – enters into with groups, individuals and households. The contract specifies a target output. Arrangements vary with respect to the distribution of output (both target and above target), degree of access to land by the contractor and various other features of the contract. There has been a good deal of spontaneity about the spread of the system after the Third Plenum of the 11th Central Committee of the Chinese Communist Party gave approval to it in December 1978. There was no single blueprint or model guideline comparable to the 'Model Regulations for an Agricultural Producers' Co-operative' and the 'Model Regulations for an Advanced Agricultural Producers' Co-operative' of the 1950s. As a result a great many alternative forms of contracting has been in practice. One must neglect numerous differences on less than crucially important aspects in order to arrive at a finite number of types of contract.

Before attempting a schematic classification of the main types of contract under the responsibility system it may be useful to describe them for Sichuan, the province that both pioneered the system and experimented with radical methods. By the middle of 1982, Sichuan had eight main forms of the responsibility system in operation.[23] Some of them were quantitatively so insignificant that it appears they were becoming increasingly unimportant over time. Else it is hard to understand why a type that encompasses less than a half of 1 per cent of the teams would head the list in an official presentation of the main forms of contract. Clearly the classification refers to an earlier period during which this form was more prominent. Thus, the classification also provides a hint or two on the changes in relative importance of the various types of contracts.

The shares shown below refer to the proportion of production teams practising the forms in June 1982. Generally teams are completely specialised in a particular form of contract. However, in certain cases a given team practises more than one form. This is particularly true for teams simultaneously operating in several sectors. Thus, a team simultaneously involved in farming, fishery and forestry may use one method for farming and another (usually contract along specialised line, the first type listed below) for fishery and forestry. The shares shown below are, in such cases, based on a classification of teams according to the dominant form. The eight forms may briefly be described as follows:

1. Contract along specialised line. Under this system the team is divided up into *groups* along specialised lines, e.g. crop production, forestry, fishery, upkeep of tractors and equipment, and so on. Output and input quotas are fixed. Bonuses and penalties generally amount to 100 per cent of the quantities in excess of the quotas fixed in the contract. In other words, the entire output above quota is retained by the group and the entire cost above the target is paid by the group. The quota output is turned over to the team which, after deductions for taxes, collective accumulation and welfare funds, distributes it collectively on the basis of work points earned by the different groups. Work points are in turn proportional to outputs. Only 0.38 per cent of the teams in Sichuan practice this method.

2. Contract with labourers. Under this system land is equally divided among the members of the labour force of the team and contracts made with individual labourers. Output quotas and costs are fixed. Bonuses and penalties are 100 per cent. Quota outputs are collected by the team and distributed among the labourers in proportion to earned work points which in turn are proportional to outputs. This method is practised by 7.19 per cent of the teams in Sichuan.

3. *Bao chan dao hu*. Under this system land is divided among households on the basis of equal amounts per capita (making allowance for quality differences as far as possible). Output quota, input target and labour (i.e. work points) are stipulated in the contract. Bonuses and penalties are 100 per cent, i.e. above quota (shortfall in) output and saving of (excess over) target cost are entirely retained (paid) by the household. The quota outputs are collected by the teams and distributed among the households according to work points after deductions for welfare, accumulation and taxes. This method of contracting is

prevalent in 17.06 per cent of the teams in Sichuan.

4. *Bao gan dao hu*. This is another form of contracting with individual households. By now this is the most widely prevalent system all over China. In Sichuan 64.46 per cent of the teams practise this method of contracting. Under this system land is divided among households on the basis of equal amounts per capita just as in the case of *bao chan dao hu*. Each household is required to pay a share of the team's taxes, make a contribution to accumulation and welfare funds and take up a share of quota sales to the state. All the remaining output is retained by the households. There is no calculation of work points as collective distribution is abolished. Nor is there a system of food ration.

5. Contract on a per capita basis for the direct production of food. Under this system a certain proportion of land – upto a limit of 60 or 70 per cent – is distributed among the households on the basis of an equal amount per capita. On this land the households produce food for self-consumption. This is to replace food ration which is abolished. The remaining land is used to produce for the fulfilment of procurement quota. After deductions for tax, accumulation and welfare any surplus from this production is distributed among the workers on the basis of work points earned. This part of the land can be cultivated under a variety of systems, for example, direct management by teams and contracting out to groups and individuals. By the middle of 1982, 3.35 per cent of the teams in Sichuan were using this method.

6. Different types of contracts for irrigated and unirrigated land. Under this system a team contracts out the cultivation of irrigated land only to *work groups* and of unirrigated land to individuals and households. This is in recognition of the fact that greater flexibility is desirable in order to create conditions for the improvement in yield in land that is less productive. This system is adopted by 3.97 per cent of the teams in Sichuan.

7. Contracting with groups. The system is similar to *bao gan dao hu* except that the team enters into contracts with *groups* rather than households. Groups retain all output after contributing to tax, accumulation and welfare funds and taking up a share of procurement quota. This system prevails in 2.26 per cent of the teams in Sichuan.

8. Short-term seasonal contract for specific farm operations, not directly linked to output but to 'pieces of work' (e.g. a given amount of weeding or harvesting). This is being practised by 1.32 per cent of the teams in Sichuan.

An attempt has been made in Table 3.1 to provide a schematic classification of the above eight types of contract. The rows provide the

TABLE 3.1 *Types of contract under responsibility system in Sichuan*

<table>
<tr><th rowspan="2">Form of contract →
Contract with ↓</th><th colspan="2">Comprehensive access to land</th><th colspan="2">Access to a part of land</th><th colspan="2">Without access to land</th></tr>
<tr><th>All output retained after compulsory payments</th><th>Bonus part of above target output retained; rest distributed according to work points</th><th>Part of land distributed to produce food ration</th><th>Unirrigated land distributed; irrigated land used to produce for quota</th><th>Specialised line contract</th><th>Seasonal/short term contract for fixed work</th></tr>
<tr><td>Worker</td><td colspan="2">(2)
7.19</td><td></td><td rowspan="2">(6)
Unirrigated
3.97</td><td rowspan="2"></td><td rowspan="3">(8)
1.32</td></tr>
<tr><td>Family</td><td>(4)
64.46</td><td>(3)
17.06</td><td>(5)
3.05</td></tr>
<tr><td>Group</td><td>(7)
2.26</td><td></td><td></td><td>(6)
Irrigated
(3.97)</td><td>(1)
0.38</td></tr>
</table>

NOTE The number within parenthesis in each rectangle is the serial number of the contract type listed in the text. The other number shows the percentage of teams practising the system represented by the rectangle in Sichuan in June 1982.

classification of contractors into individuals, households and groups. The columns first classify the contracts into three broad categories on the basis of the comprehensiveness of access to land by the contractor. First, we have the forms of contract that provide comprehensive access to the contractor. At the least the security of access to land is as great as in the case of guaranteed tenancy over a number of years. In practice, there is an attempt on the part of the current leadership to make the rural population feel like 'de facto owners' of the land that has been contracted out. Next, we have the types of contracts that provide access to only a part of land (contract types 5 and 6). Finally, we have those minor types of contract that entail no access to land. These include contract types 1 and 8 shown above.[24]

It is clear that the classification shown in the table is incomplete due to the lack of information on the shares of the sub-classes of some of the types shown. Thus, for example, contract type 2 could be further divided into those which allow the contractors to retain all output after compulsory payments (*bao gan dao lao*) and those which require the quota output to be distributed according to work points earned (*bao chan dao lao*).

It is, however, clear that the forms of contract that allow individual workers and households to have comprehensive access to and control over given amounts of land constitute an overwhelming proportion of the total. In Sichuan types 2, 3 and 4 together account for 88.71 per cent of the teams. Moreover, much of contract type 5 (about 65 per cent of the land at the command of the teams practising this type) probably uses a system of contracting that represents comprehensive access to and control over land.[25] Similarly, the unirrigated land under contract type 6 belongs to the same category. Assuming that the teams under different types of contract have, on the average, the same amount of land one would conclude that in Sichuan 95 per cent of the land is cultivated under a system of contracting which assures comprehensive access to and control over land by individuals and households.[26] As will be demonstrated below, the system resembles peasant agriculture with fixed rental tenancy with security of tenure.

The situation in Sichuan does not appear to be qualitatively different from that in China as a whole although there are regional differences in the composition of contracts under the responsibility system. *Bao gan dao hu* alone accounted for about 70 per cent of the teams in China as a whole by mid 1982.[27] This is clearly the fastest growing and the overwhelmingly important type of contract in China. In Yunnan it accounted for more than 84 per cent of the teams.[28]

To get some idea of the rapidity with which the more radical forms of the responsibility system came to be adopted one might refer to the case of Mi Mu Commune in Xindu county in Sichuan. The year by year account of the adoption of the system by the 107 teams looks as follows:

1979 54 teams started the system of fixed amount of farm work for fixed amount of work points.
1980 53 teams practised the system of fixed amount of farm work for fixed amount of work points.
54 teams practised contract with work groups.
1981 105 teams practised contract with work groups.
2 teams practised contract with individual labourers and households.
1982 10 teams practised contract with work groups.
97 teams practised contract with individual labourers and households.

It is important to understand that there is a great variety of practices in actual operation, far more than the relatively neat account of the eight types described above. Let us give some examples. Of the 84.2 per cent of the teams practising *bao gan dao hu* in Yunnan, 20.4 per cent use this method in agricultural production while sidelines are contracted out along specialised lines (type 1 in the above list). The remaining 63.8 per cent have adopted *bao gan dao hu* for both agricultural production and sidelines. Again in Yunnan two broad categories of *bao gan dao hu* were reported to exist.[29] Under what is known as lesser *bao gan dao hu* – the less extreme form conforming to the account above – the team collects from households contributions to agricultural tax, accumulation and welfare funds and to state procurement quota. It also retains a few team-level enterprises in non-crop activities. Under the system known as the greater *bao gan dao hu* – the more extreme form – team members only make a small contribution for welfare and cadres. There is no collective accumulation, tax, quota for sales to state or team-level enterprise. No doubt the spectrum between these two types is more or less a continuous one.

It is also useful to note that there are certain radical experiments that go beyond the eight broad types described above. In this category belongs the separation of economic and administrative functions of the commune and the consequent delinking of the three tiers of the commune system. This will be discussed in detail in a subsequent section.

Contracting with households

It is clear that contracting with households has become the main form of the responsibility system in China. However, its spread seems to have faced successful resistance in some areas, particularly among the advanced communes.

> There is no need for the rural areas around the suburbs of Shanghai, said leading members from the city, to adopt the system of fixing output quotas on the basis of households. The lèvel of collective economic development is high and the tasks confronting agriculture are to continue to develop production and better serve the city.[30]

After making an inspection tour of the rural areas early in 1981, Premier Zhao Ziyang instructed that different forms of the responsibility system should be adopted to suit different levels of development. His recommendations were as follows:[31]

> – Advanced regions (where the collective economy is relatively consolidated, production develops year by year and peasants' lives improve annually) should mainly adopt the system of responsibility for a special line of production under a contract. The peasants should voluntarily organise themselves into groups based on a division of labour and specialisation and undertake tasks given by the production teams.
>
> – Regions in an intermediate state should adopt the system of assigning output quotas to individual able-bodied labourers under the unified administration of the production teams. (More or less similar to the piece-work wage system in factories).
>
> – Poor and backward regions should introduce the system of fixing output quotas based on households.

Thus, a contract of type 1 discussed above was recommended for the advanced regions. For the intermediate area type 2 was recommended although it is puzzling that it was compared with 'piece-work wage system in factories'. For the poor and backward areas the recommended varieties of contract were *bao chan dao hu* (BCDH) or *bao gan dao hu* (BGDH).

It is not difficult to understand why the collective farmers in advanced areas would be unwilling to go back to a system that basically resembles peasant farming. These teams are relatively highly mechanised. There would be diseconomies of too small scale if the unit of operation were suddenly reduced.[32] There would also be practical difficulties in splitting up the smaller equipment and assets among households. Even so, specialised lines contract was being practised by no more than 5 per cent of the teams by the end of 1981 in China as a whole. In a province like Sichuan its quantitative significance has virtually vanished. This implies that in some provinces – particularly in the agriculturally prosperous ones – the proportion of teams practising this method may still be quite high.

As already indicated, contracting with households has by now encompassed over three-quarters of the teams in China. According to all available indications it is still growing and will perhaps continue to do so for some time until a hard core of advanced teams and those (like plantation crops) which cannot adopt the structure of peasant agriculture efficiently remain the only ones outside this system.

Of the two main forms of contracting with households, BGDH is by far the more widely prevalent and rapidly growing form. Indeed, it appears that BCDH is gradually losing out to BGDH although the former had preceded the latter in terms of temporal sequence. In justifying this trend it has been argued in the official press that *in principle* there was little difference between the two systems while there was a great deal of practical advantage in BGDH because it avoids the unnecessary two way movement of quota ouput.

In the absence of complete information on the standard forms of legal contracts it is difficult to know with certainty if the difference between the two systems is nominal or of substance. We shall try to compare the two systems in a hypothetical example of a team, using whatever is known about the method of operation of the two systems. It should be emphasised that our understanding of the detailed practices of the two systems is sometimes based on fragmentary information. Also, in view of the great diversity of form each system takes in practice, it is unlikely that our stylised examples would apply universally.

Let us assume that our hypothetical team has three households, *A*, *B* and *C*. They are equal in size (say four members in each) and have the same amount of land (say six *mou* each) contracted out from the team.[33] Their productivities differ due partly to the difference in their labour endownment, partly to skill differences and partly to differences in the ability to finance the purchase of inputs (including the endowment of capital inputs).

Table 3.2 shows the situation in the case of BCDH under the following assumptions: (a) The quota outputs are the same for all three households (3000 jin) since land in quantity and quality is about the same. The quota or target is set in the contract in such a way that all are able to fulfil it and the more productive households are able to exceed it easily. The quota is below the level of average output. This seems to

TABLE 3.2 *A hypothetical case of bao chan dao hu (BCDH)*

	A	*B*	*C*	*Total*
Quota output (jin)	3000	3000	3000	9000
Actual output (jin)	3000	4500	6000	13 500
Team's sales to state (jin)				
Basic quota[a]				1350
Premium quota[b]				900
Team's sales in free market[c] (jin)				1050
Food ration (jin)	1600	1600	1600	4800
Tax, welfare, accumulation and reserve fund in kind (jin)	300	300	300	900
Distributed cash collective income (yuan)[d]	160	160	160	480
Value of total distributed collective income (cash and food ration valued @ 0.1 yuan/jin)	320	320	320	960
Income from sale of above quota output in free market (yuan)		300	600	
Total family income (yuan)	320	620	920	

[a] Assumed price per jin = 0.1 yuan
[b] Assumed price per jin = 0.15 yuan
[c] Assumed price per jin = 0.2 yuan
[d] This is found as follows:

$$0.1\,Q_1 + 0.15\,Q_2 + 0.2\,Q_3$$

where Q_1 = basic quota
Q_2 = premium quota
Q_3 = free market sale

For simplicity of calculation contributions towards tax, welfare, accumulation and reserve are netted out in kind so that the entire revenue from sales is distributed.

conform to what is known to be the actual practice except that, in reality, not all households are always able to fulfil the quota. We shall discuss the case of unfulfilled quotas later. (b) Actual output of *A* is the same as the quota, of *B* 50 per cent higher and of *C* 100 per cent higher due to factors noted above. (c) According to the terms of the contract, quota outputs are turned over to the team while the above-quota outputs are completely retained by the households (100 per cent bonus.[34] (d) The team sets aside 10 per cent of the quota output (in kind) as provision for tax and contribution to welfare, accumulation and reserve funds. The remainder is sold. A basic procurement quota–amounting to 15 per cent of quota output–is sold to the state at a basic procurement price of 0.1 yuan per jin. Another quota of 10 per cent of quota output is sold to the state at a premium price of 0.15 yuan per jin. Per capita food ration is

400 jin (per family 1600 jin). The rest is sold in the free market where the price is assumed to be 0.2 yuan per jin.[35] (e) The revenue from sales constitutes the distributed 'collective income' as provisions for tax, accumulation, welfare and reserve have already been made. Since work points are proportional to fulfilled quota outputs the three households earn the same amounts of work points and receive the same 'collective income', a part of which is in the form of food ration. The latter is converted into cash value at the ration price which is the same as the basic procurement price. (f) The above quota outputs, which are retained by the households, are sold in the free market.

Table 3.3 shows the outcome in the case of BGDH under identical conditions with respect to production. It is assumed that each household makes the same contribution to the team's fund for taxation, accumulation, welfare and reserve as under BCDH and that the team's procurement quotas are divided among the households in the same proportion as the land they contracted out. It is further assumed that each household makes a provision for food consumption which is the same as their food ration under BCDH and it is valued at the basic procurement price.[36]. The remaining outputs are sold in the free market.

It is now possible to analyse the characteristics of the two systems and compare them. The first fact to note is that the outcomes in terms of family incomes and income distribution are identical under BCDH and BGDH under the assumptions made above. We shall later examine the circumstances under which the two systems would result in different outcomes.

TABLE 3.3 *A hypothetical case of bao gan dao hu (BGDH)*

	A	*B*	*C*
Actual output (jin)	3000	4500	6000
Contribution in kind towards team's tax, accumulation, welfare and reserve fund (jin)	300	300	300
Retained output (jin)	2700	4200	5700
Provision for consumption (jin)	1600	1600	1600
Sale to state			
Basic procurement (jin)	450	450	450
Premium procurement (jin)	300	300	300
Sale in free market (jin)	350	1850	3350
Value of sales (yuan)	160	460	760
Value of self consumption (@0.1 yuan per jin)	160	160	160
Total family income (yuan)	320	620	920

Both the systems resemble fixed rental tenancy. The payment of rent would arise due to:

(i) the contribution made to the team's tax, accumulation, welfare and reserve funds; and
(ii) the concealed payment due to sale to the state at prices below that in the free market.

Evaluating (i) at the market price and adding (ii) to it, the total rent turns out to be 120 yuan for each of the three households. This amount is invariant with respect to actual output. For household A rent is 20 per cent of the 'potential value' of output.[37] For B rent is 13.3 per cent of the potential value of output and for C only 10 per cent. Note, however, that under a less than 100 per cent bonus BCDH would no longer be a fixed tenancy. The ratio of rent to potential value of output at the margin would no longer be zero but would vary inversely with the rate of bonus.

Both the systems reward households more than proportionately for the differences in their performance in terms of productivity. This seems to be inevitable under BGDH due to the combination of (i) fixed rental on land, and (ii) the opportunity of higher prices being available only to those who are able to achieve progressively higher levels of productivity. Under the usual case of BCDH – such as the one shown in Table 3.2 – the same result obtains. Thus, the ratios of income and productivities of the pairs of households compare as follows under both systems shown in the Tables 3.2 and 3.3:[38]

Pair of households	*Ratio of income*	*Ratio of productivity*
B/A	1.94	1.50
C/B	1.48	1.33
C/A	2.88	2.00

While this result seems to be inevitable under BGDH the outcome under BCDH would be different depending on a number of factors, some of which may be enumerated as follows. First, BCDH would protect a demographically disadvantaged poor household far better as the household would qualify for a larger aggregate food ration. Thus, consider the possibility of household A having an additional member (who is not in the labour force).

Under BGDH the only way this family can consume the same per capita amount of food would be by partially defaulting on premium procurement. If as before one values self-consumption at the ration price, the value of *A's* income would fall further and income disparities widen. Under BCDH family *A* would qualify for an additional 400 jin of food ration which, according to our convention, would add an additional 40 yuan to its income. As a result the team's sale in the free market would decline by an equivalent amount, resulting in a decline in per family distributed collective cash income of 26.7 yuan. The net result would be an increase in *A's* income (by 13.3 yuan) and a decline in that of *B* and *C* (by 26.7 yuan each) resulting in the following income disparities:[39]

B/A : 1.78
C/B : 1.51
C/A : 2.68

The poorest family is better off under BCDH than it would be under BGDH and the disparities between its income and that of the richer ones would be significantly lower.

A second source of difference between the outcomes of BCDH and BGDH has already been noted, namely, the possibility of less than 100 per cent bonus on above-quota output under BCDH. By making the bonus a gradually declining proportion of above-quota output one could make income disparities lower than the disparities in productivity. Short of introducing a progressive income tax there is no comparable instrument available under BGDH.

Summary and conclusions

Since 1979 China has been experimenting with a wide variety of forms of contracts between the team on the one hand and households, individuals and groups on the other. By 1982 it was very clear that the overwhelmingly dominant form of contracting was with households. Other forms appear to have been relegated either to the prosperous and productive teams, which found it both unnecessary and undesirable to adopt such a system, or to those teams which were engaged in specialised practices unsuitable for family based farming.

Contracting with households has two main forms of which *bao gan dao hu* (BGDH) is by far the more widely practised one. This is essentially a system of guaranteed tenancy – peasant control of land – at a fixed rent. The possibility of access to more remunerative prices only at increasingly higher levels of output has the effect of making the marginal tax rate of the system vanish. Reward for higher productivity is more than proportionate to the difference in productive efficiency. In this sense the principle of distribution goes beyond the officially endorsed one of 'to each according to his work'.

The other type of contracting with households – *bao chan dao hu* (BCDH) – also resembles a system of guaranteed, fixed rent tenancy in the main form in which it is practised. Indeed, in the form in which it is usually practised, it need not lead to an outcome that is, in any significant way, different from that under BGDH. However, in principle and/or under conditions of poverty caused by unfavourable demographic conditions, it can provide better protection to the poorer households.

Official policy pronouncements strongly dispute that the system amounts to the dismantling of the collective and the restoration of individual farming. The document summarising the National Conference on Rural Work Convened by the CPC Central Committee at the end of 1981 based such a defence on the following points:[40]

(i) Land continues to be publicly owned and its sale is not permitted.
(ii) The collective still administers the utilisation of land, large-size farm tools and water conservancy facilities.
(iii) Some production teams also engage in agricultural capital construction. (Note that it is not claimed that all teams are engaged in such activities to some extent.)
(iv) Production teams retain a part of the output to 'provide for the members of revolutionary martyrs' families, soldiers' dependents and people who have financial difficulties'.

The above characteristics are hardly inconsistent with a basically peasant farming system. Land is nominally owned by the state even in the non-socialist countries and a peasant need not have formal ownership of land as long as he has access to returns from it. In a typical South Asian country peasants buy the services of large-sized farm tools and irrigation facilities which are owned by the public authorities. Public and collective authorities frequently dictate cropping patterns.[41] Some amount of capital construction by public or co-operative authorities and a levy on household output are quite consistent with peasant farming and are widely observed in contemporary non-socialist Asia. Under BGDH and BCDH peasants have the essential benefit of ownership of land in so far as they are the recipients of the factor income of land after the payment of a fixed rental. They can own implements. In Sichuan some peasant households were reported to own power tillers.

Households can obtain production loans from banks. Hiring of wage labour is not permitted. Mutual exchange of labour is encouraged. One, however, wonders how easy it is to identify clearly the borderline between hired labour and exchange labour.

It may be argued that if the system is in effect a form of peasant farming then it is an extraordinarily egalitarian one in so far as the amount of per capita land, in quality units, is the same for each household. This, however, is true only for a given team. Between teams – more importantly between areas with different land/labour ratios – there must exist a substantial difference between peasant households in terms of land endowment.[42] Such a difference is compounded, first, due to the differences in labour and other resource endowments between households and, secondly, by the disproportionate increase in income for those having higher output due to the regressive fiscal structure embodied in the system of rent and procurement.

The effect of the reforms on the distribution of income must still be regarded as an empirical question to be verified on the basis of factual evidence. If, however, such evidence shows an increase in inequality, one could interpret it as a success achieved by the Chinese policy-makers in their quest to 'curb the tendency towards egalitarianism'.

Clearly the system is highly oriented towards the promotion of individual incentive. Previously the system of taxation and procurement was such that a collective unit paid a considerably lower rate of average tax by increasing its output.[43] The system of contracting with households has brought this down to the level of households. One should expect a positive effect on production of such a shift in incentives on the assumption that incentives at the level of the collective units are not enough unless there is a mechanism to allow such incentives to percolate down to individual households. The implication is that, with the possible exception of the handful of advanced teams, the teams in rural China failed to develop such a mechanism.

SEPARATION OF ECONOMIC AND POLITICAL POWER

The 1982 Constitution published in draft form at the Fifth National Peoples Congress and finally adopted in December 1982 stipulates the reinstatement of township governments and the stripping of the communes of all political, administrative and non-economic powers and functions. Even before the draft Constitution made the proposal, reports had become public about the experimental separation of government administration from the economic functions of the commune. These experiments were being carried out in three counties of Sichuan. The authors visited such experimental cases in two of these counties, namely, Qionglai and Guanghan.

In July 1982 two members of the Commission for Legal Affairs of the National People's Congress Standing Committee said in a published article:[44]

> once the Constitution has been formally adopted by the National Peoples Congress, the government will conduct experiments on a larger scale than the current trials done is several counties. Experiences will be summed up and on this basis, concrete laws and policies will be formulated. It will take several years to complete this reform step by step in the light of local situations.

The draft Constitution was formally adopted by the National Peoples Congress in the beginning of December 1982. The stage has now been set for the nationwide replication of the model tried out in the three counties in Sichuan. It is, therefore, important to understand the true extent of these reforms.

Reasons behind the change

In official discussions four main advantages are claimed for the new system and these are cited as the reasons behind their adoption. First, it is conducive to the independent management of the rural collective economic organisations:

> Under the . . . system of combining government administration with commune management, too much administrative interference makes independent business accounting difficult. For instance, before the system has changed, government imposed unpaid labour required from the Xiang and People's Commune in Sichuan Province averaged 10 per cent of its total amount of labour every year. Furthermore, the commune itself also used the labour power and funds of the production teams without remuneration, thus interfering with team production and distribution.

The second advantage claimed for the change is related to the vast expansion of enterprises engaged in non-stop activities in recent years. It is claimed that in many such enterprises economies of scale are so great that:

> trans-commune and trans-regional economic joint enterprises, such as

> agricultural–industrial–commercial complexes and other companies dealing with seeds, plant protection, agrotechnology and farm machinery have emerged . . . An agricultural–industrial–commercial complex may embrace several communes, or even factories and other enterprises in the urban area. Therefore, maintaining a common government administration and commune management is obviously not beneficial to the growth of production.

Thirdly, it is claimed that the commune cadres hold too many posts and are not able to give due attention to economic work. Because they are simultaneously government administrators and economic managers, their attention is divided.

> It is hard to establish a strict responsibility system in their work. The separation of the two will enable the local government to supervise and give guidance to the grass-roots level through planning, finances, taxation, bank loans and commodity pricing. It will free grass-roots rural economic organisations to manage their own production and business affairs.

Finally, it is claimed that the new system would strengthen political power at the local level.

> As a result [of the institution of the responsibility system], the tasks of mediating disputes, maintaining public security, tax collection, village construction and providing welfare facilities have become heavier. They require stronger local political organisations . . . However, under the present system, when the busy farming seasons come, commune leaders have to devote all their energy to production. Their work as political leaders cannot but be weakened. The separation of the two will lead to the establishment of township governments and villagers committees that can devote all their time to political power building and administration. This will contribute to peace and stability.

One cannot evaluate these claims in the abstract. One must know what actual changes have taken place. To do so one must look at the experiments carried out in the three counties of Sichuan.

The experiments in Sichuan

The above account appears to suggest that the change amounts to no more than taking away the administrative and political functions from the top tier of the three-tiered commune organisation and leaving the rest of the commune, including all the economic linkages among the three tiers, unchanged. If the experiments in Sichuan, which are meant to serve as prototypes of the coming reform, are any guide then the changes must be regarded as of much greater consequence.

Let us take the example of Guanghan county in Sichuan, about 40 kilometres north of the provincial capital, Chengdu. The county had twenty-three *xiangs* (administrative entities below *xien*, or county), 265 villages and 2459 production teams. In October 1980 the new experiment was started in a limited number of communes and in September 1981 it was extended all over the county. The main changes were as follows:

(a) The communes ceased to exist. Their administrative functions were taken over by xiang governments. These governments were not necessarily co-extensive with the former communes. For example, the administrative functions of the particular commune visited by the authors were divided among three xiang governments. The economic enterprises of the commune were organised into a joint corporation (in the case visited by the authors, the Jinan Joint Corporation managing twenty-eight enterprises formerly run by the commune).
(b) Brigades were converted into companies at the village level operating their enterprises.
(c) The teams were renamed agricultural co-operatives and adopted various forms of the responsibility system.

Each enterprise directly managed by the Jinan Joint Corporation retains 20 per cent of its profits for 'expanded production'. Thirty per cent of the profits are retained by the Corporation for new investment and other purposes. The remaining 50 per cent of the profits are distributed among the share holders who are mainly the agricultural co-operatives (former teams) and villages (former brigades).

The shares representing the value of fixed assets at the time of the formation of the Corporation were allocated among the co-operatives and villages. Half the shares were divided on the principle of an equal amount per person and the other half on the basis of an equal amount per unit of land. These shares cannot be redeemed although they may be sold.

The Corporation has issued new shares on the expanded assets since its formation. These new shares can be purchased by anybody including individuals and households. Most such shares are, however, owned by the co-operatives and the villages. Officials claimed that the private ownership of shares was discouraged and that only 1 per cent of the shares were held privately. Shares earned a fixed rate of dividend of 12 per cent which is several times higher than the return on saving deposits.

Workers are drawn from the co-operatives although recently recruitment has also been made from the towns.[46] Workers are paid wages according to piece rates. Workers drawn from the co-operatives retain their basic affiliation to the co-operatives by paying 5 per cent of their wages as a contribution to the latter's accumulation and welfare funds.

Enterprises can also be set up at village level (under the joint companies managing the former brigade enterprises or as enterprises sponsored jointly by several co-operatives), at the level of the co-operatives or even at the level of households. The authors did not collect direct information on the joint companies (i.e. the companies now managing the former brigade-level enterprises) but it appears that the disposal of their shares and profits among the co-operatives follows the same general principles as in the case of the Joint Corporation.

Qionglai is another county in Sichuan which started to experiment in 1980. Here also the administrative functions of the commune were taken over by the newly created xiang government. Our attention was focused on the Phoenix Joint Corporation which managed the enterprises that had been under the brigade of the same name. What happened to the former commune-level enterprises is not clear.[47] It was, however, clear that the Phoenix Joint Corporation was itself some kind of an apex body rather than being affiliated to one. The Corporation has under it the following four companies:

(i) Oil and Cereal company. This is concerned with the production of oilseeds and cereals. It was formed by the merger of the five teams that had belonged to the erstwhile brigade. The 201 households with 852 persons and 345 workers who belonged to the five teams are all members of this company which supplies labourers to the other companies listed below and to the Corporation. In this sense, this is the basic company of the system.

(ii) Industrial Company. It manages brick production, the brewery, the chemical plant and other industrial enterprises.

(iii) Commercial Company. Its responsibility is to market the products produced in the enterprises managed by the Corporation and the companies.

(iv) Sideline Company. It manages non-oil cash crops and collective sideline activities.

The agricultural company, i.e. the Oil and Cereal Company, practises contracting along specialised lines and contracting with individual workers. The other companies also practise the responsibility system by contracting along specialised lines. The Corporation enters into contract with various companies which in turn enter into contract with workshops and groups. Workers are paid according to piece rates in workpoints at their teams (which are merged into the Oil and Cereal Company).

Households can own shares of the Corporation which have a high fixed rate of dividend of 20 per cent. Nearly 88 per cent of the households owned some shares, the range of ownership per household being 200 yuan to 2000 yuan. More than sixty households each owned more than 1000 yuan worth of shares.

Both in Guanghan and Qionglai the rates of output and income growth have been very high. Industrial growth has been the major source of overall growth. We have deliberately avoided giving details of output performance[48] because it would be hard to claim that it was due mainly to the kind of institutional change under discussion. The role played by assistance from the government and the extent to which performance was due to other independent factors are impossible to determine.

Some conclusions

It should be clear that the reform does not merely amount to the taking away of the administrative and political functions from the highest tier of the three-tiered commune organisation. It amounts to the abolition of the three-tiered organisation as it has existed over nearly a quarter of a century. The communes have ceased to exist; their administrative and political functions have been taken over by the xiang governments and their economic functions have been reorganised in the form of corporations.[49] The economic enterprises at the brigade level have also been formed into corporations or companies. The three levels have effectively been delinked and the teams have been converted into autonomous co-operatives.

The linkage between the co-operatives and the higher level corporations through the holding of shares exists because of the need to distribute ownership among those who historically accounted for the accumulation. Similarly, the practice in some places – as in the Phoenix Corporation in Qionglai – of paying the workers in terms of workpoints in their teams is an accounting device to facilitate the collection of contributions to teams from these workers. The teams appear to have little freedom to redistribute such payments among the workers. The linkages among the three levels by way of promoting capital construction, accumulation and redistribution have been severed. Indeed, it is hard to argue that the three levels continue to exist in any meaningful functional sense.

In the past brigades looked after capital construction that transcended team boundaries and communes looked after capital construction that transcended brigade boundaries. This was matched by an automatic ability of the higher levels to mobilise labour from the lower units. For example, a commune could ask teams to contribute labour for commune-level capital construction. The workers would receive workpoints in the teams. The system would amount to a proportional taxation on all team members' collective income. Now the mechanism has been abolished. The only way to organise such capital construction would be the conventional one followed in contemporary developing countries, namely, the xiang, county or higher level of government to undertake the work and finance it from its own revenue.

The cost of providing local public administration and defence through a network independent of the economic organisation may increase efficiency. It has, however, been admitted in official writings that there has been an increase in the demand for these services and that this increase is a direct result of the spread of the responsibility system.[50] Also the new system will undoubtedly increase the cost of providing these services. This cost will have to be met through the conventional instruments of public finance which have a limited manoeuvrability in a low-income country.

The adoption of the new Constitution in December 1982, with the provision for the nationwide replication of the three-county experiments in Sichuan, signals another wave of sweeping change in rural China in the coming years. It is quite possible that in its wake the formal structure of the three-level commune organisation, that survived the responsibility system at least in name, will be wiped out.

AN INTERIM EVALUATION OF THE RESPONSIBILITY SYSTEM

Too little time has elapsed since the responsibility system was instituted in rural China to permit a thorough factual analysis of the effects of the reforms. However, there are important reasons why one is justified in attempting an interim evaluation, especially of the effect on production. If there is truth in the official indictment of the preceding system then incentives and discipline had broken down completely. Quick and dramatic results of the reforms would then be expected. Indeed, numerous claims have been made in reports about the performance of the responsibility system in different localities. These reports are replete with claims of more than 100 per cent increase in output over a three-year period (1981 over 1978) attributed to the institution of this system. In his speech at the Central Committee Party School Du Runsheng, Vice-Minister in charge of the State Agricultural Commission, tried to estimate the average gain in output due to the responsibility system in the following words: 'I found that in areas where the two forms [of the system] have been instituted, production has increased by an average of 30 per cent. A few production figures have doubled or even tripled.'[51]

By 1981 the responsibility system had spread to more than 90 per cent of the teams across the nation and the two forms of comprehensive contracting with households (BCDH and BGDH) had been in operation in more than two-thirds of the teams. If, as is implied by the official pronouncements, the incentives and enthusiasm for production have been radically transformed in such an overwhelming proportion of the teams then the resulting output should certainly show a discontinuous jump between 1978 – the year immediately preceding the institution of the system – and 1981.

For both 1978 and 1981 official communiqués on fulfilment of national economic plans claimed that many localities in China were hit by drought and other natural disasters. For a country of China's continental dimensions nothing else seems normal for an average year. It appears reasonable to assume that any variation between the two years with respect to these circumstances was small.

Tables 3.4 and 3.5 contain some indicators of agricultural growth in China in recent years with a measure of overall growth of agriculture since 1952. According to the official estimates the value of output at constant prices increased at an annual rate of 5.64 per cent between 1978 and 1981.[52] This is about the same – 5.62 per cent – as revealed by our estimates of output value based on the average export prices for the years 1978–80.[53]

Clearly the rate of growth in agricultural output in the three years since the institution of the responsibility system has been substantially higher than the long-term rate of growth. Over the period between 1952 and 1978 the rate of growth in agricultural output was 3.25 per cent per year according to the official index reported in Table 3.4. The long-term *trend* rate of growth in grain output has been about 3 per cent per year.[54] The rate of growth experienced by the agricultural sector in the three years since the institution of the responsibility system was, therefore,

TABLE 3.4 *Growth of output and income*

	1957	*1965*	*1978*	*1979*	*1980*	*1981*
1. Index of agricultural output value at constant price (base 1952)	124.8	137.1	229.6		256.1	270.7
2. Index of agricultural output value at export price (base 1978)			100.0	110.86	112.60	117.82
3. Average per capita income of rural households (current yuan)			133.6	160.2	191.3	223.4
of which:						
Collective distribution			88.5			116.2
Family sideline			35.8			84.5
Remittance, relief & irregular receipt			9.3			22.7
4. Average per capita income of rural households (at 1978 price)			133.6	157.7	181.6	210.5

NOTES 1. Official estimate by the State Statistical Bureau 'at comparable prices' reported in *Beijing Review*, No. 48, 1982.
2. Estimate by the authors using average export prices of 1978–80 and production figures from official Chinese sources.
3. Information supplied by Mr He of State Statistical Bureau on 4 August 1982 at a meeting at the CASS, Beijing.
4. This is obtained by deflating 3 by the index of retail prices in the countryside supplied at the meeting mentioned under Note 3.

nearly three-quarters higher than the growth rate over more than a quarter century since 1952.

However, the rate of growth since the institution of the responsibility system was by no means an historically unprecedented short-term rate in the post-liberation period. In many ways the period that one is reminded of as being closely comparable is that of readjustment beginning in 1962. The rate of growth in agricultural output value in the four years after 1961 averaged well over 10 per cent per year. One should add that this partly reflected the dismally low output in the years leading to 1961 and that, calculated over a normal base, the rate of growth in the years thereafter would be lower.

One notable fact about agricultural growth since the institution of the responsibility system is that the output of grains has increased at a low rate – much lower than the rate at which it grew over the long period and at a small fraction of the rate at which the agricultural sector grew. Land

TABLE 3.5 *Agricultural Production and Inputs*

	1978	*1981*	*Annual compound rate of increase*
Annual production of crops (million tons)			
Grain	304.75	325.02	2.17
Cotton	2.167	2.968	11.05
Oil-bearing crops	5.218	10.205	25.06
Sugar-cane	21.117	29.668	12.00
Jute and ambary hemp	1.088	1.260	5.01
Tea	0.268	0.343	8.57
Pork, beef and mutton	8.563	12.609	13.77
Pigs sold to the market (million heads)	170.49	194.95	4.57
Chemical fertiliser production (million tons)	8.693	12.390	12.54
Large and medium tractors in use (thousand)	557	792	12.45
Hand tractors in use (million)	1.37	2.04	14.14
Power driven drainage and irrigation machines (million hp)	65.58	74.98	4.57

SOURCE *Beijing Review*, No. 27, 1979 and Nos. 20 and 35, 1982.

area under grains reportedly declined by 6 million hectares between 1977 and 1980.[55] It appears that the doctrine of 'grain as the key link' was backed up by numerous administrative dictates in the past. This resulted in too much emphasis on grain production irrespective of the suitability of land. It also seems that the grain ration used to be less for those engaged in non-grain producing activities than for those producing grain.[56] These disincentives came to an end after 1978. The increase in the purchasing price in 1979 was generally lower for grains than for cash crops. As a result of all these factors grain area declined and output increased at a low rate. In official discussions this has been cited as an example of efficient readjustment. For example, it was reported that in one area the non-labour cost of producing a half kilogramme of rice declined from 7.26 fen in 1976 to 2.27 fen in 1980 and 1981 mainly due to the discontinuation of rice cultivation on unsuitable plots on which cultivation was forced in the past.[57]

The growth rates in the output of cash crops (such as cotton, oil seeds, sugar-cane and tea) and meat have been far above the overall rate of growth in agriculture. Incentives were shifted sharply in favour of these products and it is, therefore, not surprising that their outputs grew much faster.

The rate of growth in yield of grains per hectare must have been higher than that of output as the area under these crops is known to have fallen despite a modest rate of increase in output. Although direct estimates of area are not available for them, it seems probable that the growth rate in yield of most cash crops per hectare was lower than that in their output as the land diverted away from grains must have gone into these crops.

An important point arising out of the above is the possible role played by the increased procurement and purchase prices in promoting agricultural growth. Table 3.4 shows that the per capita income of rural households increased by 57.6 per cent between 1978 and 1981 even after allowance is made for the increase in retail prices in the countryside.[58] Over the same period agricultural output value at constant prices increased by only about 17.9 per cent. The geometric difference between the two – 33.7 per cent – is a little less than the rate of improvement in the terms of trade of the agricultural sector, which was 36 per cent over the same time period.[59]

In China it is customary nowadays to subtract from the earnings of a collective unit the effect of increased purchase prices and other physical factors and claim that the residual is due to greater enthusiasm promoted by the responsibility system among the peasants.[60] One might argue that a separation of enthusiasm from prices is not justified in so far as the enthusiasm was largely due to the price incentive. What is more important to note is that such a massive incentive in the form of a 36 per cent improvement in the sectoral terms of trade of agriculture over a three-year period would almost certainly have promoted enthusiasm and incentive under the older collectivised form. Collective units might have been promoted to greater productive efforts and might have been able to generate greater surplus for the absorption of more modern inputs if such opportunities had been available to them.

There are convincing precedents within collective experiments of a similar outcome. In the case of the Soviet Central Asian Republics, the greater productivity and prosperity of the rural economy appears to have been based on the rejection of the doctrine of 'primitive socialist accumulation' in the case of their main product, cotton. The favourable terms of trade introduced in the mid 1930s created an unprecedented prosperity in the rural economy of these republics within the framework of collective agriculture.[61] One need not argue that incentives through the older collective organisation would have achieved equivalent results and that they would have been easy to organise. The point merely is that the claim that the 'residual' increase in output was due entirely to private incentives under the responsibility system is exaggerated.

The distribution of income

During the field visit in Sichuan and Yunnan we came across a good deal of data on the distribution of income among members of teams, and the distribution of average income among collective units belonging to a higher level of collective (e.g. teams of a brigade, brigades of a commune and communes in a county). These data invariably pertained to what is known as 'distributed collective income'. It includes the value of output on land contracted out to the households.

The practice itself is somewhat odd, especially under the *bao gan dao hu* contracts which do not even have a quota output except the implicit norm on the basis of which the procurement quotas are determined. This is a qualitative departure from the definition of collective output under the system prior to the institution of the responsibility system. In the past collective income referred to the income derived from the collectively produced and distributed output. Today the bulk of it is produced on contracted out land and retained by the households outside collective distribution. Thus while under the old system the collective unit had exact knowledge of distributed collective income, under the present system what goes under this name is at best made voluntarily known by the individual households. Although most teams still appear to have the information, one has little basis for thinking that its reliability is the same as in the past.

Even on the basis of the changed definition, collective distributed income in rural China in 1981 amounted to only 52 per cent of household income.[62] The remainder consists of family sideline (38 per cent) and remittances, relief and irregular receipts (together amounting to 10 per cent). To base one's judgement about the degree of egalitarianism on the distribution of the so-called collective income would be unjustified. This is particularly so in view of the absence of any knowledge about the relationship between the patterns of the distribution of collective income and that from sidelines and other sources.

Information on the distribution of family income should, however, be available from a survey of 18 529 peasant households carried out by the State Statistical Bureau all over China. Information on per capita income and its sources in Table 3.4 (item 3) is derived from this survey.[63] Unfortunately, the data on the distribution of income from this survey have not been published. Once it becomes available interesting insights may become possible on this important question which has, for a long time, been discussed on the basis of indirect and partial evidence.

Some fragmentary information from the survey of households in Yunnan province is available. This has been reproduced in Table 3.6. An analysis of change over time is not possible because nothing is known about the past distribution of income in rural Yunnan even on the basis of partial data or indirect evidence. Nor can a clear judgement be formed about the current degree of egalitarianism in the absence of information on the average income or income share of each group. One merely notes that the distribution reveals considerable – though perhaps not excessive – inequality.[64]

While available empirical evidence does not provide much help in identifying the direction and magnitude of change in income distribution, the presence of a number of factors unleashing forces of greater inequality has been noted. The most important is the system of reward that makes the difference in payments to households more than proportional to the difference in their productivities. This has been discussed at length in a previous section. In China, as in any other country of continental dimension, differences between regions have always been high.[65] Ample evidence of substantial difference between collective units is also available.[66] Nothing is known to have happened to reduce these inequalities. And yet, without a firm empirical basis, it would be hazardous to arrive at a judgement on the direction of change in the distribution of income. Too many changes have taken place encompassing such varied aspects as the magnitude and variety of sideline activities, the commitment to engage in 'collective activities', the spread of the private market and the opportunity for non-farm

TABLE 3.6 *Distribution of net collective and private income of 610 households in Yunnan*

Range of income in Yuan	*Number of households in 1980*	*1981*
Above 300	29	54
201–300	105	147
121–200	278	267
80–120	143	106
Below 80	55	36

SOURCE Provincial Statistical Bureau of Yunnan quoted in *Yunnan Ribao*, 24 April 1982.

employment. It would be impossible to trace the income distribution effects on purely *a priori* grounds through this maze.

The policy-makers appear to be aware of the possibility that the responsibility system has adversely affected the weaker and poorer households. Various kinds of measures have been devised to provide such families with protection. The package that is used in Fengyang county, Anhui province to assist the bottom 9 per cent of the households, who have less than 700 jin of grain ration and less than 50 yuan of cash income per capita, is probably representative of such measures. These are as follows:[67]

(1) The households are exempted from compulsory procurement so that they are able to sell their products at premium, or negotiated, or free market prices;
(2) School fees are waived for the children;
(3) Registration fees for medical visits are waived;
(4) Free service is provided for the insemination of sows;
(5) Credit co-operatives provide loans at low interest;
(6) Preferential treatment is accorded in the allocation of fertiliser and construction material; and
(7) State relief is given.

The quantitative magnitudes of all these measures in terms of coverage and as a proportion of income of those covered are not known. Many of these methods closely resemble the conventional income redistributive measures adopted in the non-socialist developing countries. This indicates the changed focus of redistributive measures in rural China – moving away from dependence on the system of payment towards relief and welfare measures.

Macroeconomic aspects

We shall begin with a description of the system for state procurement of agricultural output. The team is the basic unit on which the procurement quota is levied. As discussed above, depending on the form of contract, the quota is either fulfilled directly by the team or transferred to individuals, households or groups.

There is a basic procurement quota that must be fulfilled at *a basic price per unit fixed by the state.* Next, there usually is an additional quantity specified – a secondary quota that must also be fulfilled – for which a higher purchase price is offered. The premium on this secondary quota is 50 per cent of the basic procurement price for grains and oil-seeds and 30 per cent for cotton.

There is a third category of sale to the state after the two quotas are fulfilled. For this kind of sale the price has to be negotiated and agreed upon. It has been claimed by some officials that there is yet another quota for this kind of sale. This appears puzzling. If there is a requirement to fulfil this quota then in the negotiation about price the seller would have little role to play. If, on the other hand, there is no need to fulfil this quota then the seller would not sell at a price below the free market price and the difference between the negotiated sale to the state and the free market sale would vanish.

Finally, after fulfilling the procurement quotas, the seller can sell any surplus quantity in the free market. There is by now an extensive network of such markets both in rural and urban areas. Prices in the free market are substantially higher than the basic procurement price and significantly above the premium procurement price. The volume of sales in these markets has grown phenomenally in recent years. In most cases 'negotiated sales' to the state have practically become indistinguishable from the free market.

Table 3.7 summarises the available information on different prices. The purchasing price of farm and sideline products (column 3) has been increasing steadily since the early 1950s except during the decade 1965 to 1975. These prices have increased particularly rapidly since 1979. It is not stated clearly if the purchasing price of farm and sideline products (column 3) merely includes sales to the state or also sales in the free market. It is doubtful if there is any comprehensive accounting of prices and quantities in the mushrooming private markets all over the country.[68] It therefore seems almost certain that the purchasing price only refers to state purchases. In view of the fact that the free market price is higher than any procurement price and of the sharply rising share of the free market in total sales, the weighted average price of all sales must have risen even faster in recent years than is shown by the data in Table 3.7.

The retail price of industrial goods in rural areas has been remarkably constant over the three decades. A mild increase over the pre-Cultural Revolution period was followed by a decline during the Cultural Revolution. It has remained stable since then.

The index of the agricultural terms of trade, therefore, shows a steady increase over the entire period. However, the rate of increase steadily decelerated from 1952 through 1978. For the various sub-periods the

TABLE 3.7 *Some price indicators (Indices with 1950 base)*

Year	*Retail prices (1)*	*Cost of living of workers and staff members (2)*	*Purchasing price of farm and sideline products (3)*	*Retail price of industrial goods in rural areas (4)*	*Retail price in the countryside (of capital, industrial and agricultural goods) (5)*	*Index of agricultural sector's terms of trade (6)* = [(3) ÷ (4)] 100
1952	111.8	115.5	121.6	109.7		110.8
1957	121.3	126.6	146.2	112.1		130.4
1965	134.6	139.0	187.9	118.4		158.7
1975	131.9	139.5	208.7	109.6		190.4
1978	135.9	144.7	217.4	109.8	125.4	198.0
1979	138.6	147.4	265.5	109.9	127.4	241.6
1980	146.9	158.5	284.4	110.8	132.1	256.7
1981	150.5	162.4	301.2	111.9	133.1	269.2

SOURCE Columns 1 to 4 up to the year 1979: *Economic Readjustment and Reform*, China Today Series No. 3 published by *Beijing Review*, Beijing 1982, p. 215. The figures for 1980 and 1981 and column 5 supplied by a State Statistical Bureau official at a meeting at the CASS on 4 August 1982.

rates of improvement have been as follows:[69]

1952–7	3.3 per cent per year
1957–65	2.5 per cent per year
1965–75	1.8 per cent per year
1975–8	1.3 per cent per year

After 1978 the rate of improvement has been a staggering and unprecedented 10.8 per cent per year. The biggest rise was in 1979. On 1 July of that year the state purchase price of grain was increased by 20 per cent. The procurement prices of other agricultural products were increased more sharply.

Although state procurement prices have increased sharply, the retail prices of publicly distributed food have remained virtually unchanged. In recent years some increase has occurred in the prices of only the non-staple foods. Perhaps the following prices in Beijing are an indicator of the long-term stability in the distribution prices of the major products procured from agriculture or produced from the procured agricultural goods (yuan).[70]

	Rice (Kg)	*Flour (Kg)*	*White Cloth (Metre)*
1952	0.296	0.34	0.84
1980	0.304	0.37	0.84

The constancy of retail prices for public distribution, combined with the sharply rising purchase prices, has resulted in a large deficit in state trading in food and agricultural goods. As Table 3.8 shows, the 'subsidy on grain and oil-seeds' – presumably measured to be equal to the loss in state trading in these two commodities alone – amounted to 14.5 per cent of total state revenue and 3.7 per cent of national income.

Even before 1979 state trading and distribution of farm products had been gradually transformed over a long period from a major source of surplus to a modest deficit. In the 1950s and 1960s this was a main source of investible surplus for the economy. This declined steadily over time and was gradually replaced by the rising profit in the industrial sector as a source of surplus. In the industrial sector the rise in wages was kept below the rise in output per worker.

In the period after 1978 the industrial sector could no longer make up for the rising deficit in state trading in agricultural products. Indeed, it appears that the urgency of creating jobs in the urban areas and permitting an improvement in the living standards of the workers led to an increase in the wage bill in state and collective enterprises (44 per cent between 1978 and 1981) far in excess of the increase in the value of industrial output over the same period (23 per cent).[71]

It is, therefore, not surprising to find that public investment has declined sharply in recent years. At current prices the rate of decline is as much as 21 per cent in 1981 over 1980 (see Table 3.8).

In recent years Chinese policy-makers have been arguing that the rate of accumulation was too high in the past, that a lot of investment was unproductive and that a reduction in the rate of accumulation was desirable. The following quotation from a recent article by the Deputy Director of the Institute of Economics of the Chinese Academy of Social Sciences indicates the change in policy since 1979.[72]

> Accumulation is gradually being reduced to a more appropriate level, the efficiency with which it is used is being improved and the distribution of the accumulation fund is becoming more rational. The measures taken to achieve these ends include: a reduction in the rate of growth of heavy industry; cutbacks and restrictions on capital construction; increases in urban wages and rural incomes; a readjustment of the internal structure of production and especially of heavy industry; and acceleration of housing construction and urban development; an acceleration of development in science, education and health services; a lowering of production costs; a reduction of enterprise losses; and an improvement in enterprise profitability.

TABLE 3.8 *Some macroeconomic data (billion yuan)*

	1980	*1981*
Subsidy on grain and oil-seeds	11.39	14.32
Total purchase by state of agricultural and sideline products	84.22	95.50
The value of state purchase of agricultural and sideline products at 1978 prices	64.38	68.93
Additional receipt by agriculture due to price increase since 1978	19.84	26.57
Increase in income of urban employees over 1978 (more employees, higher wages and bonuses)	14.00	19.00
Total capital construction investment	53.94	42.79
National income	366.00	388.00
State revenue	108.52	106.43

SOURCE State Statistical Bureau estimates published in *Beijing Review*, No. 48, 1982 and supplied directly to the authors. National income consists of value added in the five sectors: agriculture, industry, commerce, construction, and transport and communication.

While most of these measures are desirable in themselves, it is very hard to argue that a reduction in reinvestible surplus is in itself a desirable objective for a country like China trying to accelerate its growth rate. The reduced investible surplus should be seen as the cost the society must bear in order to achieve whatever objectives may have prompted it to adopt policies that have caused such a reduction.

In China prices have been recognised to contain a great deal of irrationality. Consider the following extract from a recent statement by Liu Zhoufu, Director of the National Price Bureau:[73]

> It is true that, for complex and historical reasons, the present pricing system has many irrational elements. Sometimes, products whose supply is constantly in excess of demand are highly priced and provide their manufacturers with large profits, while goods which are in short supply are priced too low and their producers lose money as a result. For example, cotton textiles are fixed at low prices whereas chemical fibres are much too high. This has prompted textile mills to go into chemical fibre goods with a vengeance to the neglect of cotton cloth. Such a situation is definitely detrimental to the planned, proportionate development of the national economy.

It would be useful to analyse the rationale behind the procurement prices currently in use. There are several aspects of these prices that would be of interest, for example, the extent to which they reflect relative scarcities and the effect they have on the distribution of income.

It is not easy to identify the yardsticks for relative scarcities. One possible set of indicators would be free market prices. But information on them is not available and, even if it were, one might argue that free market prices were much distorted due to the operation of the public distribution covering a large segment of the overall market for the product.

The other set of indicators – the one chosen in this case – relates to the relative export prices China received for these commodities. These, too, are subject to numerous difficulties. Nothing is known about the quality difference between an export and the corresponding commodity sold to the state (although exported goods have been domestically procured). In principle, one would like to compare not the average export prices but the marginal export revenues.[74] The ratios of the latter would generally be different from the ratios of the former depending on the elasticities of demand for different exports. These objections are important but not an overriding reason for abandoning the exercise when the objective is no more than to identify only the most glaring irrationalities, if any.[75]

With the exception of those for rice (which is a major export) and groundnuts (which is a relatively less important export) the basic procurement prices of all other commodities are fairly high proportions of export prices and for wheat and cotton actually higher (see Table 3.9). This means that the premium procurement prices for these commodities are much higher than the export prices.[76] Cotton, an import substitute, appears to be in an extraordinarily favourable position.[77] The same is true to a lesser extent of wheat, another import substitute. Rice, an export, is most seriously discriminated against. Groundnuts, another export, is nearly equally discriminated against.

Quite apart from the irrationality of the relative prices, one would like to know the income redistributive effects of the procurement prices. Table 3.10 shows the ranking of the provinces of China according to per capita industrial and agricultural output value. The provinces specialising in the cultivation of rice are concentrated at the bottom. The incomes of these provinces – particularly of the peasants there – must have been adversely affected by the discriminatory price for rice. A good part of rice must be exported for the use of consumers in the richer northern provinces. More than a million tons (a million and a half tons in unhusked unit) have been exported abroad annually during the late

TABLE 3.9 *Procurement and export prices* (Yuan per ton)

Item	*Basic procurement price: Yuan/ton*	*Percentage of premium on above quota sale*	*Average export price 1980*	*Basic procurement price as percentage of average export price*
Wheat	326.4	50	293.74	111.1
Unhusked Rice	248.2	50	422.86	58.7
Maize	215.2	50	244.22	88.1
Cotton	2996	30	2142.00	139.9
Oil-bearing Crops:				
Groundnut	672	50	1054.86	63.7
Sesamum	1166.4	50	1271.51	91.7
Rape-seed	714.6	50	785.67	91.0

NOTE Export prices are from the FAO, *Trade Year Book*, Vol. 34, 1980. Dollar values have been converted by using the 1980 exchange rate of $1 = 1.53 yuan. For rice the export price has been reduced to two-thirds and a further deduction of 5 per cent for processing cost made to arrive at the 'export price of unhusked rice'. The procurement prices refer to a somewhat later date; but their increase since 1980 has been very modest, less than 5 per cent per year. It is possible that basic procurement prices have changed little between 1980 and 1981 and that the increase in overall purchasing price has been due to the rising shares of purchases at premium and negotiated prices.

TABLE 3.10 *Per capita total industrial and agricultural output value in 1981 (yuan)*

Rank	*Province/Region*	*Per capita output value*	*Cropping pattern*	*Rank*	*Province/Region*	*Per capita output value*	*Cropping pattern*
1	Shanghai	5558		17	Shaanxi	544	wheat/corn
2	Tianjin	2880		18	Inner Mongolia	540	
3	Beijing	2629		19	Gansu	528	
4	Liaoning	1524	corn/kaoliang/soybean	20	Ningxia	528	
5	Jiangsu	1128	wheat/rice	21	Qinghai	526	
6	Heilongjiang	1058	corn/kaoliang/soybean	22	Jiangxi	511	rice/tea
7	Jilin	860	corn/kaoliang/soybean	23	Henan	501	corn/kaoliang/wheat
8	Zhejiang	860	rice/tea	24	Anhui	499	rice/winter wheat
9	Hubei	764	rice/wheat	25	Sichuan	473	rice
10	Shandong	739	corn/kaoliang/wheat	26	Guangxi	431	rice
11	Shanxi	690	wheat/corn/millet	27	Yunnan	407	rice
12	Hebei	637	corn/kaoliang/wheat	28	Tibet	398	
13	Guangdong	634	rice	29	Guizhou	303	rice
14	Xinjiang	580					
15	Hunan	577	rice				
16	Fujian	552	rice				

NOTE Those provinces for which the cropping pattern is not shown are either predominantly industrial or with limited cropping potential.

1970s. The transfer of income on these quantities must have been substantial. There is also an internal transfer of resources away from the peasants to the urban consumers within the rice producing provinces.

SOME LESSONS OF THE CHINESE EXPERIENCE[78]

After the victory of the revolution in China a thorough-going land reform was completed by 1952. According to all available evidence, it resulted in a very egalitarian redistribution of rural income and the generation of a high rate of surplus for national investment.[79] However, as is common practice with revolutionary socialism, the Chinese leadership looked upon egalitarian land reform as merely a brief interregnum marking the transition towards the collective organisation of agriculture. Thus within five years of the completion of land reform – by the end of 1957 – private farming and land ownership as the partial basis of income distribution were virtually abolished. By then 96 per cent of the peasant families had been organised into advanced co-operatives under which land and other means of production ceased to be privately owned and the collective product came to be distributed entirely on the basis of work performed.

The arguments in favour of such a rapid transition towards collectivisation can be divided into two broad categories: those based on considerations of efficiency and those claiming that it would facilitate greater egalitarianism and a quicker transition to socialism and, ultimately, communism. The first set of arguments emphasise economies of scale, the greater ease in generating high rates of investible and marketable surpluses to facilitate industrialisation and the mobilisation of labour to undertake capital construction. In the Soviet case these considerations – indeed the narrower ones pragmatically contributing to the needs of rapid industrialisation – were decisive. Even in the Chinese case many of the arguments were based on considerations of efficiency and the technical transformation of agriculture. Thus Mao Zedong, in his famous report 'On the Question of Agricultural Co-operation' in July 1955, argued that socialist industrialisation was incompatible with peasant agriculture because the latter would neither generate the required surplus nor create sufficient demand for the output of industry. But Mao also argued the case for collectivisation on grounds of equity:

> As is clear to everyone, the spontaneous forces of capitalism have been steadily growing in the countryside in recent years, with new rich peasants

> springing up everywhere and many well-to-do middle peasants striving to become rich peasants. On the other hand, many poor peasants are still living in poverty for lack of sufficient means of production, with some in debt and others selling or renting out their land. If this tendency goes unchecked, the polarisation in the countryside will inevitably be aggravated day by day. Those peasants who lose their land and those who remain in poverty will complain that we are doing nothing to save them from ruin or to help them overcome their difficulties. Nor will the well-to-do middle peasants who are heading in the capitalist direction be pleased with us, for we shall never be able to satisfy their demand unless we intend to take the capitalist road.[80]

The argument that egalitarian peasant farming after land reform is an obstacle to the distributional goals of revolutionary socialism needs to be understood more clearly. At first, it would appear puzzling. A sufficiently egalitarian peasant farming system could do away with wage labour and thus eliminate exploitation in the Marxist sense of the appropriation of surplus value. By continued enforcement of a land ceiling and by avoiding fiscal measures that make payments disproportionate to effort or output it should be possible to ensure this particular objective.

However, the two kinds of bourgeois rights that Marx talked about in the *Critique of the Gotha Programme* are preserved under this kind of peasant farming as sources of inequality. The first of these rights refers to inequality in the distribution of rental income among peasant households due to an unequal land and resource endowment. In a vast country like China anything remotely resembling strict equality in the distribution of land and assets would be impossible to ensure, however thorough the land reforms might be. To curtail this right, one must begin by collectivising land and other assets and then gradually transfer their ownership from lower levels of collectives (e.g. teams) to higher levels (e.g. brigades and communes) until the level of ownership by all the people is reached.

The second type of bourgeois right arises out of the principle of relating earnings to ability in so far as the latter is not proportionate to need. On this Marx was quite explicit.

> One man is superior to another physically or mentally and so supplies more labour in the same time, or can labour for a longer time . . . Further, one worker is married, another not; one has more children than another, and so on and so forth. Thus with an equal performance of labour, and hence an equal share in the social consumption fund, one will in fact receive more than another, one will be richer than another, and so on. To avoid all these defects, right instead of being equal would have to be unequal.[81]

Let us now examine these efficiency and equity arguments against the continuation of the post-land reform egalitarian peasant agriculture in the context of achieving the goals of revolutionary socialism. The economies of scale argument is exaggerated in the context of a typical Asian agriculture characterised by a low degree of mechanisation. Indeed, it is doubtful if there is any significant economy of scale in farming activities (excluding capital construction). In the mobilisation of labour for capital construcion there are significant economies of scale that can be taken advantage of under collective institutions. However, such advantage is at best a practical one; in principle, it should be possible to organise such activities by promoting co-operation among equal peasants. In terms of the mobilisation of investible and marketable surpluses, again, there are clear practical advantages of collective institutions. It is far easier to collect a marketable surplus from a few collective enterprises than from a vast number of peasants.[82] A collective organisation, like that of the Chinese commune, provides a framework for a simple system of concealed tax on lower collective units (e.g. teams) through the drafting of labour (who are given work points by their teams) for work at the higher collective units (e.g. communes).

While the substitution of peasant farming by collective farming provides some of the advantages of a practical nature, noted above from the standpoint of efficiency, it has to face a very basic problem of efficiency in the organisation of production, namely, the setting up of an incentive system. The nature of agricultural work is such that, as one moves out of the organisational framework of a peasant family into that of a collective, the evaluation of performance, the institution of a system of payments, the organisation of management decisions and related matters become exceedingly difficult. The problem becomes much greater with the rising level and size of the basic accounting unit. As the size of the basic accounting unit increases, supervision and evaluation of work becomes very difficult and the cleavage between payments and performance becomes large. The organisation of incentives on a conventional basis becomes impossible.

From the standpoint of equity collective agriculture, in the historically practised forms, has little advantage over egalitarian peasant farming. The two kinds of bourgeois rights that are the sources of inequality under private peasant farming are also preserved under collective agriculture. The bourgeois right arising out of unequal access to land and productive assets need not be any greater under private farming than under a system of collectives in which the basic accounting unit is relatively small (e.g. an average team in the Chinese communes consisting of about twenty-six households). For such a small community in a homogeneous location it should always be possible to make land reform so egalitarian as to provide each household with roughly an equal amount of land and assets per person. The second type of bourgeois right is preserved under collective agriculture in so far as payments are based on the work performed (i.e. according to the socialist principle of 'to each according to his work').

Indeed, both in the Chinese communes and in the Soviet kolkhozy evidence has been found that income from the personal plot is more equitably distributed than collective income.[83] The present writer has tried, in a different context, to explain this phenomenon as follows:

> The distribution of income in the socialised sector, *in principle*, is proportional to the individual members' capacity to work. Individuals differ in terms of such capacity. In the socialised sector such differences in capacity result in larger income differentials because individuals work with relatively large amounts of capital and other resources. Thus the resulting distribution can be as unequal as individuals are in terms of ability. In the non-socialised sector there are such severe limitations on the volume of means of production per person that the differences among individuals' capacity to work cannot be fully translated into differential results of work. As a consequence, the distribution of income can be less unequal than that of the ability to work.[84]

For a sufficiently egalitarian peasant farming system, under the usual kind of land and capital constraint observed in a typical Asian country, the same result would obtain in comparing the outcome of egalitarian peasant farming with the alternative of collective agriculture. In this context it is useful to remember that in China the main gain in terms of improved rural income distribution was achieved by land reform and that since then further gain during successive phases of collectivisation has been small.[85]

Bourgeois rights can be restricted under the system of collective agriculture by raising the level of the basic accounting unit and by the gradual replacement of the capacity to work by need as the principle of payment. These, indeed, were tried in some advanced communes in China. It is, however, clear that these practices directly conflict with the conventional principles of organising an efficient system of incentives. Both these restrictions on bourgeois rights result in the deviation of compensation from effort to such a degree that the material basis for efficient production breaks down unless the human agents of production cease to respond to the usual assumptions of being actuated by self-interest (including the interest of the family and, perhaps, the immediate clan). Marx himself was so keenly aware of this problem as to realise that 'right can never be higher than the economic structure of society and its cultural development conditioned thereby'.[86] The precondition of successfully curbing bourgeois rights is to bring about such a basic change in the attitudes and responses of the members of the labour force as to make them cease to behave in accordance with the standard assumption of orthodox economics that individuals, households and groups work for higher material consumption. In spite of the brief periods of experimentation in China this is by and large an uncharted path. No human society has yet succeeded in organising itself on this basis for a substantial length of time and/or on a sufficiently wide scale.

For collective agriculture to provide significantly greater equality than a highly egalitarian, post-land reform, peasant agriculture bourgeois rights will have to be curtailed to such an extent as to make it impossible to set up an efficient system of incentives (in the absence of sufficient preparatory work in effecting a basic change in human behaviour of proportions not experienced by any human society to date). This will render the collective system a far less efficient organisation for productive efficiency in comparison with peasant agriculture. Attempts at hastening the path towards higher levels of collectivisation, prompted either by considerations of expediency or by doctrinaire belief in the urgency or feasibility of curbing bourgeois rights, could easily create such great problems for productive efficiency as to require a backward step in the direction of restoring much of the elements of egalitarian peasant farming as the only available method of ensuring efficiency. Recent experiments in China with the responsibility system indicate evidence of this. The lesson seems to be that revolutionary socialism should look upon egalitarian peasant farming, ushered in by a post-revolution land reform, as more than a temporary state of agricultural organisation and one should begin the transition towards collective agriculture only after the necessary subjective and objective conditions have been fulfilled. A sufficiently egalitarian peasant farming system is non-exploitative in the Marxist sense of eliminating the appropriation of surplus value. The bourgeois rights preserved under it can be modified significantly by using fiscal policy. In any case, the existing forms of collectives are not able to curb these rights much more significantly.

NOTES AND REFERENCES

1. These figures are for a somewhat later date, namely 1980, at which China was reported to have 135 million rural households, 5.15 million production teams, 7000 000 brigades and 52 000 communes.

2. This figure, pertaining to the year 1978, was provided by the Institute of Agricultural Economics of the Chinese Academy of Social Sciences (CASS). As discussed later, there was little change in this regard between 1976 and 1978.
3. In Dazhai, the proportion was estimated to be 12 per cent around the mid-1970s. See ILO, *Poverty and Landlessness in Rural Asia* (Geneva 1977) p. 280.
4. In 1975, private plots amounted to 6.4 per cent of arable land according to a Chinese Communist Party document quoted in Jürgen Domes, 'New Policies in the Communes: Notes on Rural Societal Structures in China, 1976–1981', *Journal of Asian Studies*, February 1982.
5. 'The nation's total agricultural tax accounted for 12 per cent of actual farm output in 1952 and it now (1975) has dropped to only 5 per cent.' Wei Min, 'China's Tax Policy' in *Beijing Review*, No. 37, 1975. The reference is to direct agricultural tax.
6. For a detailed discussion on these topics, see D. P. Ghai *et al.* (eds.) *Agrarian Systems and Rural Development* (London: Macmillan, 1979) chapter 8.
7. The index shows the ratio of the index of purchasing price of farm products to the index of retail price of industrial goods in rural areas. Both the indices are from *Economic Readjustment and Reform*, Beijing Review Special Feature Series on China Today; No. 3 (Beijing, 1982) p. 215.
8. Note, for example, the following excerpt from Chen Yonggui's report at the Conference:

   > corrections must be made resolutely in the few places where *san zi yi bao* (the extension of plots for private use and of free markets, the increase of small enterprises with sole responsibility for their own profits or losses, and the fixing of farm output quotas for individual households with each on its own – Tr.) has been practised and where land has been distributed to individuals. Firm criticism should be made of capitalistic activities carried out under the signboard of the collective and the collective economy of the people's communes should be switched back on to the correct path and consolidated and strengthened . . We should . . . promote the growth of the economy at the commune and brigade levels so as to create conditions for the gradual transition.

   Beijing Review, January 7, 1977, pp. 13 and 15. A footnote on p. 15 further explains:

   > At the present stage, the rural people's communes generally take the form of three-level ownership, that is, ownership by the commune, the production brigade and the production team, with the last as the basic accounting unit. When the time is ripe, this will gradually pass over to the system of ownership with the brigade or even the commune as the basic accounting unit and, in the distant future, to ownership by the whole people.

9. Hua Guofeng did so at the National Finance and Trade Conference on 7 July 1978.

10. Article 7 of Chapter 1 of the 1978 Constitution. This Constitution was replaced by yet another new Constitution adopted in December 1982.
11. The leadership of this movement came from Deng Xiaoping and his followers (notable among them being Zhao Ziyang, then the head of the party organisation in Sichuan). Deng was fully rehabilitated at the July 1977 plenum of the Party Central Committee.
12. Yan Ling, 'The Necessity, Possibility and Realisation of Socialist Transformation of China's Agriculture', *Social Sciences in China*, Vol. III, No. 1, p. 116.
13. For example, *Beijing Review*, No. 9, 1982, p. 9 reports that the Guangxi Regional People's Government discovered that the policy of five guarantees was not being implemented in some places.
14. Jürgen Domes, 'New Policies in the Communes', *Journal of Asian Studies*, Feb. 1982, quotes Sichuan People's Broadcasting Station of 22 January 1979 and Renmin Ribao of 31 January 1979 as evidence.
15. It should be noted that these prices are far from what free market prices would be since most of these goods are distributed through ration shops at administered prices. The prices in the private markets are the result of the interactions between residual demands and supplies.
16. Sidney Shapiro, *Experiment in Sichuan* (Beijing: New World Press, 1981) p. 14.
17. *Beijing Review*, No, 26, 1981, p. 3.
18. Peng Zhen's report at the 23rd session of the Fifth National People's Congress Standing Committee, *Beijing Review*, No. 19, 1982, p. 26.
19. We visited some of these experimental cases in July 1982.
20. Song Dahan and Zhang Chunsheng, 'Important Change in the System of People's Communes', *Beijing Review*, No. 29, 1982, pp. 15–17.
21. This was done in the autumn of 1979. Early in 1980 Dazhai brigade was divided into three production teams (*Beijing Review*, No. 16, 1981, p. 27). In February 1979, Chen Yonggui lost his leadership of China's agriculture ministry.
22. Yan Ling, 'The Necessity, Possibility and Realisation of Socialist Transformation of China's Agriculture', *Social Sciences in China*, Vol. III, No. 1 (March 1982), pp. 118–19.
23. This is based on an exposition given to the delegation on 21 July 1982 at Chengdu by Mr Ling Kaefung, Division Director, Office of Agricultural Affairs, Provincial Government of Sichuan. This is the single most detailed classification we have encountered.
24. It is very hard to know if this is strictly the case with certain kinds of contract of type 1. However, the quantitative insignificance of this type perhaps makes it unnecessary to worry about this point.
25. Perhaps this type of land belongs to a more extreme category of contract than type 4, in so far as it appears that no contribution is made by their users to tax, welfare and accumulation funds.
26. Thus, under this assumption, types 2, 3, 4 and unirrigated part of 6 would have 92.7 per cent of land. To this add 65 per cent of the land under type 5 (which would have 3.05 per cent of land).
27. This information was provided at the Chinese Academy of Social Sciences,

Beijing. According to them *bao gan dao hu* was practised by 40 per cent of the teams by the autumn harvest of 1981 and by 70 per cent of them by June 1982. By the latter date *bao chan dao hu* was being practised by about 5 per cent of the teams. The extent of contracting with individual labourers was not separately reported but, together with contracting with groups of labourers, they represented 12–13 per cent of the teams by the end of 1981. Thus, nationwide comprehensive access to land by individuals and households would probably amount to over 85 per cent.

28. This information was supplied by Mr Yang of the Provincial Committee for Agricultural Affairs in Yunnan.
29. This was reported by the accountant of the Gao Qiao Team of Pu Chao Brigade in the outskirts of Kunming.
30. *Beijing Review*, No. 34, 1981, p. 19 reporting on a meeting the Party Secretariat had with provincial Party leaders in Beijing in September 1980 'where the responsibility system was discussed, differing opinions were expressed and reports were given on the local situation by the participants'.
31. Ibid, p. 19.
32. It is not being implied that we necessarily believe that there are important economies of scale with respect to size of farm in China in an *ex-ante* sense. All that is being said is that given a particular level of mechanisation it would, *ex-post*, be difficult to adapt to a smaller size of operation.
33. The assumption of equal size of all households is not necessary. This is made for simplicity. The alternative would be to show all other measurements in per capita terms.
34. From official writings it appears that less than 100 per cent bonus is possible under BCDH. We have not come across such an actual case. Such a case would clearly make BCDH different, in terms of substantial outcome, from BGDH.
35. This seems to be a reasonably accurate description of the system of procurement for grains. However, in some places a third kind of sale to the state was reported. The price of it was reported to be negotiated with the state.
36. One might object to this and suggest that food should be evaluated at the free market price, the only price at which additional quantities can be bought and sold. Our decision to use the basic procurement price (the same as ration price) is to ensure the use of the same price as under BCDH. Later we shall demonstrate the outcome that would obtain as a result of the use of the free market price.
37. For comparability, output must also be evaluated at the free market price for the purpose of determining the rate. We call this the 'potential value of output'. Note that this method of valuation is different from that adopted in Tables 3.2 and 3.3 to arrive at family income.
38. In the present comparison food ration under BCDH and self-consumption under BGDH are valued at the ration price. For the outcome when the free market price is used see the next note.
39. Note that a similar, though less extreme, result obtains if the food ration under BCDH and self-consumption under BGDH are valued at the free market price. The ratios of incomes and productivities corresponding to this

situation (with equal family sizes) would be as follows:

Pair of households	*Ratio of income*	*Ratio of productivity*
B/A	1.63	1.50
C/B	1.38	1.33
C/A	2.25	2.00

40. *Beijing Review*, No. 24, 1982, pp. 21–7.
41. An outstanding example is the Egyptian co-operative system.
42. We were told – in Sichuan and elsewhere – that labour weak families are encouraged to contract less land per capita. The collective, however, makes up for their food ration.
43. See A. R. Khan, 'Taxation, Procurement and Collective Incentives in Chinese Agriculture', *World Development*, Vol. 6, No. 8, 1978.
44. Song Daham and Zhang Chunsheng, 'Important Change in the System of People's Communes', *Beijing Review*, No. 29, 1982, pp. 15–17.
45. These points and the following quotations are from Song Dahan and Zhang Chunsheng, 'Important Change in the System of People's Communes', *Beijing Review*, No. 29, 1982.
46. Remissions from income tax for three years and indirect taxes for one year are available to enterprises employing educated urban youth to the extent of a minimum of 50 per cent of the labour force. The Corporation takes advantage of this provision.
47. This is an unfortunate gap in our investigation and is due mainly to our inadequate understanding of the scope of change in Qionglai, which was the first of the counties undergoing current reforms that we visited. There are the following possibilities: (a) The commune-level enterprises were divided among the brigades or (b) they were put under a separate, parallel joint corporation. In any case, the main difference from the Guanghan experiment is that the apex corporation is at the level of the former brigade, not the former commune.
48. To give some idea of the claimed rates of growth one can cite the following figures: In Guanghan county total output value increased by 2.7 times (presumably at current prices) between 1976 and 1981. At the Phoenix Joint Corporation in Qionglai per capita income from all sources increased from 163.1 yuan in 1977 (186.7 yuan in 1978) to 673.8 yuan in 1981 (again, presumably, at current prices).
49. In the article by two members of the Commission for Legal Affairs of the NPC (Song Dahan and Zhang Chunsheng – see note 44) only an oblique reference is made to this important change. 'During the experiment in Sichuan Privince, some communes have changed into agricultural–industrial–commerical complexes and some production teams into agricultural producers' co-operatives.'
50. See Song Dahan and Zhang Chunsheng, 'Important Change in the System of People's Communes', *Beijing Review*, No. 29, 1982, p. 17.
51. *Beijing Review*, No. 30, 1981, p. 19. The two systems he was referring to are *bao chan dao hu* and *bao gan dao hu*.
52. Needless to say that such estimates between two points are overly influenced

by the levels at the terminal points. However, estimates of trends are ruled out over such short periods.

53. Relative prices in China are substantially different from international prices and perhaps have less rationale than the latter. Also, they have undergone changes in recent years. We, therefore, wanted to have an alternative estimate that would be free of the 'distortions' of domestic prices.
54. See D. Ghai, *et al.*, *Agrarian Systems and Rural Development*, chapter 8. Such trend estimates for agricultural output value are not available because estimates of output value are available only for selected years.
55. *Beijing Review*, No. 6, 1982, p. 5.
56. *Beijing Review*, No. 11, 1979.
57. *Beijing Review*, No. 35, 1981.
58. The information on per capita income is based on a survey of 18 529 peasant households conducted nationwide by the State Statistical Bureau.
59. The denominator of the terms of trade index is the index of the retail price of *industrial* goods in rural areas (call it P_m) *while the index of retail price of all goods* in the countryside (call it P_r) is used to deflate income to obtain *real* income. P_r contains agricultural goods for which the rate of increase in price was greater than that in P_m. Thus the increase in P_r was greater (compare columns 4 and 5 of Table 3.3). The rate of increase in real income (57.6 per cent) was, therefore, lower than the product of the rates of increase in real output value (17.9 per cent) and improvement in terms of trade (36 per cent):

$$1.179 \times 1.36 = 1.60 > 1.576$$

60. At a briefing session a county official in Yu Xi explained the 75 yuan increase in per capita rural income as follows: 15 yuan due to increase in purchase prices, 14 yuan due to reduction in cost and the remaining 46 yuan due to greater enthusiasm. Such characterisations are quite common.
61. See A. R. Khan and D. Ghai, *Collective Agriculture and Rural Development in Soviet Central Asia* (London: Macmillan, 1979) chapter 2.
62. See Table 3.4. This was 66 per cent in 1978. Note, however, that in 1978 this consisted of *collectively* distributed income whereas in 1981 this largely consists of income from produce on land contracted out from the collective.
63. Inquiries made of the officials of the State Statistical Bureau revealed that the survey was originally held in 1978 and repeated every year. It was claimed by these officials that the survey represented the major ecological zones in each province roughly in proportion to their population. Nothing much could be found out about definitions, concepts and methods except that the survey was largely based on self-enumeration. The State Statistical Bureau had only asked for the averages from the provincial bureaux and not for the distribution at the time of our discussions with the officials. It was a puzzle that the size of the sample remained exactly the same – the identical households presumably – over the years.
64. Under plausible, but by no means verified as accurate, assumptions that the average incomes of the groups are respectively 370, 280, 180, 113 and 70 yuan (which are internally consistent in so far as their weighted average is 203 yuan, the average income for all households) the Gini coefficient turns

out to be 0.22. This, though nothing more than an arbitrary illustration, is enough to show that the inequality, under any plausible set of assumptions, would be moderate.

65. For example, see E. B. Vermeer, 'Income Differentials in Rural China', *The China Quarterly*, March 1982 and Table 3.10 of this chapter.
66. See A. R. Khan, 'The Distribution of Income in Rural China', in ILO, *Poverty and Landlessness in Rural Asia*, Geneva, 1977.
67. This was quoted from a field report at a meeting attended by the authors by Mr Ni Xinyi of the Institute of Agricultural Economics of the CASS in July 1982.
68. This is the impression formed after visiting such markets in Chengdu and Kunming. There was no evidence of a systematic collection of price and quantity data.
69. These periods can be given the following approximate titles: the First Five-Year Plan; Great Leap Forward and the subsequent adjustment; Cultural Revolution; and the interregnum after the Cultural Revolution.
70. *Economic Readjustment and Reform*, China Today No. 3 (Beijing: Beijing Review Special Feature Series, 1982) p. 206.
71. *Beijing Review*, No. 17, 1982.
72. Dong Fureng, 'Relationship Between Accumulation and Consumption', in Xu Dixin *et al.*, *China's Search for Economic Growth* (Beijing: New World Press, 1982), p. 100.
73. *Economic Readjustment and Reform*, China Today No. 3, p. 207.
74. The rationale behind such measures of relative scarcities is to be found in I.M.D. Little and J. A. Mirrlees, *Project Appraisal and Planning for Developing Countries* (London: Heinemann, 1974).
75. Attention is also drawn to the problem of comparability of periods to which procurement and export prices refer. See note to Table 3.9.
76. This is perhaps an indication of the overvaluation of the rate of exchange for yuan (in 1980 about 1.53 per dollar). The rate fell rapidly in later years.
77. One might argue that for import substitutes the relevant comparison should be with import prices. This would not alter the calculations radically. The basic procurement price would be 130.2 per cent of import price for cotton and 96.2 per cent for wheat. Ranks would be unaltered.
78. This section is based on a part of the author's paper presented at the 18th International Conference of Agricultural Economists: A. R. Khan, *Institutional Organisational Framework for Egalitarian Agricultural Growth*, Jakarta, August–September, 1982.
79. See Charles R. Roll Jr, *The Distribution of Rural Incomes in China: A Comparison of the 1930s and 1950s*, Harvard Ph. Dissertation, 1974; and A. R. Khan, 'The Distribution of Income in Rural China', in ILO, *Poverty and Landlessness in Rural Asia*, Geneva, 1977.
80. Mao Zedong, 'On the Question of Agricultural Co-operation', in *Selected Readings from the Works of Mao Zedong* (Beijing: Foreign Languages Press, 1971).
81. Karl Marx, *Critique of the Gotha Programme* (Beijing: Foreign Languages Press, 1972).
82. Note that under household contracting the quota is still levied on the team which transfers it to the households.

83. See A. R. Khan and D. P. Ghai, *Collective Agriculture and Rural Development in Soviet Central Asia*, for similar evidence in the Soviet Central Asian Republics and Keith Griffin and Ashwani Saith, *Growth and Equality in Rural China*, ARTEP, Bangkok, 1981 for that in the Chinese communes.
84. A. R. Khan and D. P. Ghai, *Collective Agriculture and Rural Development in Soviet Central Asia* (London: Macmillan, 1979).
85. See A. R. Khan, 'The Distribution of Income in Rural China', in ILO, *Poverty and Landlessness in Rural Asia*, Geneva, 1977.
86. Karl Marx, *Critique of the Gotha Programme* (Beijing: Foreign Languages Press, 1972).

4 Employment and Incomes in Rural China: The Impact of Recent Organisational Changes

EDDY LEE

The organisational changes that have occurred in rural China since 1978 have been rapid and far-reaching, affecting almost every aspect of the production and distribution system. It is possible that the cumulative impact of these changes will be a qualitative transformation of the system of collective agriculture, centred around the three-tier commune system, that has been characteristic of rural China since 1956. This chapter will, however, eschew the larger questions and will instead focus on one set of issues – employment, work organisation and related topics. Employment will form the organising concept from which the recent organisational changes in China are viewed and evaluated. The chapter will draw upon the notes from a field trip to China in July/August 1982.

The next section contains a brief description of the salient features of employment and labour allocation as it existed until 1978. There then follows a discussion of the arguments that have been advanced for a reform of this system while in the subsequent section we describe the types of transition that have occurred since 1978. The main features of the new system that is emerging will then be discussed, followed by an analysis of the potential effects of this new system on future employment and income distribution. The conclusions are contained in a short final section.

EMPLOYMENT AND LABOUR ALLOCATION UNTIL 1978

A key feature of employment in rural China was the limited mobility of labour between communes and also between communes and the urban economy. Each commune was thus to a large extent the basic unit within which employment was generated and labour was allocated to alternative activities. The amount of employment available, the type and intensity of tasks, the payments system and the level of remuneration were all determined within the framework of the three-tier commune system. It should be noted, however, that this did not imply significant inter-commune variations in methods of work organisation. Although the returns to labour and the structure of employment varied widely due to the same factors which resulted in inter-commune differences in income levels, there was a framework of work organisation which applied to the whole commune system. Thus the description that follows applies to this common framework.

A basic aspect of employment and labour allocation within the commune system was the overwhelming predominance of collective activity. The size of the private sector was regulated through land allocation, restrictions on private non-farm activities and the minimum requirements for participation in collective agriculture. The total area for private plots was in general restricted to between 5 and 7 per cent of total cultivated area and was allocated to households on a per capita basis. This, in the context of the extremely low land/man ratios in China, meant minuscule plots of no more than 0.05 mou per had (or 0.25 mou[1] for a household of five) and the total labour absorption for crop production on private plots was thus very limited. At the same time non-crop and non-agricultural private activities such as cottage industry, trading and other services were prohibited.[2] Thus the alternatives to work in collective activities were very limited and the predominance of collective employment was ensured by the requirement that almost all able-bodied adults had to participate in collective work. Differences in the returns to labour in private and collective activity were thus of limited relevance in determining the allocation of labour between the private and collective sectors, since an effective ceiling was imposed on private activities.

Within the collective sector the allocation of labour amongst agriculture, sideline activities and industry was determined at the level of the commune. The rate of collective accumulation and investment determined the size of the industrial sector and hence the number of jobs in commune and brigade enterprises. These employment opportunities were typically distributed on the basis of some notion of need; labour recruitment by commune and brigade enterprises gave priority to poorer and labour-weak families. The rest of the commune labour force were absorbed in collective agriculture, sideline activities and in capital construction. The latter was essentially a device to mobilise surplus labour into productive activity especially during the agricultural slack season. Apart from these there were virtually no other sources of employment. As mentioned earlier, inter-commune mobility of labour was non-existent. There were some, but very limited, opportunities to work in enterprises run by the county (or in urban enterprises) and there was some conscription into the Peoples Liberation Army. Thus, in general, out-migration was not a factor which affected rural employment.

It is difficult to establish with any degree of precision the effects of this system of employment and labour allocation on efficiency in production and labour use or on equity in the distribution of income. Data on labour input by activity and the returns to labour by activity do not exist. Nonetheless some features can be surmised and these will be highlighted in so far as they relate to the evaluation of recent changes in the system.

On overall employment generation the record has been remarkably good. In the first place the commune system guaranteed employment and thereby also an entitlement to collective output. Whether this represented 'full employment', measured either by the resulting marginal productivity of (and returns to) labour or by the amount of work available throughout the year, or instead represented the outcome of work-sharing arrangements is difficult to tell. However, there are indications that the system has been remarkably successful in absorbing the huge increase in China's rural labour force in the post-liberation period. An authoritative assessment of the process concludes as follows:

> China's undeniable success in absorbing new cohorts of rural workers, however, has brought with it a substantial decline in the marginal product of labour. Although the rising number of workdays per farm labourer has prevented output per man–year from declining, both output per man–day and total factor productivity in agriculture were considerably lower in 1975 than in 1957.[3]

According to Rawski's estimates the number of persons employed in the rural economy increased from 231.5 million to 328 million between 1957 and 1975, while at the same time the number of days worked per employed person also increased substantially, from 159 to 206 days per year. Output per man–year also was estimated to have increased – from 232 yuan in 1957 to 255 yuan in 1975. These are, by any standards, stupendous achievements in labour absorption (or employment generation). At the same time, however, it is important to note that according to Rawski's estimates output per man–day declined from 1.46 yuan in 1957 to 1.24 yuan in 1975. From an overall standpoint this process could be seen as one whereby labour was 'mobilised for tasks with a low and declining – but positive – effect on farm output',[4] a sensible policy if the opportunity cost of this labour was low. 'From the peasants' viewpoint, the falling value of each workday brought about by a rising man/land ratio meant that, with migration and private plots closely restricted, increased collective labour was the only way to protect existing living standards; to attain higher incomes further extra work was unavoidable.'[5]

Labour allocation at the macro level was determined within the planning system which determined the relative sizes of the collective and private economy; within the collective economy the planning system also influenced the allocation between agriculture and industry (through its control over material supplies) and also between different crops in agricultural production.[6] Apart from this the level of labour absorption within the commune system was also influenced by the distribution of material inputs (including machinery), production norms which specified factor-proportions and the pricing and procurement system. Within the communes labour allocation was determined by the extent of non-agricultural employment that could be created within the constraints of the planning framework, the choice of technology and the scale of farm management (i.e. whether at brigade or team or work group level). The latter two factors influence the efficiency of production, labour requirements and the returns to labour.

For the individual household the range of choice in labour allocation was very restricted. Non-farm jobs were desirable but were exogenously determined and would be accepted where offered. Labour allocation to the small private sector was (on the side of labour supply) determined by the residual labour time available after meeting obligations of collective work and on the demand side by the maximum labour requirement in private activity that was consistent with yielding returns to labour higher than in collective labour. Given the very small size of the private sector the system was probably 'demand determined', with maximum labour requirements being below the available supply of labour time after meeting commitments to collective labour. The choice of how any excess labour time was to be used was thus essentially between additional input of labour (above the compulsory requirements) into collective work or leisure. In addition to the number of days devoted to collective work, the intensity of work per unit of time was also another variable in the household labour-allocation decision. Both these variables are affected by the payments and incentive system within the communes and we therefore turn to an examination of these.

The distinctive feature of the payments system within communes was the use of work points instead of money as the unit of account. Work points were earned against each day of work (or piece of work under piece rate systems) but the value of these work points in terms of yuan were not known *ex ante*; the value was determined only at the end of the accounting period (usually the harvest) by dividing the net distributed collective income by the total number of work points earned by all who participated in collective work.[7] Thus although the average value of a workday is sometimes referred to as being equivalent to a wage rate, the important difference between a cash-based wage system and the work point system needs to be borne in mind.

The *ex ante* indeterminancy in the value of a work point affects the individual's decision on the amount of labour to supply to collective work in two ways. First, there is the interdependence problem – the value of a work point earned by any individual is also inevitably affected by the labour supply decision of others (the amount as well as intensity or sincerity of their work effort). Except in the case of a strictly enforced piece rate system (or with perfect motivation and social consciousness) the possibility exists for the same work points being earned for different intensities of work or different productivities of work. The total number of work points could thus be 'inflated' by the less hardworking or less productive, thereby lowering the value of the work point for all workers in the final distribution. The greater is this effect the lower will be the supply of genuine units of labour time since it lowers the expected return to labour. This is sometimes known as the free rider problem. Secondly, the individual labour supply decision will also be affected by the diminishing total factor productivity that has been observed to prevail in China. This implies that there would be a stronger tendency for diminishing returns to labour to set in than is the case under the usual assumption of labour input being increased with other factors being held constant. Beyond a certain point earning more work points will raise total earnings at a diminishing rate. Given the fact that the work point system yields a final distribution linked to average rather than marginal product, there is a corresponding tendency for the willingness to supply additional effort (or labour time) to slacken off once the marginal product falls below the expected average product.[8]

The other aspect of the work point system which has a major influence on labour supply decisions is the high proportion of net collective income which was distributed on a per capita basis. Typically about 60 per cent of the disposable collective income was accounted for by per capita food grain distribution. This was essentially a system of ration entitlement charged against work points earned in collective work. A norm of per capita grain entitlement was established and households paid for this per capita distributed grain with work points earned, with the ration price of grain being the rate of conversion from grain to work points. Households not earning enought work points were, in principle, required to make good the deficit from subsequent earnings, but in practice this was rarely enforced. This is probably the source of derogatory references to this system as having been analogous to 'eating from one big rice pot' and 'egalitarianism'. It should be noted, nonetheless, that the system was, in principle at least, not egalitarian since there was no unconditional per capita distribution[9] and the system did not by any means cover the entire distributed output.

The rationing system also affected individual incentives through its effect on the real value of work points, that is, the transformation possibilities from work points into cash or an ultimate basket of consumption. The work points earned by a worker could thus be seen as consisting of two parts: the first part (up to the value of the per capita ration entitlement) was in the nature of ration coupons which would not normally be traded; and the second part was freely convertible into cash. Given the element of subsidy implicit in the difference between the ration and sale price of grain, the first part of work point earnings would be more highly valued and this would tend to lower on the margin the propensity to contribute additional effort. (An additional factor working in the same direction was the high relative price of 'incentive goods' such as bicycles, watches and radios.)

Another feature of the work point system which also had an important effect on individual labour supply decisions was the very narrow differentials in work point ratings (roughly equivalent to wage rates in other systems). A large proportion of communes operated a time rate system (i.e. work points were earned on the basis of time spent in collective work) supplemented by a system of work assessment designed to allow for differences in work performance. The differentials in work point ratings fell within a narrow band and were revised only infrequently. The narrowness of the differentials can be seen in the fact that the work point system has been described as an inverted pyramid with about two-thirds of workers earning the maximum work point rating.

All these features of the payments system within communes, when seen purely as a system of material incentives, probably tended to limit the amount and quality of labour contributed to collective work. Whether or not this actually operated, however, would depend on how successfully this was offset by 'correct' motivation and social consciousness. Apart from this, however, there were also external influences which affected individual incentives.

One set of such factors was the pricing system and its effect on collective incentives and the returns to labour. The procurement prices and agricultural taxes affected the level and value of disposable income of a commune and hence also the average and marginal output per worker in collective work. Similarly, the controls on country fairs and regulation of the free market in rural areas would have reduced the scope for disposal of output from private activity and depressed the potential returns to labour from private activity. Another influence on the individual supply decision was the policy on mechanisation and the diffusion of modern inputs. This would have tended to raise labour productivity and lower the disutility of labour and both these factors would have increased the propensity to supply additional labour.[10] Labour displacement would have to be offset against this, but the impression is that on balance labour displacement was not a significant problem. In any case, any such labour displacement would have resulted in greater labour mobilisation for activities such as capital construction or, where such alternative uses of labour did not exist, in increased work sharing.

The outcomes of this system in terms of employment and income distribution were, in all likelihood, highly positive. As we have seen, employment generation was extremely high and this was accompanied by a moderate rise in total earnings per worker and in per capita rural incomes over the whole period. At the same time, the distribution of income did not exhibit extreme inequalities. Within an individual commune the intra-team distribution was generally very equal as a result of the egalitarian payments system. Whether this remained true for a commune as a whole depended partly on whether or not higher level units constituted the Basic Accounting Unit and partly on the size of the commune and its inter-team diversity in natural endowments. In any case, within a basic accounting unit the payments system ensured that inequality was kept within very narrow limits. In the first place communal ownership ensured that differences in asset endowment were not a source of income differences. Second, differences arising from a differential endowment of labour power were kept within limits by the egalitarian features of the payments system. Finally, there is also some evidence that the private sector within communes, by providing an outlet for the labour of dependants and secondary workers, acted as an additional equalising factor.[11]

The outcome of the system in terms of efficiency criteria (such as the rationality of labour allocation, efficiency of labour use, labour productivity and output growth) is less clear-cut. The trend rate of growth of agricultural output has been reasonable in comparison with other large and densely populated agrarian economies. But this in itself only begs the question of whether or not a faster rate of growth would have been possible under a different system of payments and work organisation. Similarly, we have noted earlier that there was a general tendency for total factor productivity in Chinese agriculture to decline and that output per man–day had been declining too. Yet it is difficult to decide on the basis of the available evidence whether this reflects a basic tendency towards diminishing returns due to ecology, factor proportions and given technological possibilities or, at least in part, reflects the negative impact of the institutional and incentive structure on productivity and output. However, be this as it may, there appears to have been no doubt in the minds of the current leadership when they inaugurated the new policies after 1978. The diagnosis was that the commune system as it existed was seriously flawed and that the chief defect was the payments system and incentive structure. This was seen as having acted as a brake on output growth by seriously impairing individual incentives to work. We therefore turn to examine these arguments for reform before discussing the nature and effects of the changes introduced.

ARGUMENTS FOR REFORM

No systematic analysis of the failings of the past system and the consequent need for reform is available. Rather we have only the new catch phrases used in the drive for reform (which apparently encapsulate the ills of the past system) and the nature of the new institutions which have been introduced to rely on as sources. It would be interesting, nonetheless, to reconstruct from these fragmentary indications what specific elements of the old system were believed to have been the source of trouble.

The keynote for reform seems to be a frustration about the levels of increase in rural living standards that have been achieved. The performance of the commune system on this score has been frequently castigated, especially the performance during the period when the Gang of Four were in the ascendency. There has been not only an expression of dissatisfaction at the growth rates in output and rural incomes that have been achieved, but also a repudiation of the achievements claimed in the past statistics. In some cases the latter amount to claims of actual statistical fraudulence (as in the case of Dazhai Brigade) and figures on production statistics, especially those on accumulation, were said to have been padded to show more favourable achievements than had actually been the case.

Arguments of this type imply the belief that output growth in rural China has been kept below its true potential because of serious mismanagement. According to this view a serious problem of 'excess capacity' was believed to exist. This is implicit in the anecdotal evidence which has been provided on cases of neglect of communal farm machinery and hence underutilisation of capacity. Similarly, references to 'surplus labour' in the rural areas imply serious underutilisation of labour, even though labour had been over-mobilised into activities yielding low returns. As mentioned earlier, there is evidence that total factor productivity had been declining, as had output per man–day, but these facts are not sufficient by themselves for establishing the 'excess capacity' hypothesis. A related bit of evidence – that material inputs, especially farm machinery, increased more rapidly than the growth of output – also suffers from the same difficulty. The crux of the problem is that diminishing total factor productivity can be due to either basic diminishing returns to agriculture or mismanagement, or both. If it is diminishing returns which has been operating strongly then the charge of excessive application of material and labour inputs would need to be evaluated mainly in relation to the opportunity cost of these inputs. In the case of labour it is clear that the opportunity cost was very low and that the increased labour mobilisation was justifiable from a social (or macroeconomic) standpoint since it generated positive, though declining, marginal product. Moreover, in a case of diminishing returns with limited alternative uses of 'surplus' labour the element of work sharing implicit in this 'excessive' mobilisation has to be viewed positively.

It is, therefore, difficult to decide, purely on macro evidence, how much credence to give to these criticisms of the old system. However, more specific points have been made by way of pinpointing the source of the malaise. The most important of these is the criticism of the incentive structure. The previous payments system has been portrayed as being excessively egalitarian and was likened to 'eating from one big rice pot'. This was held to be the cause of low work motivation and hence low productivity and output growth. The low morale of workers could then be seen as the explanation of diminishing output per man–day as well as the neglect and underutilisation of farm machinery and wasteful application of variable inputs.

The charge of 'egalitarianism' under the old system centres on the high proportion of total output distributed on the basis of need instead of work. It also refers to the narrow spread in earnings which is seen as not allowing sufficient differentials for different intensity and quality of work. The result of these two features is then seen to be the very loose and tenuous link between effort and reward, a fact thought to be conducive to irresponsibility and low effort by workers. Implicitly this ascribes major importance to the 'free rider' problem in collective payments systems and asserts that moral incentives have failed to operate. The latter belief is also reflected in statements about the 'social relations of production' being instituted too far in advance of the 'forces of production'. Several other points have been made in this vein. For instance, the tight control of private activity is seen as having been mindlessly doctrinaire and as having thwarted opportunities for productive use of labour as well as having contributed to apathy. The high relative price and deliberate restriction on the supply of incentive goods such as bicycles and radios can also be seen as part of the reason for the alleged collapse of worker motivation. It has been said that accumulation was excessive and was inefficiently deployed. This lowered the collective distributed income of workers without giving much expectation of future benefits (because of inefficient use of the investment funds), hence contributing further to lower morale.

Apart from the adverse effects on individual incentives it has also been claimed that there was serious economic mismanagement associated with the old system. It is important to note that this is quite distinct from the defects in the payments system, although the two points are often made together. One aspect of mismanagement that is repeatedly stressed is the arbitrary 'commandism' which is said to have been widely prevalent. Production decisions such as the choice of the cropping pattern and pattern of input use were said to have been arbitrarily imposed on production units without considering local conditions and the knowledge and views of the lowest level production units. Glaring examples of this were said to be the strong bias in favour of grain production and the imposition of production norms and related 'fixes'.

This was believed to have been the source of a serious misallocation of resources and hence kept output below its full potential. This, of course, could also be seen as a factor which could have aggravated the fall in the morale of workers, since it would have reduced the element of 'social participatory motivation' and also reduced the reward from effort to below what was perceived to have been possible according to the expectations of the workers themselves. Other aspects of mismanagement that have been mentioned are the excessively high rate of accumulation, wasteful use of investment funds, over-mobilisation of labour, and underpricing of material inputs and their excessive use. Also, to judge from subsequent reforms, there must have been a feeling that the private sector was curbed to a greater extent than necessary. Possibly it was felt that income-generating activities were needlessly foregone through actual prohibition or indirectly through the excessive mobilisation of labour into low productivity collective activities.

Most of these ills were attributed to the rigidities of the three-tier commune system. The charge of commandism would imply that intra-commune democracy was poorly developed, perhaps even difficult to ensure within the given institutional structure. One aspect of this is contained in the criticism that the communes were too large and represented an over-centralisation of decision-making powers. The same has been said of the brigades and even teams. It has also been said that the system was over-bureaucratised in that there were too many cadres. Another aspect of the supposed rigidity of the commune system is that it did not allow for inter-commune or cross-commune economic organisations and activities to emerge. No organisational forms other than the three-tier units could be formed and this ruled out flexible responses to local economic opportunities through alternative economic groupings, within as well as across communes. This could be either groupings of households to undertake cottage industry production or larger grouping between several teams or brigades.

It is, of course, virtually impossible with the available information to evaluate how much of the economic case for reform outlined above is valid. It would be interesting, however, to spell out the relationship between the validity or otherwise of the economic case for reform and the expected effects of the reforms themselves. If the economic case for reform is essentially correct then the introduction of more effective individual incentives can be expected to restore and even raise worker morale, thereby raising total output and labour productivity. Output would rise because the 'effective' labour unit (or labour input in terms of standard efficiency units) would rise and more efficient use would be made of land, machinery and other inputs. The 'slack' in production would be taken up in the short run and this would constitute a sharp but once-for-all gain. In the longer run the prospects for sustaining these output and productivity increases would depend on the possibilities for reversing the trends towards diminishing total factor productivity. It should be noted, however, that an observed increase in output and labour productivity would not necessarily be conclusive proof that the economic case for reform was correct. This would be so only if other things were held constant and the most important other factor in this regard would be the terms of trade facing agriculture and its impact on collective incentives. On the other hand if, contrary to the economic case for reform, more fundamental factors making for declining total factor productivity have been operating then we would expect different results from the reforms. The introduction of stronger individual material incentives would not lead to improved labour productivity all round. Labour productivity will increase only if the system also manages to shed surplus labour and allows the stronger and more skilled workers to work more and earn more. The effects of this shedding of labour would be mitigated to the extent that new employment opportunities are created in rural non-farm activities or in a liberalised private sector. The growth of such employment opportunities would determine whether labour is in fact elbowed out or only leaves voluntarily.

THE TRANSITION TO THE NEW SYSTEM

Although the arguments for reform described in the previous section focused on the payments system and individual incentives, the reforms that have been introduced have encompassed a wider range of changes. It could, of course, be argued that all the changes that have been introduced ultimately affect individual incentives, but this would be to lose sight of the important distinction between measures directed primarily at collective and those directed at individual incentives. It is possible to improve collective incentives (and thereby individual incentives) without tampering with the payments system which determines individual incentives.

The changes that have been introduced include changes in the payments system within communes, in collective incentives (through the terms of trade for agriculture), in the balance between collective and private economic activity, in the administrative structure of communes and in the promotion and organisation of rural industries. In what follows we shall deal with each of these changes separately in order to examine their distinct implications for employment and labour allocation.

The first major change was in the terms of trade facing agriculture. Procurement prices have increased substantially since 1978 and the terms of trade moved in favour of agriculture.[12] This was accompanied by changes in procurement policy and in the production guidelines regarding cropping-mix derived from procurement targets. Apart from the raising of the procurement price, there was also a relaxation of procurement targets for poorer communes,[13] some measure of liberalisation of above-procurement quota sales on the free market and a relaxation of procurement targets for grain, which allowed greater freedom to collective units to determine cropping patterns. All these changes will lead to an increase in rural incomes due to the price effect as well as through increased output through the induced supply response. In the process, regardless of whether or not changes are made to the payments system, the returns to labour will rise and this will have a corresponding effect on labour supply and allocation. Labour input in 'efficiency' units will increase although this need not be reflected in the number of persons at work or in the total man–days of labour input. The increase in labour supply in efficiency units will occur because the collective distributed income and hence the value of work points will rise, except where all the increases in income as a result of the increase in prices is retained for accumulation.

A main thrust of the reforms, however, has been on the payments system and individual incentives within the communes. The main features of this system have been discussed in the previous chapter so only their position within the whole range of reforms will be briefly touched upon here. These changes have been described as the introduction of a 'responsibility system' which essentially represents a shift to a system of payment according to work. One aspect of this is to reduce or eliminate the proportion of collective distributed income which is distributed on some principle of need or as part of an egalitarian food rationing system. This implies a widening of earnings differentials within the communes since the 'base' of egalitarian distribution is removed. Furthermore, the 'inverted pyramid' structure of work points which dampened income differentials from collective work has been largely removed. Under the most prevalent forms of the responsibility system work point calculations have been abolished and hence the control on earnings differentials through the system of work point ratings for different workers has disappeared. The upshot of these changes is that the share of incremental income going to an individual worker will rise to 100 per cent, whereas previously it was lower than this to the extent that part of incremental income had gone to egalitarian distribution as well as being absorbed in a compressed 'wage structure'. The expected incomes for additional work of those workers who had previously withheld labour because of the redistributive features of the old system will rise and hence their effective labour input in efficiency units will also rise. By the same token those workers who enjoyed a 'free rider' element in their incomes will face reduced expected incomes and will have to react through increased effort to preserve their previous income. However, those who enjoyed a redistributive element in their incomes although they had worked to their fullest ability (such as weaker or less skilled workers) will face an unavoidable drop in their incomes.

The net effect of these changes on output, however, will depend on the extent of worker demoralisation and of actual work shirking that existed as well as the scope for increasing output through increased labour input. The higher the demoralisation the greater would be the expected increase in work efficiency and output on the part of previously discouraged workers. At the same time a high degree of demoralisation will also imply a wide prevalence of work shirking by the 'lazy' (otherwise there would be no cause for demoralisation). Both demoralisation and laziness imply a slack in labour input which could be taken up by the improved incentives. But whether or not this leads to increased output will depend on whether the slack in labour input had been a constraint on output growth or merely represented the limits of labour input. The latter case would be the diminishing total factor productivity situation discussed earlier.

Another important change affecting employment and labour allocation was a shift in the balance between private and communal economic activity. Several measures were introduced to increase the size of the private sector in the rural areas. The maximum percentage of total land that could be devoted to private plots was increased from 7 per cent to 15 per cent. Simultaneously, several restrictions on the range of activities in the private sector were lifted. Restrictions on the crops that could be grown on the private plots were removed and opportunities for free market sales of the produce from private plots have been improved through the lifting of restrictions on country fairs and markets. Thus, any demand constraints on production in the private plot arising from the restrictions on the disposal of output have been removed. In addition restrictions on non-crop and non-farm private sector activities have been lifted. For instance, restrictions on the number of chickens that can be raised, the rule that only hogs and not sows could be raised and the prohibition on the ownership of draught animals have all been lifted. Similarly, sideline occupations are now being encouraged and promoted. Households are now free to form enterprises for handicraft, other cottage industry and workshops for repair and servicing where previously all non-agricultural enterprises had to be within the structure of commune and brigade industries. Assistance in terms of technical know-how and marketing are now to be given to these 'enterprises jointly run by individual households' by the commune and brigade enterprises. Indirect control over the private sector through the stipulations on minimum compulsory participation in collective activity have also been relaxed. The current situation is that one or two members of a household can be exempted from collective labour and can participate full time in private sideline activities.[14] The only condition for being eligible for this exemption from collective labour is that the household should have surplus labour.

These measures aimed at liberalising and expanding the size and range of activities in the private sector could, from the point of view of employment and labour absorption, be seen as a means of transferring the burden of job creation to individual households, whereas this function had previously been very largely with the collective. Individual households are now allowed and even encouraged to generate 'self-employment' in private sideline occupations, a process which has parallels in the urban sector where self-employment has also come to be encouraged.

The changes with regard to household activities in the private non-farm sector are in fact part of larger changes which have been presaged in the experimental counties in Sichuan. Households not only are free to organise enterprises themselves but also are free to invest as stock-holders in the former brigade and commune industries which have been converted into corporations or joint-stock companies. These organisational changes in commune and brigade enterprises are, in fact, the heart of the virtual abolition of the erstwhile three-tier commune structure, but their important effect on the private economy and individual incentives needs to be noted. The main impact is on the balance between private and collective accumulation. The commune and brigade industries were a major source of accumulation in the old three-tier commune system and this accumulation relied on two basic mechanisms. One was through a high rate of reinvestment of the surplus of these enterprises. The second was the payments system in the Commune and Brigade Enterprises (CBEs) which kept wages at the level of average earnings in collective agriculture. The workers in the CBEs drawn from the teams were in fact paid within the same payments system which operated for the basic accounting unit (BAU) and earned work points in the same way as other members of the BAU. The BAU was paid, as a collective unit, by the CBEs and in turn paid workers within its own work point system. In this way the usual wage gap between agriculture and industry arising from productivity differentials could be controlled through the payments system and this 'wage suppression' allowed the high observed rate of accumulation of the CBEs. Wages in state industries were much higher than the agricultural 'wage' and hence the transfer of labour from agriculture raises aggregate disposable income, reduces surplus and creates a need to increase the supply of wage goods. In contrast, the transfer of labour from agriculture to industry (CBEs) within the old commune system did not have to contend with these disadvantages and hence industry could accumulate and grow at a high rate.

The new wage system in rural industry has tended to widen the gap between agricultural and industrial wages within the rural areas. In essence the change has been motivated by the same concern to link payment more directly to work that has characterised the reforms in agriculture. Specifically, this has meant a shift to a full piece-rate system supplemented by bonuses and penalties based on a comparison of actual performance with a production norm. There has also been a tendency to shift over to a system of cash wages paid monthly. However, the details of this new payments system in CBEs still vary considerably. For instance, in the two experimented counties (Qionglai and Guanghan) the two corporations have different payments systems in the CBEs. In the corporation based on the former Feng Huang Brigade, workers in the CBEs are still paid close to the agricultural wage. A system of work point accounting still prevailed and the average value of a workday was still the same for agricultural and industrial workers. However, workers in industry have 10 per cent more workdays and receive a bonus which is twice as large as that of agricultural workers. In the Jinan Joint Corporation of Guanghan county, on the other hand, the change has gone much further. Fifty per cent of the workers in industry are paid cash wages and these have been graded in relation to wages paid in state enterprises. The other 50 per cent receive half of their earnings in terms of a monthly wage and the remaining half as a settlement at the end of the year. In addition, two types of bonuses boost the earnings of workers. One is the bonus at the enterprise level: an enterprise exceeding its annual production quota (or norm) is paid a bonus which is divided among all workers.[15] The other is a 'piece-rate bonus' where, in the specific example given, a particular shift of ten workers in a chemical plant earned 0.20 yuan for each kilogramme by which they exceeded the quota of 50 kilogrammes per shift. It should be noted that for a given enterprise the first type of bonus is analogous to a 'collective incentive' in so far as the individual workers are concerned and even the second example is still not a case of a pure individual incentive. Thus, in general it is interesting to note that, except in cases where the nature of the product or the production process makes it possible to assign output to individual workers, the type of pure individual incentive aspired to in the reforms to the payments system in agriculture will not be attainable. Therefore, an element of the same problem with collective incentives could also prevail unless it is argued that the nature of work in industry is such that uniformity of performance per worker is easier to monitor and enforce than in agriculture.

These changes in the organisational structure of CBEs have occurred in the context of increased emphasis on growth and labour absorption in rural industries. In a majority of the communes visited there has been a spurt of growth in output and employment in rural industries and this has been particularly spectacular in the experimental counties in Sichuan. This is an intensification of a trend which pre-dates the reforms. In the mid-1970s to late 1970s, CBEs became an engine of growth in the rural economy, with a growth rate of 18 per cent per annum and the share of rural net output originating from CBEs increased to 15 per cent by 1979.[16]

The cumulative impact of all these changes from the standpoint of labour allocation is to alter the range of choice that is available as well as the relative returns from different activities. The expansion of private agriculture and the liberalisation of non-farm private activities means more scope for applying family labour into such activities. If the level of labour input into such activities had been limited by the demands of collective work, then it is likely that the marginal returns to labour had been higher than in collective agriculture and that the expansion of private activity was thus consistent with the labour allocation aspirations of households. Against this, however, must be set the fact that the marginal returns to labour in collective work for a large proportion of individuals would also have been raised by the reforms. Unfortunately no data are available on what has happened to the relative returns to labour in the two sectors as a result of the recent changes. A further complication is that the returns to labour as well as opportunities for employment in CBEs have also risen as a result of recent developments.

Thus returns to labour are likely to have risen all round but no data exist for it to be possible to tell how relative returns have changed among activities. Yet another complication is that the division between private and collective agriculture becomes blurred with the shift to *bao gan dao hu*. In the extreme case, where the latter implies contracting for collective land by a household against only the payment of a fixed sum for tax, accumulation and the welfare fund, the distinction between the private plot and collective land contracted in by the family is slight. The difference probably lies in the fact that the contract for collective land is intended to be adjusted periodically, is subject to tax, accumulation levies and procurement and its economic use has to be under the guidance of unified production plans. The latter (based on information for Sichuan) refers to unified practices concerning seeds, irrigation and the use of farm implements still managed by the collective. The private plot, on the other hand, is free from such restrictions and may be used even for concentrating on non-farm activities such as pig raising. In addition, the disposal of output from the contracted-in collective land has still to be within the framework of the state's procurement policies (i.e. sales at the basic procurement and premium procurement have to be made and only the excess production after meeting these obligations may be made in the free market), whereas after the recent changes the disposal of output from the private plot is free of restrictions. Thus, even in the case of extreme *bao gan dao hu* there are differences between collective land and the private plot and it should be noted that these differences are stronger in the less extreme forms of the responsibility system. Under *bao chan dao hu*, for instance, a system of work point accounting still operates and a rationing system with a redistributive element still remains intact. Another important difference to bear in mind is that the average size of a plot of collective land contracted in by a household is much larger than the private plot; on average it would tend to be more than six times as large. This, of course, implies very different possibilities for labour absorption.

Thus far we have concentrated more on market rather than administrative reforms. The former are those reforms which have had their primary impact on collective and individual incentives and where we have touched upon administrative reforms they have been only with reference to changes which have resulted in greater freedom for economic association and decision-making for households, thereby affecting individual incentives. But the question of administrative reform is also important in spite of the fact that it has tended recently to be overshadowed by the market reforms.

It has been observed that in the past 'discussion of economic reform in China focused almost exclusively on administrative forms of decentralisation rather than decentralisation through the market'.[17] It focused on issues such as the transfer of industrial and commercial enterprises to local management and was characterised by the retention of a high degree of centralised control of economic policy instruments to achieve distributive goals and to prevent the emergence of 'subordinate autarchy' which would result in the loss of inter-regional specialisation and economies of scale. There was also a heavy reliance on non-market mechanisms to limit inequality both in rural and urban areas.[18] Viewed in this light, the recent reforms can be seen as preserving a basic continuity in the macroeconomic framework. The overall agricultural planning system still remains intact with its production targets, input allocations, procurement system and 'unified production plan' which guides production techniques and relative input use. Similarly, the growth and operations of CBEs still remain within the framework of material supply planning and the system of allocating inputs. Even the free market in grain remains a very small part of the production system. In 1979 out of a total grain production of 332 million tons only 5 to 6 million tons were sold at free market prices. This represented only 10 per cent of the total marketed surplus.[19] Thus 'annual plans continue to be central to resource allocation, investment and production in agriculture'.[20] The allocation of critical inputs to the level of counties is still determined by these annual production plans.

The locus of the rural reforms has thus been at the level below the county. The administrative reforms affecting the three-tier commune system, for instance, could be seen as a transfer of administrative functions to the xiangs (the administrative unit below the county) without necessarily leading to greater decentralisation in economic decision-making to lower-level economic units. It is not clear that the new joint corporations in the two experimental counties enjoy any greater economic autonomy than the former commune and brigade-run enterprises. New organisational forms have no doubt emerged but it is not obvious that these new entities have a more autonomous role, as economic units, within the macro planning system.

It is below the level of the communes that most of what could be characterised as administrative reforms have taken place and these changes could, in fact, be seen as decentralisation to progressively smaller units down to the household. The steps in the transition process have followed this decentralisation paradigm. Apart from the two experimental counties the commune system has remained intact and the changes have consisted of decentralisation within the commune. One important change was to lower the level of the Basic Accounting Unit. This was a reversal of the pre-1978 policy of raising the BAU from the team to brigade and even commune level. By 1981 the number of communes and brigades serving as BAUs had each been reduced by 50 per cent compared to 1978 and as a result of this only some 5 per cent of brigades remained as BAUs, compared to 10 per cent in 1978. Together with these changes the average size of a collective unit in agriculture has also been reduced. The main thrust of these changes was the reduction in the average size of teams and by 1981 the number of teams had increased by 25 per cent compared to 1978. In addition to this the size of groupings below the team was also reduced. In teams where workgroups did not exist, these were created and where work groups existed they tended to be broken up into smaller groups. The limit to this process has, of course, been the shift to a system of contracting with households which then becomes the basic unit for taking production decisions and implementing production targets. But it should be noted that, except with *bao gan dao hu*, in all these instances of decentralisation below the level of the team, the team continues to have an economic function. In the system with work groups and *bao chan dao hu* the team still serves as the Basic Accounting Unit, a system of work points with a redistributive element still operates and the team remains as the decision-making unit determining production targets and practices as well as the allocation of land to work groups or households. Even in the case of extreme *bao gan dao hu* the team has not ceased to exist. Although there is no longer a team-level payments system the team is still the unit of implementing the unified production plan, for running residual collective economic activities[21] and maintaining residual collective property such as machinery and equipment. Most importantly it is still the team which determines the allocation of land to be contracted out to households and its periodic reallocation in the light of changing circumstances within the team. It is also presumably the unit which monitors, supervises and polices the functioning of the responsibility system. In addition some of the new reforms have increased the economic role of the team by allowing the formation of enterprises below the level of the brigade. Thus in the Jinan Corporation in Sichuan province the new co-operatives running enterprises are in fact based on the former teams.

In this way, the sequence of changes in terms of administrative reforms has been a step by step approach analogous to decentralisation of economic decision-making to lower-level units up to the individual household. The usefulness of seeing the changes in this perspective may, of course, be questioned. Decentralisation to the household might sound like a contradiction in terms since it could be argued that this is indistinguishable from a system of private farming where it is also the household which is the lowest-level decision-making unit. The aim in describing the reforms in the context of decentralisation has, however, been to emphasise the essential continuity in the agricultural planning system in China and to underline that this in many important respects makes the Chinese system distinct from one of private agriculture. While the individual household now has greater freedom in economic decision-making, that freedom is not in any sense within a market system but is very much within a centrally planned one. In spite of the reforms, free markets do not exist for land, labour or material inputs, all critical elements in agricultural production. Land transactions in any form are not possible, labour hiring is not allowed, the restrictions on labour mobility still remain and the allocation of material inputs is determined by plan allocations.

What has made these administrative changes appear dramatic has, of course, been the simultaneous changes in the payments system. These changes have given the decentralised units not only greater power of decision-making but also the right to retain more of their own output. An individual household now has to pay less by way of the redistributive 'tax' inherent in the egalitarian features of the old system.[22] But in essence the economic environment in terms of the determination of prices they face or the systems of allocating material inputs and labour remain unchanged.

An important economic issue raised by these changes is that of the appropriate size of the management unit and how this relates to economies of scale. Hitherto, the collectivisation of agriculture in China has been based on the pooling of land resources and the joint ownership of major assets. Although the dominant motivation behind this was to achieve an income distribution objective, it could also be supposed that the drive to collectivise implied the belief that economies of scale could be reaped. Group farming must have been held to be superior to purely individualised (though egalitarian) farming. The changes in the size of communes, brigades and teams since the beginning of collectivisation could be seen, apart from redistributive objectives, as attempts to arrive at the appropriate size of the farm management unit from the standpoint of productive efficiency.

The recent changes in reducing the size of collective units could be seen as a revision of views concerning the importance of economies of scale. Two interpretations are possible. One is that the problems with the payments system and administration within the commune structure outweighed the advantages of economies of scale and, as such, de-emphasising the group farming element became inevitable because of the need to reform the payments system. The other is that economies of scale were not significant to begin with and the previous faith in group farming was misplaced. No information is available to decide on which of these interpretations is closer to the minds of the policy-makers. Nonetheless, the arguments for reform discussed in the previous section appear to favour the former interpretation. The case for reform emphasised not only worker demoralisation under the old payments system but also administrative problems such as 'commandism' or arbitrary decision-making by commune, brigade and team leaders. One aspect of 'commandism' was the neglect of the specifics of local conditions and the views of individual members, and this was held to have arisen because the collective units were too large and because there was little internal democracy. Hence the need to reduce the size of collective units and to allow a greater say in decision-making to individual households. The latter would allow the initiative and knowledge of local conditions of the individual farmers to become paramount in decisions on farming practices. Thus, one interpretation could be that even if technical economies of scale in production were important, the diseconomies of scale in administration arising from a lack of internal democracy outweighed them. In addition there were the problems with the payment system.

In deciding between the two possible interpretations, however, it is what happens at the level of the team under the new system which is most important. Although units larger than the team have been important with respect to capital construction projects, irrigation and large-scale mechanisation, it has been the team which has constituted the effective unit of farm management. The shift to a system of contracting with households could thus be seen as a weakening or even abolition of this farm management function of the team. In the case of extreme *bao gan dao hu* where collectively owned farm machinery and draught animals have been sold to individual households, it would appear that the group farming element and farm management by the team have disappeared. In other cases such as *bao chan dao hu* the teams still function as a payment unit and communally owned means of production have remained. In these cases the farm management functions of the team probably remain. Moreover, in those communes and teams which have resisted the change to a household contracting system, the reasons given have been based on economies of scale arguments and the imperative of maintaining communally owned means of production.[23]

Ultimately, the issue of what will become the effective unit of farm management in China will depend on what interpretation can be attached to the policy declaration that under the system of household contracting production will still remain under the 'guidance of a unified production plan'. On the one hand, this could be interpreted as the maintenance of the essential elements of group farming (or farm management) where economies of scale (or diseconomies of non-uniformity) are significant, such as the use of uniform seeds, management of irrigation and common farm machinery. Thus, it is only the other functions which are decentralised and the household contracting system could be seen as a form of piece-rate, 'putting out' system of those functions where working communally is not important for efficiency. On the other hand, it could be argued that the 'unified production plan' has no real significance and the system of household contracting has become one of individual farming based on fixed rental tenancy with the team serving as the 'landlord' and without any farm management functions. In most of the collective units visited by the author during the field trip, the team still maintained substantial farm management functions. However, it has to be noted that this was an unrepresentative sample in view of the fact that teams practising the most widespread form of household contracting – *bao gan dao hu* – were grossly under-represented. In all but one of the teams visited, some farm management functions were retained. Farm implements and irrigation facilities were still communally run and the unified production plan appeared to impinge on several aspects of farming practices. Moreover, even in the teams practising household contracting under *bao chan dao hu* the contract with households typically contained specifications on farming practices. The contract specified not simply target outputs but also other 'fixes' such as a given level of fertiliser and labour input. These fixes are clearly designed to guide relative factor inputs and to ensure uniformity of farming practices within a team.

A final point of interest regarding the reforms is how the different elements of change that we have discussed were managed. They were part of a coherent process of transition management with several interesting features. One of the first steps in the reform was the use of conventional macroeconomic instruments to create a favourable economic environment in the rural areas. This involved the use of the procurement system to shift the terms of trade sharply in favour of the rural economy. Rural incomes were thereby raised through this terms of trade effect, as were the returns to labour. The receptiveness to the reforms and experimentation was likely to have been greatly enhanced. In much the same way the stimulus to rural industry contributed to an improved economic climate in the rural areas. Amidst this improving economic climate, the reforms centred upon the payments and production system were introduced in a step-by-step fashion. A typical sequence observed on the field trip was for the level of accounting to be reduced first. This was then followed by the institution of work groups prior to the shift to household contracting. Again the system of household contracting first introduced was *bao chan dao hu* which still retained a system of work point accounting with some redistributive element. *Bao gan dao hu* was then the final stage of transition. Thus, although the changes were compressed within a relatively short period of three years, abrupt shifts were avoided and some allowance was made for adaptation and experimentation. As mentioned earlier, all but two of the collective units visited on the field trip had still not adopted *bao gan dao hu* and several had declared their intention not to do so at all. The same element of experimentation was also very striking in the case of the administrative reforms affecting the three-tier commune system. Up till the summer of 1982 only a handful of counties had instituted the changes and these counties had been officially referred to as 'experiments', and experimentation with alternative institutional forms was very much in evidence in the two such counties visited.

THE NEW SYSTEMS OF WORK ORGANISATION AND PAYMENTS

The new systems of work organisation and payments involve a departure from the system of communal production and distribution based on the team or higher level units. They all involve decentralisation to units lower than the team, that is work groups and households. In all cases access to land is the main determinant of income for the work group or household, since the reforms involve a fragmentation of the total production to work groups or households who receive a payment closely related to their own production. The system by which land is allocated is thus central to the final distribution of incomes.

The information obtained from the field on the basis on which land is distributed is summarised in Table 4.1. The striking feature is that in only one of the six collective units is land distributed on a per labour force (or per worker) basis and that too is in a unit where the work group system prevails. In all other cases at least 40 per cent of the land

TABLE 4.1 *Land distribution under various contracting systems*

Name of collective unit	*Type of responsibility system*	*% of contracted land distributed on per capita basis*	*% of contracted land distributed on basis of labour force*	*Additional feature*
1. Xu Guang Brigade, Mi Mu Peoples Commune, Xindu county, Sichuan	BCDH	40	60	
2. Phoenix Joint Corporation, Qionglai county, Sichuan	BCDH	40	60	
3. Jinan Joint Corporation, Guanghan county, Sichuan	Work groups			Equal division by work group
4. Sun Jin Brigade, Chun He Peoples Commune, Yunnan	Work groups			Land allocated to work group on per labour force basis
5. Gao Chio Team, Pu Chao Brigade, Ala Peoples Commune, Yunnan	BGDH	100		Voluntary additional contracting on 6 per cent of total collective land, also half of orchard land (7 per cent of total area) contracted out to labour-weak families
6. Team No. 7, Xiang Sui Brigade, Xiao She Qiao Commune, Yu Xi county, Yunnan	BGDH	100		

NOTE BCDH = *bao chan dao hu*
BGDH = *bao gan dao hu*

contracted out is on a per capita basis, and particularly interesting is the fact that in the only two teams practising *bao gan dao hu* the land distribution is entirely on a per capita basis. The significance of this is that, given the differential endowments of labour in households arising from demographic and life-cycle effeccts, distribution on a per worker basis will reinforce differences in earning power arising from differential labour endowments. In contrast distribution of land on a per capita basis gives labour-weak households more land per worker and thus tends to dampen inequalities arising from differential labour endowments. This would hold true so long as the land distributed on a per capita basis is not larger than the maximum area that can be worked by the labour in a given household. In this case the 'surplus' land would not add to income. However, given the very low land/man ratios in China this is a very unlikely possibility except for households with extremely high dependency ratios. It is also interesting to note that in one of the *bao gan dao hu* villages an additional redistributive element exists in the system of allocating work on half of the communal orchards[24] to labour-weak households.

Information on other features of the payments system obtained during the field trip is summarised in Table 4.2. It will be seen that those collective units still operating on the basis of work groups have essentially retained the old payments system. Work points are earned on the basis of output produced by the work group or on a piece-rate basis. The main change has been the introduction of quotas (or targets) and bonuses (penalties) for exceeding (falling below) quotas. The level of bonuses and penalties appears to be 100 per cent; thus a work group exceeding the quota keeps all the additional output to be distributed amongst its members. However, the range within which this bonus and penalty system operates is limited. The quotas are typically set on the basis of the average of the past three years production and thus bonus is earned only by surpassing the previous normal output levels. Unless output was substantially below potential, it is unlikely that a substantial increment in output is likely. Indeed, information from the field trip tends to confirm this view. In Chao Tan Brigade, the production quota was exceeded by 8 to 10 per cent on the average and in Co-operative Number 7 of the Jinan Joint Corporation the quota was exceeded by a margin of only 3.6 per cent. Therefore, in this particular case the new system operates only on marginal income and its overall impact is for this reason likely to be slight. The other change in the payments system was a reduction in the proportion of grain that was distributed as a food ration on a per capita basis. In the only case where information was

TABLE 4.2 *Distribution system*

Name of collective unit	*Contracting system*	*Basis for earning work points*	*Basis for distributing work points*	*Nature of contract*				*Cultivated land per worker (Mu)*	*Average value of workday (1981) (Yuan)*
				Quota (or target)	*Bonus (penalty) for above (below) quota*	*Labour fix*	*Other conditions*		
1. Fu Bao Brigade, Liu Jia Commune, Yunnan	Work groups	Work points per unit of output and bonus work points	Bonus distributed by work group internally					1.1	1.1
2. Jinan Joint Corporation, Guanghan county, Sichuan	,,	Work points per unit of output		Average of past 3 years output	100% bonus and penalty	38 man-days per man for paddy			
3. Chao Tan Brigade, Yuan Men Ko Commune, Sichuan	,,	Work points per unit value of output		Average of past 3 years output	100% bonus and penalty				
4. Team No. 1, Gao Chang Brigade, Gao Chang Commune Yu Xi, Yunnan	,,	10 work points per 4.5 yuan of output for tobacco 23 to 30 work points per mu for paddy						1.8	2.3
5. Sun Jin Brigade, Chung He Commune, Yu Xi county, Yunnan	,,	Work points per unit output	50% of grain distributed per capita					1.7	

6. Xu Guang Brigade, Mi Mu Peoples Commune, Sichuan	BCDH	Work points per unit of output	80% of grain distributed on per capita basis	Average of past 3 years output	100% bonus and penalty	80 days per mu for paddy		1.5	1.0
7. Phoenix Corporation, Qionglai county, Sichuan	BCDH			800 jin per mu for paddy	100% bonus and penalty			1.7	3.5
8. Team No. 8 (San Jia Cun), Long Xu Brigade, Gao Chang Commune, Yunnan	BCDH	0.7 work points per jin of grain		700 jin per mu for maize	100% bonus and penalty			4.8	
9. Team No. 7, Xiang Sui Brigade, Xiao She Qiao Commune, Yunnan	BGDH						50 jin + 3 yuan per mu paid to team. Households keep the rest		
10. Gao Chio Team, Pu Chao Brigade, Ala Peoples Commune, Yunnan	BGDH						126 jin per mu paid to team. Households keep the rest	3.3	

obtained on this point the proportion distributed on a per capita basis was reduced from 70 per cent to 50 per cent, again not a dramatic change. Thus, for those units which have introduced or continued with the work group system the change in the payments system has been slight; the old system has been supplemented by a mild bonus and penalty system.

For the three teams practising *bao chan dau hu* the same observations also broadly hold true. The quotas are set on the same basis of the average of three years' production or are high in relation to past yields per mu. In the only case where information was available on the point, 80 per cent of the grain was distributed on a per capita basis under the food rationing system. A crucial difference between this system of household contracting, however, lies in the way work points are earned. In the work group system, the old system of work point rating or piece rates is used and some operations are still done jointly. Thus, it does not allow for a direct link between production and reward for each individual worker. Under *bao chan dao hu*, on the other hand, this becomes possible through the allocation of responsibility to individual households on specific plots. Work points are earned per unit of output produced by an individual household and thus the only redistributive elements would be the food rationing system, the distribution of contracted land to households on a per capita basis and special redistributive features such as allocation of light work to labour weak households. Therefore, the work point system *per se* no longer has the redistributive function it used to have under team or work group systems of accounting.

With the two teams practising *bao gan dao hu* the work point system disappears and the households pay a fixed sum per unit of land to cover their tax, accumulation fund and welfare fund obligations. The burden of these obligations to the collective are thus levied on the basis of land contracted out from the team. The households keep the rest of the output and in fact the level of the obligatory payments is very small in relation to yields. In both the production teams practising *bao gan dao hu* the payment to the team represented about 16 per cent of yields. The contracting households have to bear the cost of production so the payment to the team would be a higher proportion of net income. Assuming that the cost of purchased inputs represents about one third of gross output, the payment would represent about a quarter of net output. If the payments to the team are seen as analogous to a rent, then the level of rents is considerably lower than that under tenancy systems prevailing in other developing countries.

It is also of interest to note that in the Gao Chio production team draught animals (horses and buffaloes) and small farm implements have been sold to households within the team and the only remaining collective economic activities are an orchard, a kiln and a mill. In this way, communal ownership of the means of production, a key aspect of group farming since the inception of collectivisation in Chinese agriculture, has been effectively abolished in the case of this team. Apart from running the collectively owned enterprises, the remaining functions of the team are limited to the maintenance of the irrigation systems and administering the land contracting system and the welfare fund.

Bao gan dao hu is now the most widely practised form of the responsibility system and it is useful to examine the case of Gao Chio team a little more closely. As it evolved up till the summer of 1982, the payments system in Gao Chio team represents about the furthest movement away from the old system that is at present envisaged by policy-makers in China. Apart from the residual collective team enterprises it has all the features of a full-fledged *bao gan dao hu* system. It is thus of interest to consider the determinants of household income and labour allocation within this team.

From the standpoint of an individual household, access to land (in addition to the private plot) is guaranteed and the principle of distribution is egalitarian. This access to land is conditional upon meeting the fixed payment to the team but this, as we have seen, is not onerous. It is not clear whether a household can choose not to contract land if it so wishes, but given the rising returns from working the land because of the increase in agricultural prices and the share of output which is retained by the cultivators, this would appear to be an unlikely possibility. There are, however, no minimum requirements for labour input into this 'collective' agriculture; the rule has been abolished and the contract does not contain any fixes specifying labour or other inputs. This, coupled with the new freedom to own farm machinery and draught animals, means that the household is free to adjust factor proportions in production.

Apart from contracting communal land, other income-earning activities open to the household are the private plot and sideline activities, setting up new household enterprises which are now permitted and wage-employment in collectively owned industry (run either as CBEs or in the form of corporations). On the supply side almost all labour time in the household can be allocated at its own discretion. Minimum labour inputs into collective agriculture have been removed and the labour conscription for capital construction projects within the old three-tier commune system no longer makes demands on household labour supply. Thus more labour time is available but whether or not this leads to greater labour input will depend on the labour absorption in the new activities. In particular, labour mobilisation for capital construction used to be a means of using labour during the slack agricultural season, and whether or not the labour released from this activity will be used for activities yielding higher returns to the household depends on how successful it becomes in generating self-employment either in agriculture or cottage industries.

In the old system labour was virtually the only source of earnings, but this is no longer true. Households can now acquire farm machinery and this can augment the labour power available to a household and can be a source of rental income. In addition, households can invest in household-level non-farm enterprises and in financial assets such as the shares of the new joint corporations created in the experimental counties in Sichuan. In the past the only outlets for savings were expenditure on the household's dwelling or acquiring a consumer durable such as a bicycle or sewing machine. The latter could be used for own-production but presumably not for commercial purposes.

Thus the determinants of income are now more varied and also for this reason there is a possibility for greater variations in income amongst households. The more hardworking, skillful and thrifty stand to earn more than households less so. In agriculture the ceiling on earnings was set by the relatively narrow range of the 'wage structure' embedded in the work point system and also by possible disincentive effects arising from the 'free rider' problem. In addition, 'augmented labour power' in the form of farm machinery and equipment now enters as a further source of income differentiation. Those households able to earn and save more can capitalise on this initial advantage by investing in complementary factors to increase the productivity of land and labour. The extent of this source of differentiation, however, will be contained within fairly narrow limits so long as the egalitarian principle of land distribution and a prohibition of land transactions is maintained. The small size of contracted-out plots puts a firm limit on the amount of mechanisation possible. Thus, households with a lower initial savings rate could still catch up to the feasible level of mechanisation obtained by those with higher initial savings capacity.

To the extent that mechanisation is labour-saving, the household can also divert more labour into private sideline activities or new household enterprises where differences in entrepreneurial skills and savings capacity will result in income differences. However, this source of differentiation is again likely to be kept within limits so long as the rule against the hiring of labour is not relaxed. Moreover, the household enterprises exist within a definite hierarchical structure and it is inconceivable that within the present economic system these would be allowed to grow to the point where they would compete with higher-level enterprises. The new possibility of investing in the shares of the new joint corporations that have emerged in the experimental communes also serves as an additional source of income differentiation. In contrast to the previous system this now allows returns on household investment which hitherto had no such productive outlets. In the case of one of the experimental counties ownership of shares in the joint corporations also gives an added edge to shareholders in that they and their relatives are given preference for employment in these industries.

The overall impression is that possibilities for increasing income inequality have been created. At the same time, the scope for a cumulative widening of income is severely limited by the egalitarian land distribution, the prohibition on land transactions with contracted land and on labour-hiring, and the limits to the growth of household enterprises. Indeed, impressionistic evidence from the field trip tends to suggest that the first round of savings from income gains in recent years has not gone into directly productive investment. In Sichuan, the substantial increases in income that have occurred in the experimental counties appear to have gone mainly into new housing or improvements to houses. Other popular items of expenditure were consumer goods such as radios, cassette recorders and watches. In Yunnan, we have already noted the case of Gao Chio team where households bought the horses and buffaloes which had been communally owned but the purchases were widely distributed. A total of fifty-four animals were sold and 70 per cent of households in the team purchased at least one animal. Information from a household survey in Yunnan indicates that in the province as a whole expenditure on consumer goods such as bicycles, sewing machines and watches increased by more than average income between 1980 and 1981. However, expenditure on 'buying means of production' also increased sharply, from 6.5 per cent of total income in 1980 to 11.8 per cent in 1981.[25] No details were available on what this item of expenditure included.

Of course, all these changes in the payments system which have widened the range of income earning opportunities would also have brought about adjustments in the labour allocation decisions of households. It is difficult to judge on the basis of the available data how the relative returns to labour in different activities have changed. If before the reforms labour input into private activities was 'demand determined', then the increased size of the private plot and liberalisation measures would have increased the opportunities for allocating more household labour to such activities. If it had been 'supply determined', then the relaxation of the obligations to provide collective labour would also have been an additional factor allowing a greater allocation into these activities. Against this has to be set the increased returns to labour from collective agriculture arising from the improvement in the terms of trade and in the share of output retained by the household. It is also possible that, apart from changes in the relative returns to labour in private and 'collective' activity, labour input to both sectors increased, either because of a labour supply-response or because there was under-utilised labour within the household. It is also relevant that the reforms to the payments system in commune and brigade industry raised the attractiveness of their jobs. The switch to cash wages and the linking of these to wages in state industries greatly enhanced the attractiveness of these jobs. It should be noted that such jobs were in great demand even before the reforms because they offered more year-round employment than in agriculture.

No systematic information was collected on changes in labour allocation and the best that can be done is to report a few fragments of information which have a bearing on the issue. In two collective units in Yunnan, the reforms appear to have increased the attractiveness of farming relative to work in commune and brigade industries. In Team No. 18 of Long Xu Brigade, Gao Chang Peoples Commune, it was reported that two-thirds of the team members who were working in commune and brigade industries had returned to farming after the reforms. In Sun Jin Brigade of Chun He Peoples Commune one of the reasons given for not adopting household contracting was that it would lead to a withdrawal of labour from commune and brigade industries. In both these cases, however, it is not known what changes, if any, had been made to wages in the CBEs. In Gao Chang Peoples Commune, it was reported that there was little demand for contracting additional land because more work points could be earned from sideline occupations. In four collective units for which data were available, the average value of a workday had increased substantially since the introduction of the reforms. In three of these cases the value of a workday had at least doubled between 1978 and 1981. A final bit of information relevant to the question of labour allocation is the dramatic increase in income from the private sector in rural areas. Data from a National Household Survey show that between 1978 and 1981 average family income increased by 67 per cent, whereas income from 'family sidelines' increased by 167 per cent increasing the share of total income from this source from 27 to 37 per cent over the period.

POTENTIAL EFFECTS ON EMPLOYMENT AND INCOME DISTRIBUTION

The effects of the reforms on total rural employment are again difficult to judge. However, several factors point towards increasing total employment. The improvement in the terms of trade and rising returns to labour can be expected to have a positive impact on labour supply and employment. Similarly, the expansion and liberalisation measures in the private sector and the expansion of rural industry are also likely to exercise a positive impact on total employment. The greater range of investment and consumption possibilities now available will also have a positive effect on the incentive to work. The cases of communes where there has been, or was expected to be, a return of labour into collective agriculture would be examples of the positive effects of the reforms on rural employment. Against these possible positive effects, however, must be set several negative ones. The first is the loss of the commune system as a guarantor of employment and as a mechanism for mobilising labour. As we have seen, with the reforms the responsibility for generating employment has now been shifted from the collective to the individual household. This creates the possibility of a loss of employment for some workers in collective agriculture. References to successful cases of implementation of the reform mention not only output gains but also the rise in labour productivity and the release of surplus labour from collective agriculture.[26] In general, to the extent that there was disguised unemployment in the old system, this could show up as open unemployment unless new employment opportunities in new household and rural industrial activities are sufficient to absorb any labour that is released. However, if the contracting with households remains on the basis of an equal distribution of land to each household, then any burden of work sharing would simply be shifted from the collective to the household and need not show up openly. An identifiable group of households with no agricultural employment available to them would not appear. If the diagnosis of the reformers on worker demoralisation under the old system is correct, then this would mean that effective labour input into agriculture in each household would increase and more labour time would now be available for other activities, since the element of time-stretching simulation of work (or work at less than full capacity) would be no longer necessary.

Some of the effects on income distribution have already been touched upon in the previous section. The new system potentially allows wider differentials in income but at the same time also contains features which will keep these differences within limits. Differences in endowments of labour will be an important source of income differences, but this is largely based on a 'life-cycle' element which is an inherent source of income differences within any system. It is thus unlikely to be a source of permanent differences or lead to widening cumulative differences in income. Differences from variations in the means of production and other assets are potentially a more powerful and lasting sources of differentiation but, as already discussed, several features of the new system will tend to keep these differences in check. Indeed, to the extent that land is allocated to households under contract on a per capita basis, income inequalities will be less than under the previous work point system.

Although the new system appears on balance to allow for wider income differentials, it does not follow that this is necessarily an inevitable outcome. It is conceivable that the improved incentives lead to a near universal enthusiasm to work and that income differences do not widen and may even narrow. For example, if the lower-income households were also the more demoralised ones under the old system, then the reforms could lead to an initial narrowing of income differences. Ultimately, the determinants of the final income distribution in the new system are more complex and difficult to predict *a priori*. Unfortunately, neither has there been sufficient reliable empirical data to provide a guide. In the two cases where data were obtained on the change in income distribution since the inception of the new system, there appears to have been a decrease rather than an increase in inequality.[27]

It is interesting to consider one of the above two cases where more detailed information is available on the impact of the responsibility system on income distribution. This is Team No. 2 of the Phoenix Corporation in one of the experimental counties in Sichuan. In this team of thirty-one households per capita distributed collective income increased dramatically between 1977 and 1981, namely, from 72 yuan to 497 yuan. The contracting system adopted in this team was *bao chan dao hu*. A work point system still operates and collective distributed income still records income from land contracted by households. As such these income statistics capture the major part of total income.[28] The major source of income increase in the Phoenix Corporation, of which the team is a part, was the dramatic expansion in rural industry and this is reflected in the occupational structure of the team where about forty-five of the sixty-eight workers have at least a part time industrial job.

The striking feature of the income change in this team is that inequality was reduced sharply – the coefficient of variation fell from 0.32 to 0.22. In 1977, nineteen out of the then thirty-two households in the team had a per capita collective distributed income of less than 300 yuan per month, but in 1981 there were no households below this income level. In the latter year twenty-six out of thirty-one households had per capita incomes of between 300 to 600 yuan, only four had per capita incomes between 600 to 800 yuan and none exceeded this income level. Thus, the income gains were widely diffused throughout the team and households which were poorer in the initial year increased their incomes very substantially indeed.

What explains the above pattern of income change? A major explanation appears to be the equal distribution of the most important new income-earning opportunities – a job in an industrial enterprise – among households in the team. All households[29] had at least one worker in the greatly expanded industrial sector.[30] Furthermore, a rough proportionality to household size appeared to have been followed for distributing additional jobs above the basic one per household distribution. Four households in the team had three workers in industry and these were the four largest households in the team (with seven to nine members).

The other striking feature is that the introduction of *bao chan dao hu* does not appear to have caused an increase in inequality in incomes from collective agriculture. In the first place the bonus element accounts for only 8 per cent of total agricultural income in the team which in turn was only 45.5 per cent of total income. Thus, it is only a minor influence on income differences. Secondly, the dispersion in the amount of bonus earned is very narrow; as will be seen in Table 4.3 it ranges from only 18 to 34 yuan per capita per household and about half the households earned a bonus of 23 yuan. It will also be noticed that there is no systematic tendency for a higher bonus to be associated with higher per capita incomes. Table 4.4 shows the distribution of contracted land per capita and at first sight this might appear to be fairly unequal; the range is from 0.7 mu to 3.5 mu. However, it will be noticed that there is an equalising tendency in that the households contracting plots smaller than 1.2 mu per capita were also those which had more workers in industrial employment. There was also no clear tendency for a larger size

TABLE 4.3 *Team No. 2, Phoenix Corporation: agricultural bonus per capita by land per capita and income per capita*

Bonus per capita (Yuan)	*0*	*18*	*20*	*21*	*23*	*24*	*26*	*27*	*30*	*32*	*34*
Land per capita (individual observation)	0	1.1	1.2	0.8	1.2	2.4	1.2	1.5	2.3	0.9	2.3
		1.64		0.9	1.4				1.4	3.48	
					1.6						
					0.8						
					1.7						
					1.0						
					2.9						
					1.0						
					1.2						
					1.4						
					1.2						
					1.9						
					0.7						
Average land per capita	0	1.37	1.2	0.85	1.48	2.4	1.2	1.5	1.85	1.78	2.3
Number of households	0	2	1	2	13	1	1	1	2	2	1
Average income per capita	423	418	364	378	421	533	372	377	631	377	454

Table 4.4 *Team No. 2, Phoenix Corporation: per capita distribution of contracted land*

Per capita contracted land	*No. of households*	*No. of workers in industry per household (individual observation)*	*Per capita income (individual observation)*	*Average per capita income*
0	4	1, 1, 1, 1	328, 344, 386, 642	425
0.7	1	2	380	380
0.8	2	1, 3	350, 352	351
0.9	2	1, 1	406, 344	375
1.0	2	3, 1	425, 356	391
1.1	1	3	374	374
1.2	5	2, 2, 1, 2, 3	419, 372, 465, 685, 364	461
1.4	3	1, 1, 1	550, 441, 353	448
1.5	1	1	377	377
1.6	2	2, 2	702, 462	582
1.7	1	1	322	322
1.9	1	1	357	357
2.3	2	1, 1	712, 454	583
2.4	1	2	533	533
2.9	1	1	544	544
3.5	1	1	329	329

of contracted land to be associated with higher per capita incomes. Thus, the case of this team does illustrate the possibility of income inequality being contained in the face of sharp increases in income if appropriate policies such as the allocation of industrial jobs on an equitable basis are adopted. It should be noted that this particular team does not represent the most far-reaching changes possible. It has not adopted *bao gan dao hu*, the payments system in rural industry has not been changed substantially, and household enterprises have not emerged.

The pattern of income change in the above team illustrates one possible configuration with regard to the balance of gainers and losers from the reforms. In this case all were better off absolutely and inequality also was reduced. But, as mentioned earlier, it is possible that the outcome could have been different in other cases. The incomes of some households only could have increased; the others could have remained no worse off absolutely but then inequality would have increased. Alternatively, one could envisage the incomes of some falling absolutely and inequality rising. In fact the arguments for reform to the payments system *per se* suggested that there would be losers as well as gainers. Other things being equal, a removal of the redistributive element in the old payments system would have had an adverse effect on those enjoying a net redistributive element in their incomes. These would have been either the weak or the lazy (the free riders); the former would be unable to do much to redress matters in the new system but the latter group could, of course, increase their supply of effort in the new situation. The gainers would be those who had been previously discouraged by the redistributive element. The reason why this pattern was not seen in the team under discussion was that other things were not constant. One was a factor applicable to the whole of rural China, the sharp improvement in the terms of trade for agriculture. This led to sharply improved collective incentives and tended to increase incomes and the return to labour across the board. The second factor was more specific to the Phoenix Corporation of which the team was part, namely the phenomenal increase in industrial production which brought about a major structural change in the economy of the team. This was a powerful source of income increase which was, as we have seen, distributed equitably. Thus, if one were to extrapolate from the outcome in this particular team, it needs to be borne in mind that only the improvement in the terms of trade would be a common element. The increase in industrial output far exceeds that for rural China as a whole and, furthermore, the reforms in the payments system had not gone as far as it has in the majority of collective units in rural China. The balance of gainers and losers could thus be very different and would depend largely on the extent to which the effects of the reform of the payments system *per se* is offset by the positive effect on income arising from the improvement in the terms of trade. In this connection it is interesting to note that in terms of transition management, the engineering of a 'boom' in the rural economy through improving the terms of trade and stimulating rural industry has probably masked the redistributive tensions which were inherent in the process of reforming the payments system. However, the 'boom' is probably not sustainable, given other macroeconomic objectives and the experience of dramatic industrial growth in a handful of 'model' counties is not likely to be one that is widely replicable.

CONCLUSION

At one level the reforms can be seen as a rapid dismantling of collective agriculture and its substitution by a system very much akin to egalitarian peasant farming based on fixed rentals. This would, however, be to lose sight of very important features of the Chinese system which distinguishes it from any system of private farming. Suffice it to recall that Chinese agriculture operates within the framework of a centrally planned economy and that the system of agricultural planning still operates. A unified production plan in principle still guides production at the level of the team and the household contracting system differs in several crucial aspects from private egalitarian farming. As the term 'household contracting' implies, the land is only contracted out and these contracts are, according to current policy statements, intended to be adjusted and reallocated periodically. Therefore, no element of proprietary (or inheritance) right is at present implied in the contracting system. Moreover, land transactions and labour-hiring are prohibited, as is construction on the contracted land. In principle the household contracting system can be seen as a decentralisation measure designed to overcome mismanagement in the old system through devolving decision-making power to units below the team, that is, to individual households. It is also designed at the same time as a reform of the payments system. Residual collective elements still remain, the most important of these being the supervision of the contracting system of household contracting and land allocation, the operation of the five-guarantee welfare system and the implementation of the unified production plan and procurement system. In some cases the team had added responsibility for team-level non-agricultural enterprises (on the Jinan Corporation model) and in others it still administers a redistributive food rationing system. It is also probably still the case that the basic inter-commune (and inter-team) immobility of labour remains in spite of the liberalisation measures with regard to labour allocation between private and collective activities. Moreover, it is unlikely that all collective units will have to shift to the *bao gan dao hu* system. Indeed, several units were encountered on the field trip which had either tried and rejected this system or signalled their intention not to dismantle a collective system which conferred many advantages.

At the same time, it is necessary to summarise those features of the old system which now seem to have disappeared in the broad sweep of the recent reforms. Several of these features were considered by outside observers to be unique features of the Chinese system which offered important lessons for other developing countries. The most important casualty has been the objective of progressively reducing the degree of inequality in rural China as a whole through the curbing of residual 'bourgeois rights'. The main instrument which had been relied upon to attain this objective was a progressively greater reliance on moral incentives and the raising of the level of the basic accounting unit. The reliance on moral incentives was intended to allow for progressively narrower 'wage differentials' in the payments system and greater distribution on the basis of need. At the same time, the heightened political consciousness associated with the acceptance of moral incentives would also permit the elimination, through raising the level of accounting, of income differences deriving from differential natural endowments between collective units. This would first reduce inter-team and inter-brigade inequality within a commune and ultimately, by raising ownership to the 'level of the whole people', reduce inter-commune inequality.

This latter aspect of redistribution was necessary because collectivisation in China was essentially based on the old social units – villages and neighbourhoods within them. Thus, land reform and collectivisation removed individual ownership of land by turning it over to production teams which corresponded to former villages or cohesive sub-groups within them. Consequently, unlike a system of state farms with wage labour, there was the problem of standardising the returns to labour between localities with different natural endowments.

Another element of the old system which is likely to disappear is team-level farm management and group farming. This had been considered important for overcoming inefficiencies associated with small individual units of land and for achieving economies of scale in production. Team (or higher) level farm management is now considered to have been a major source of inefficiency and, in some cases, even the collective ownership of farm machinery and draught animals is no longer considered essential for productive efficiency. The question of whether or not economies of scale exist can only be resolved empirically. Nonetheless, the new system of household contracting must not be equated to the situation that prevailed prior to the formation of Mutual Aid Teams. In fact, the new system is based on the cumulative benefits derived from land consolidation and communal development of infrastructure such as irrigation. As such it is not at all akin to a haphazard system of private peasant farming and its viability cannot be interpreted as proof of the absence of economies of scale. It should also be noted that the new system does not rule out all forms of group farming such as transplanting and harvesting communally. Systems of informal exchange and voluntary co-operation are not ruled out and the 'unified production planning' by teams may also seek to maintain basic uniformities in production.

The important function of the three-tier commune system as a vehicle for accumulation and for labour mobilisation for capital construction will be lost in the new system; so too will be its function as a guarantor and generator of employment and its unique role of maintaining parity between industrial and agricultural wages. However, some of these functions will be taken over by the new organisational forms emerging in rural China. The joint corporations in the experimental counties appear to have been efficient vehicles for mobilising capital for rural industrialisation, as well as for accumulation through ploughing back the profits of rural industrial enterprises. But collective accumulation for agriculture will be seriously weakened and accumulation and investment decisions will be in the hands of individual households. The burden of employment generation will also be shifted to households and there will be no guarantee of employment beyond the access to land for household contracting and private plots.

How this new system will perform in the future remains an open question. Too little time has elapsed and the evaluation of performance in this period has been complicated by simultaneous changes that have accompanied the reform of the commune system. Only observation over a longer period and further research will tell whether the new system represents an improvement in terms of productive efficiency and offers the hope of reversing the trend in diminishing total factor productivities that has been observed in Chinese agriculture. In terms of distributional consequences the evidence so far, albeit very limited, does not suggest any dramatic sharpening of inequalities and increased differentiation. However, whether or not this will continue to remain true depends crucially on how the features in the present system tending to limit inequality are maintained. In particular, the extent to which land allocations will be periodically adjusted to maintain equality of access to land will be of crucial importance. The potential contradiction in the new system lies in the possibility that it may foster proprietorial attitudes and vested interests in currently contracted land which may make the periodic reallocation of land extremely difficult to implement, however sincerely it may be desired by policy-makers.

NOTES AND REFERENCES

1. 1 mu or mou = 1/6 of an acre.
2. Such activities were regarded as constituting the 'tails of capitalism'. Even the number of draught animals, sows and poultry that could be owned were controlled.
3. Thomas G. Rawski, *Economic Growth and Employment in China* (Oxford: Oxford University Press, 1979) pp. 90–1.
4. Ibid.
5. Ibid.
6. The strong bias in favour of grains in the cropping pattern was the most striking example of this.
7. If there were no deductions for accumulation the average value of a work point would be equal to the average product of labour. However, with accumulation it would be less than the average product of labour and, depending on the level of accumulation, may approach the marginal product of labour.
8. This, however, also depends on the relative returns to labour in the collective and private sectors. The return to labour in collective activity below the expected average product may still be higher than marginal product in the private sector and hence the labour supply to collective activity need not slacken off.
9. However, in some communes 40 per cent or more of the grain ration used to be an unconditional need-based distribution. In Dazhai Brigade it was 100 per cent. See A. R. Khan, 'The Distribution of Income in Rural China', in ILO, *Poverty and Landlessness in Rural Asia* (Geneva, 1977) p. 280.
10. It should be noted, however, that this would be true only if the introduction of these inputs also raised net distributed income. If 'output ceased to increase or its maintenance at high levels required large quantities of inputs that had to be purchased from outside (such as tractors for deep ploughing or chemical fertilizers, weedicides etc.) the value of the workpoint would fall'. See K. N. Raj, *Agricultural Growth in China and India: Some*

Reflections on the Role of Price and Non-price Factors (Trivandrum: Centre for Development Studies) Working Paper No. 152, November 1982.
11. K. Griffin and A. Saith, *Growth and Equality in Rural China* (Bangkok: ILO–ARTEP, 1981) pp. 44–51.
12. See Chapter 3.
13. These measures were encountered on the field trip to Yunnan province.
14. Information supplied during a briefing at the Chinese Academy of Social Sciences.
15. The bonus was probably divided equally among all workers but the point was not clearly established during the field trip.
16. IBRD, *China: Socialist Economic Development* (Washington DC: World Bank, July 1981).
17. N. Lardy, *Economic Growth and Distribution in China* (Cambridge: Cambridge University Press, 1978) p. 26.
18. Ibid.
19. IBRD, *China: Socialist Economic Development*, p. 37.
20. Ibid., p. 42.
21. This was the case in Gao Chio Team, Pu Chao Brigade, Ala Peoples Commune in Yunnan.
22. Or receive less subsidy.
23. This, for instance, was the case in Sun Jin Brigade, Chun He Commune, Yu Xi county in Yunnan.
24. This is relatively light and irregular work which could be performed by secondary workers in a household such as old females or mothers with young children.
25. Data supplied by Yunnan Provincial Statistical Bureau.
26. Information supplied during a briefing at the Chinese Academy of Social Sciences.
27. See Chapter 2.
28. There was only one household enterprise at the time.
29. Except the five-guarantee household which is excluded.
30. Income from industry accounted for 54.5 per cent of total collective income of the team in 1981.

5 China's New Population Policies

ASHWANI SAITH

This chapter is concerned with certain aspects of China's single child family programme (SCFP) with particular reference to its operation in the countryside. This programme marks a profound change in the population control policies adopted by China, and is unique to the experience of developed as well as developing countries. The SCFP has been fashioned with a keen eye to inter-sectoral, inter-regional and inter-community differences, and even within these variations, room has been left for interpreting and implementing general provincial guidelines in the light of local specificities. Nevertheless, these remain variations around the general theme of a policy which represents a fundamental break with past efforts at coming to grips with the vexed population question. The SCFP has an enormous developmental significance both when considered within the Chinese context itself as well as when viewed through the window through which other developing countries eagerly, and often expectantly, scan China's development experimentation. As such, much interest attaches to the success or failure that this programme is meeting even in its early stages of implementation, and information is building up from a variety of sources on this score. But apart from documenting regional and community variations in the population norms adopted, the central focus has really been on the rate of adoption of the SCFP by couples; their subsequent ability to keep within their pledges; on the behaviour of various demographic variables; and on the specific incentive and disincentive structures that have accompanied the SCFP to assist its adoption and implementation.[1]

The purpose of this chapter is to extend the scope of the discussion on the SCFP by considering some of its wider, even though latent, social and economic consequences, and by setting this broader discussion explicitly in the extended context of the new economic and institutional policies being implemented in rural China. Especially at this early stage, it might be useful to explore some broader dimensions of the phenomenon, if only to draw specific attention to several additional aspects which need to be monitored more closely. Otherwise there might be some danger of interpreting success or failure exclusively in terms of the numerical impact of the SCFP on population growth, while ignoring its social consequences. It must be recognised, however, that it is not always possible or valid to link some 'consequence' to a 'cause' rooted in the SCFP. The programme is being implemented as part of a much wider programme of economic reform in rural China and hence most of the social consequences are likely to have multiple and interacting causes. A further problem is that this chapter, while developing arguments at a general level, in largely based on field observations and materials obtained on three short research trips into rural China beginning in 1979, as well as on the published findings of other researchers inside and outside China. This caution is necessary, otherwise there is a risk of treating what are often speculations and extrapolations as conclusions meant to apply across the board.

Like most other socialist countries, China is a target chaser: in the period of the Great Leap Forward, the slogan was to catch up with Britain within fifteen years; the current exhortation is to attain the magic number of US $1000 GNP per capita by the year 2000. This target is attainable if annual growth averages 6.8 per cent, 7.5 per cent or 8.1 per cent, assuming respectively that there is a zero population growth rate over the period, or that couples have on average 1.5 children, or two children. Such growth and population targets would not be credible in most Third World developing countries, but in China, the record has been good enough for both targets to be taken fairly seriously. At the national level there is one package of policies which attempts to raise the rate of growth of the economy in the medium and long term through wide-ranging institutional and economic reforms, while there is another package centering on the SCFP which is directed towards reducing the growth rate of population, thereby accelerating the per capita growth rate further. Since both the 'growth reforms' and the population policies are widely regarded as drastic in their reorientation, it is useful to consider the performance of China in the spheres of economic and population growth in the recent past. Are the new policies to be understood in the context of a dismal record on these fronts which calls for strong medicine?

Let us first consider the demographic experience. Since 1949, China's population has doubled, implying an average annual growth rate of about 2 per cent. This average hides some strong patterns in the behaviour of the rates of births, mortalities and natural growth. In the year of the Revolution, the total population stood at 541.7 million, both the birth rate (36/1000) as well as the mortality rate (20/1000) were very high, yielding a natural growth rate of 16/1000. Since then, both the birth and mortality rates have dropped dramatically, with the decline in the latter preceding that in the former. This allows a separation of two relatively contrasting periods each marked by a distinct pattern. In the first of these periods, covering the years from 1949 through the late 1960s, we observe a remarkable decline in the mortality rate, which plummets from its initial level of 20.0 to 8.3 per thousand by 1968. However, though the birth rate wobbles about somewhat, it maintains a very high level, and in 1968 is found to stand at 35.8 per thousand, which is almost the same as it was in 1949. The main characteristic of this period, consequently, is that the rate of natural increase rises steadily and after peaking at 28.5/1000 in 1965, stands at 27.5 in 1968. The second period covers the years 1969 to 1979: the mortality rate continues its decline, and reaches the low level of 6.2; the birth rate also begins its descent and comes down steadily to 17.9/1000. The result is that the rate of natural increase is more than halved over a decade, and in 1979 shows the level of 11.7/1000. Only by rather special criteria could such a growth rate be interpreted as anything but low in the modern era, especially in the context of the developing economies. However, one other significant set of statistics needs to be stated: in the years 1980 and 1981, the trends seem to have been reversed. The birth rate rose to 20.9 in 1981; the mortality rate to 6.4; and the rate of natural increase moved up to 12.0 in 1980 and to 14.5 in 1981. We will return to this feature later on; here we need only emphasise that at the point in 1979 when new economic and institutional policies were beginning to be recommended and adopted in the countryside, the experience with regard to demographic trends had been a satisfactory one. Certainly there was no cause for complacency, but nor is there reason for panic.

Let us now turn briefly to some indicators of the performance of the economy with regard to production, consumption and income. Using Perkins' estimates for the period 1952–74, we find a remarkably high annual growth rate of GDP (at 1957 prices) throughout the span; indeed, in what has come to be described as 'the lost decade', namely, 1966–76, the years of the Cultural Revolution, industry grew at an average annual rate of about 9 per cent in real terms; agriculture at upwards of 3 per cent; and GDP at about 6.5 per cent. When we look at the official Chinese statistics for per capita annual spending (at comparable prices with 1952 as base) we find impressive increases once again. On both sides of the disturbed years 1958–64, the performance is excellent in a comparative perspective embracing China's own past performance, or the contemporary trends in other relatively successful and comparable developing economies. One feature is that the non-agricultural population does consistently and considerably better than the peasants, but even the latter record per capita increases in real spending of 2.5–3 per cent per annum over the 1965–79 period. These figures have to be read in the light of the high rates of accumulation that have been maintained over the period. The rate rises from its level of 21.4 per cent in 1952 to 27.1 per cent in 1965, to 33.9 per cent by 1975, and peaks at 36.5 per cent in 1978, after which it drops in the phase of economic readjustment to a level of 30 per cent for 1981. It is striking that in the period 1975–9 the rate of growth of real spending accelerates to about 6 per cent per year, while the accumulation rate is held at an average of about 35 per cent.

The conclusion could be drawn that as of 1979, the rates of growth of consumption as well as accumulation were not unsatisfactory in terms of their levels. No doubt the subsequent downward readjustment of the accumulation rate will lead to a short-term increase in the rate of consumption, but this change cannot be justified strictly in terms of any sluggishness in the immediately preceding years. So also, when we consider the production performance of a variety of articles, the story is no different. Coal, electricity generation, crude oil and steel all show fantastic increases throughout the period since 1949, as do consumer durables such as bicycles, sewing machines and wrist watches. The crucial category of food articles does not perform too badly either, with grain output for 1980 standing at 2.8 times the level in 1949, a period during which it will be recalled the population doubled. Pork, beef and mutton do far better, with aquatic products taking up an intermediate position.

The preceding discussion should not, however, be allowed to create the impression that the Chinese economy was, or is, free from economic problems or that the growth trajectory adopted in the pre-1979 period was near optimal. Indeed, one might argue that while the aggregate growth performances were flattering, they were also to some extent deceiving since they hid imbalances in the structure of production. Thus, perhaps the range of consumer goods was too restricted both in town and countryside, the balance between heavy and light industries was too heavily weighed in favour of the former. Perhaps the process of technological change was too clumsy and haphazard; perhaps the efficiency of production could have been improved through stricter and better systems of management. Thus, both in the efficiency and direction of resource use, high growth rates of aggregates might have glossed over serious problems. Or, on another tack, it could be argued also that the high growth rates of the past could not have been maintained in the future without the readjustment and the reforms now under way in China. But equally, it might also be contended that while some of the problems mentioned above were clearly real, they could have been solved within the contours of the old strategy. One would then have to search for alternative explanations for some of the new policies, including the dramatic single-child family. The alternatives would generally need to postulate an ideological reorientation involving rather changed social and political priorities on the part of the Chinese leadership. The new emphasis on policies for increasing per capita consumption levels in the short run would then be ascribed not to the need to make up for failures of the past, but to an independent desire or political imperative to win favour with the Chinese masses and to buy support for the ideological reorientation. Reality is likely to be a complex amalgam of these various possibilities, and it is beyond the scope of this chapter to attempt to tackle this difficult question. For our purpose it is enough to note that China's SCFP and other supporting policies must be viewed as efforts to achieve an exceptional rather than just an outstanding growth performance. They have little in common with the Malthusian fears that account for birth control policies in poor non-socialist Third World countries.

WHY CONTROL POPULATION GROWTH?

If the economic performance of China has been satisfactory so far – at least in so far as growth indices are concerned – then what is the need for additional strong measures to control population growth? To some extent, this question is misleading since it ignores the fact that the impressive per capita growth rates are themselves the product – in part, in the latter period – of the successful earlier measures to slow down the growth rate of population by curbing birth rates. Thus previous success only emphasises the need for continuing the population control policies rather than questioning their necessity. But the question as to why the SCFP became imperative still remains to be answered, since the earlier successes were achieved without this measure. In this and the following sections we will try to summarise the logic underlying the policy.

The central relationship between the growth of population and output constitutes the pivot around which the changing official positions have hinged. Hence, it might be useful to make a few brief comments on this theme. In the early Maoist framework, more people were equated with more hands and virtually axiomatically with increased output. Thus there was a direct identity between the strategic thinking regarding the use of a large stock of population on the one hand, and that regarding policies relating to regulating new inflows into this stock. The concrete expression of this thinking was the key concept of 'labour accumulation', a one-off process through which large parts of the Chinese countryside were transformed, and the benevolent circle of self-sustaining local development initiated. That this was an appropriate strategy for taking advantage of population as a stock variable is not really open to serious question, despite its several latter-day critics. What was clearly dubious was to conclude, as was indeed done, that in a socialist system there was no necessity to regulate population at all, and that all inflows into the stock of population could always be productively absorbed. Thus, the equation of the policies with regard to population as a stock and as a flow was a mistake which reflected the supremacy of ideology over pragmatism, of theory over practice. Of course, this mistake was subsequently rectified in the Maoist period, and serious and strong policies of population control were instituted. In the post-Mao period, however, while the emphasis on this aspect has been much increased, there are some new dimensions which need mention.

The first provides a good illustration of the working of the ideological pendulum: far from Mao's people = hands = production equation, we see the emergence of the notion of an 'optimal population size' for China in the current debates between Chinese demographers. The three criteria used for arriving at the magic number are: extrapolations of past trends of economic development; an analysis of food resources, diet patterns and nutrition norms; and the ecological balance and fresh water resources. The three criteria yield figures for the optimal population size (100 years ahead) of 650–700 million, not more than 680 million, and 630–650 million respectively. The reader is told that 'methodologically, the problem of determining the desirable population size is therefore a problem of multi-criteria policy decision'. Three alternative paths to achieving this optimum are offered: the first, and strongest requires the universalisation of the single-child norm by 1985, the relaxation of this norm to the replacement level fertility of 2.16 children per woman between 2000 and 2020, leading to the final level of 700 million in 2070.

In the second, the total fertility rate should be brought down to 1.5 children per woman by 1990, relaxed to 2.14 between 2025 and 2040, resulting in the 700 million target being reached 120 years from the start in 1980. The third is a correspondingly less demanding version. It is suggested that 'the ideal programme would be the first one'; but in case this is found impossible, the second alternative provides the bottom line. The winner in this exercise is clearly the one-child family programme. Ricardo and Malthus might both have approved in different ways, though one wonders what sarcasm Marx or Mao might have unleashed on such an exercise. It is difficult to regard such exercises as being anything other than games in numerical ideology.

The second, more interesting, new dimension is to do with new thinking about policies for making best use of the stock of population. The Maoist strategy of labour accumulation has been all but given up; new rules prohibiting the employment of workers without direct payment by the employing unit more or less put an end to the practice, since this move meant that such units would have to pay wages related more to average productivity than to the marginal productivity of additional labour within any specific work situation. The new policy of diversification of the rural household economy, including especially new activities undertaken by households on a private basis, is also rooted in the objective of maximising labour absorption with minimal inputs of capital from the collective or state units involved. The repudiation of Dazhai as a model as also of the old man who would move a mountain, have everything to do with the ideological reorientation which underlies this altered approach to tackling the unchanging problem (and opportunity) of a large stock of rural population relatively underemployed on account of a shortage of accompanying means of production, including land. One might be tempted to argue that the new strategy has given up one way by which this stock could be fully utilised. But this would be erroneous, since in reality one way of utilising labour has replaced another: labour accumulation was the strategy adopted by Mao within the collective framework of the rural commune, whereas economic diversification of household-based production is the corresponding strategy of the present leadership. This is designed to dovetail with the new rural production responsibility systems based essentially on individual peasant household production systems. Thus, surplus labour still gets employment, but within a sharply different pattern of resource use and within distinctly different production relations, thereby providing an implicit critique of technological determinism.

When considering the 'flow' relation between population and production, the central, overriding theme is that high population growth rates imply directly lower accumulation rates. This broad argument is hardly new in China or elsewhere, though it might be useful to dwell briefly on the specific manner in which it is presently articulated in the Chinese context. Three arguments can be identified separately; we consider each in turn.

Costs of food production

This constitutes, perhaps, the main argument, and points to the increasing resource costs of increasing agricultural production, in general, and of increasing marketed supplies of foodstuffs from within the total output. Let us begin by using a simple development relationship: that between the growth rates of food production and of income. In the equation below, f represents the annual rate of growth of food production; p stands for the annual rate of growth of population; y denotes the annual rate of growth of per capita income in real terms; and e represents the income elasticity of demand for food. Then, we have:

$$f = p + ey \qquad (1)$$

Let us assume a value of 0.6 for e; the value depends upon the level of income and thus represents a weighted average across sectors and regions, and could not be regarded as being too implausible one way or the other. Let us also consider the rates relating to the first path leading to the target of $1000 per capita by 2000, namely, $p = 0$; $y = 6.8$. It follows then from equation (1) that food production must increase at 4.1 per cent per year in order to be consistent with the levels adopted by, or assigned to, the other variables in the equation. This is a very tall order when considered over two decades. Further, we know that population is likely to grow at between 1 and 2 per cent; let us assume 1.5 per cent. If y remains at 6.8 per cent (a rate not far off past achievement), then the required growth rate of food production increases to 5.6 per cent per year; and if y rises at say 8 per cent, then f takes on a value of 6.3 per cent. Thus, in the context of China's ambitious growth plans, even a small increase in the growth rate of population would greatly increase the relative burden on the rural sector to deliver the goods. It is in this light that the agricultural resource relationships have to be viewed.

Against these high required growth rates for food production it should be noted that the total output of grains (including coarse grains and potato equivalents, but excluding soyabeans) increased by about 2.4 per cent per year over the 1952–77 period, though in view of the declining growth rate of population over this period, per capita grain output would express an increase in the latter part of the period. Comparisons with 1949 as base and 1979 as the end-year would yield higher growth rates, but the basic orders of magnitude would not be significantly altered, and neither would the significance of these rates when compared with the requirement that food production increase by over 4 per cent in the 1980–2000 period. Since GDP per capita grew at about 6 per cent over the period, it follows that the bulk of the adjustment necessary to bring about equilibrium (in an *ex post* sense) in (1) would have had to be borne by a lower *de facto* value of e. This indeed has been one of the charges of the present leadership against the previous one: peasant and worker consumption grew at too low a rate. But if this is not to repeat itself in the future, agricultural growth rates will have to rise dramatically. It is here that the strategy runs into further pressures. Let F stand for food output; L for land; I for inputs; and P for population. Then the identity (2) follows.

$$(F/P) = (L/P) \times (I/L) \times (F/I) \qquad (2)$$

We have noted the slow rise of (F/P) above. Equation (2) shows the difficulties facing China in raising this rate. As population rises, the area of land available per person declines, and even after adjusting for increased irrigation and for multiple cropping, Tang computes an increase in a 'land input index' of just 17.4 per cent over the 1952–77 period.[2] This already reflects considerable man-made extensions and improvements, since in area terms alone, the per capita land availability drops from 2.60 mu in 1949 to 1.55 mu by 1980. Further extensions depend heavily on the expansion of highly resource expensive irrigation and water control projects. Thus (L/P) in (2) does not hold out great hope for a quick and cheap way of expanding food production. The response has been to intensify agricultural production through higher applications of modern and traditional inputs.

Again, relying on Tang's estimates,[3] the current input index (covering seed, feed, insecticides and fertilisers) rises from 100 in 1952 to 659 in 1977, while the capital and labour input indices rise to 251 and to 155 respectively. With the exception of labour (where the input is clearly underestimated for not having taken into account the increased utilisation of labour along with the greater size of the agricultural labour force), all indices are well ahead of the one for land input. Clearly, (I/L) registers very sharp increases over the period. But the dismal end to the story is provided by the behaviour of (F/I). The rises in (I/L) are largely offset by a strong decline in (F/I), or the output/input ratio, reflecting steeply diminishing returns to inputs. Tang's total factor productivity index drops by nearly 20 per cent over the period.[4] One could argue that even this presents an optimistic scenario for the future, since all the early and easy slack resources have been used up and further gains must be obtained in more unfavourable structural conditions.

The question is also complicated by regional and sectoral distribution issues. Consider, for instance, a situation characterised, not unrealistically, by three types of regions. Region *R* is rich, has a high average productivity, but which yields low returns to additional applications of modern or traditional inputs. Yet, because it is rich, it offers a much greater proportion of its incremental output for sale on the market. By contrast, Region *P* is poor, has a low average productivity, but a much higher marginal one than *R*; however, it tends to want very much to consume a high proportion of its additional product. The third Region *N* is new land which has low average but very high marginal productivity. Here, the marginal propensity to consume, or to retain additional output is also very low, but the problem is that opening up the area involves very heavy infra-structural expenditures on the part of the state. Developmental objectives might demand that state resources be channelled into *P*, but from the point of view of equation (1), this would raise e to a high level while also constricting the flow of supplies to urban areas. On the other hand, both *R* and *N* would be resource expensive in a different way. Given the crucial importance of grain procurements by the state, *R* and *N* are likely to win out, as indeed they might have done in the Chinese context. But this means too that one cannot be too optimistic about the future behaviour of (F/I).

Additionally, whatever the food production growth rate, it is imperative to allocate some of the increment for raising the consumption levels of the peasantry. This further intensifies the problem of marketed surplus, and the resource costs of generating it in enough quantity.

The policy response to this problem has been threefold. First, incentives for rural production and intensification of resource use have been greatly increased through substantial rises in purchase prices for the rural sector. Secondly, there have been wide-ranging and profound institutional reforms designed to create a new set of production relations which 'would bring the enthusiasm of the masses into full play'. These include the new rural production responsibility systems, the extension of the role of private household economic activities, etc. The nature and the impact of these are the subject of other chapters, and fall outside the bounds of this one. But the third policy response has been to intensify efforts to control the growth rate of population, especially in the countryside.

Social costs of raising children

It is pointed out emphatically by family planning officials that additional children mean additional bills for the state. It has been estimated that on average the costs to the state for the provision of health, primary and middle school education and other subsidies for a child during the age of 0–16 is one-third of the total cost of 1600 yuan, 4800 yuan or 6900 yuan, depending upon whether the child is in a rural area, in a medium or in a large-sized city. These figures exclude implicit food subsidies. These sums could have gone into accumulation, it is pointed out. While the general argument is no doubt true, two qualifications need to be made. First, even holding the level of services provided constant, it is unlikely that the marginal costs of providing such state social services are the same as the average ones; in reality, the former are likely to be well below the latter. Secondly, it would be unrealistic to assume that the level of services would not in fact be lower in the event of a resource constraint, though it is clearly as unrealistic to expect such a disagreeable or cynical assumption to be given any formal status in an *ex ante* formulation.

Capital costs of employment provision

An analogous argument is made for the employment of the child once it reaches the age of sixteen and becomes eligible for employment. For a million yuan of fixed assets, heavy industrial enterprises can employ ninety-four workers; state-owned light industrial enterprises, 257 workers; non-material production units, 800–1000; and the various types of service companies which have been recently established, up to 2000 jobs. But the expansion of such service sector units must bear some relation to the rest of the productive sector, and hence, sooner or later, the easy options of labour absorption become exhausted. And in a context where technological modernisation calls for capital deepening, rather than widening, too rapidly increasing a labour force could become an unproductive burden on the overall efforts for development.

In sum, then, each of the three groups of arguments discussed emphasises the heavy drain that a high growth population imposes on the rate of accumulation, though in terms of the motivation underlying the SCFP, one must not overlook the fact that a lower population growth rate would permit a higher growth of per capita consumption at any given accumulation rate. Indeed, the consumption factor might well be more important than the accumulation one since another part of the new strategy explicitly transfers resources from the accumulation to the consumption fund.

LAGGED IMPACT OF DEMOGRAPHIC EVENTS

The reasons for population control discussed thus far relate to the link between population size and economic growth. Given the conclusion that this link militates in favour of restricting population growth, several other factors become relevant which add to the urgency of achieving this objective. Past demographic events create waves which cause cyclical fluctuations after intervals lasting a generation. In the current Chinese context, three such events need to be noted.

The first relates to the age structure of the present population. At present, 50 per cent of the population of China is below the age of twenty-one, and as much as 63 per cent below twenty-nine. This basic fact intensifies the necessity for immediate control. Secondly, at present, the babies born in the two population booms of 1953–7 and 1963–71 are either entering marriageable age, or are married and still in a crucial period of family formation. If birth control policies are not successful with them, a new, magnified wave will be transmitted into the future. These booms can be traced to the periods when the case for population control in China was ideologically repudiated or was ignored to some extent. The third demographic event is a contemporary one: before 1981, the prescribed minimum age for marriage was twenty-five for males and twenty-three for females; this has subsequently been lowered to twenty-two and twenty respectively. This means that at a stroke, a much higher proportion of the boom babies are suddenly eligible for marriage, thus accentuating the second factor mentioned above.

These factors do not in themselves provide any rationale for restricting population growth; however, should such a case be accepted, these factors tend to accentuate the importance of tackling the problem without delay, since not doing so would only pass on the problem in an exaggerated form to future generations. The timing of these demographic factors is on the whole independent of the other forces calling for the regulation of the growth of population, but in conjunction with these forces, they strengthen the arguments for drastic measures of control to a considerable extent.

CAUSES OF HIGH POPULATION GROWTH

We have been concerned so far with the costs of a high growth rate of population and with reasons making it likely that these rates might be unusually high at the present juncture, owing to some special demographic characteristics of the present population. But this takes it for granted that Chinese fertility behaviour would automatically make for a high growth of population. This brings us to the reasons underlying such behaviour, especially viewed in terms of a couple making decisions about the size of family they would wish to have. Since this topic has been discussed extensively in the literature, we will restrict outselves to a quick summary treatment, developing arguments only where they have not been adequately emphasised. In particular, we will look for factors which explain why the government – or society – has a diametrically opposed position to that adopted by most Chinese couples with regard to desirable family size. The focus will be on the rural sector.

1. Underdevelopment and poverty

Four separate reasons, whether active or contributory, can be mentioned here. First, even in non-socialist poor countries, the income of a rural household depends to a considerable extent on the size of its labour force, including children. This remains true in a modified form in rural China, where an additional, extremely powerful link between household size and household income is provided by the rule that at the age of sixteen, the child enters the labour force of the team, and is entitled to share work opportunities and income on the same basis as the rest of the team's labour force. Economic returns are therefore guaranteed at the average rate, thus providing exceptionally lucrative and easy terms for entering the labour market. Secondly, in rural areas, there is much greater scope for labour utilisation whether within the collective or the household sectors, i.e. the demand for labour is quite buoyant. Thirdly, the cost to the couple, or to the household, of producing additional labour power is very low. This is partly due to the high degree of self-provisioning that takes place in those rural areas which enjoy highly diversified economies, as in the south of China, and more importantly to the high proportion of cost that is borne by the collective in the form of implicit food subsidies, free provision of a variety of other necessities, including housing, private plots, education and elementary health services. Lastly, and paradoxically, the one failure of the collective system of social provisioning provides a powerful reason for increasing family size. Most collective units in the countryside do not provide pensions upon retirement; it is the moral and indeed legal duty of the children to support their parents in their old age. As such, in China, as in the rest of the poor world, children are viewed as sound insurance policies, especially when the premiums to be paid are so low, and the returns underwritten. The returns are further guaranteed by the absence of the option of out-migration for children once they grow up. Of course, since they are guaranteed employment in the countryside at average rates anyway, the incentive to migrate is also very low. Additionally, even after their children are married, Chinese parents generally manage to retain a very high degree of control over them. Especially in regions where there is a housing shortage married children are clearly dependent upon their parents for accommodation.

2. Feudal–patriarchal society

The hangover of the old days still persists, often strongly enough to blur the new socialist vision. This factor, which works especially in the countryside, operates through the powerful preference for male off-spring. This preference on the part of individual couples is hardly irrational, since they must exist and operate within the society they are part of, even if they do not sometimes share all of its expressed values. For one, the 'pension' argument referred to above applies really only in the case of sons, since daughters still tend, in general, to move to the husband's home after marriage. For another, the woman's position is weakened in household and society if she does not have any sons. But underlying as well as overriding it all is the high premium that the social and economic system attaches to the male in virtually all walks of life. Hence it could be fairly argued that this attitude prevails at least in part on account of the inability of the socialist system to eradicate inequalities between opportunities available to men and to women at home, at work, at school and university and in politics.

3. Erroneous ideological position

Tian Xueyuan argues that after the mid-1950s, when attention was still paid to population control, Chinese population theory took a wrong turn.

> Influenced by Soviet views, China's population theory took it as a dogma from the very beginning that continuous growth was the socialist law of

> population. All ideas which contravened this dogma were denounced, and population theory became very one-sided. The theory that the more people a nation has, the more production there will be, the more production there is the more accumulation there will be, and the more accumulation there is, the faster development there will be became the orthodox population theory in China. As a result, population policy took very much the same course.

Indeed, the first baby boom dating from 1957 has been explicitly linked in Chinese discussions to the rejection of Ma Yinchu's 'New Population Theory' arguing in favour of population control, while the second boom is linked to the years when 'the Cultural Revolution got out of hand'.

4. 'Egalitarianism'

It is also argued that the old 'egalitarian' Maoist policies created further incentives for having more children rather than for working harder for achieving a higher level of living. The denunciation of 'bourgeois right' interfered with the full application of the socialist distribution rule of 'to each according to one's work'. The specific policies identified here are those concerning the 'egalitarian' rules governing the distribution of foodgrains, and the per capita basis of distribution of private plots and housing land. Indeed, Tian Xueyuan declares that 'the equal per capita allocation of housing and of living subsidies for the less well-off wage-earners in the cities was another factor pushing population growth'.

5. Absence of penalties or disincentives

In keeping with the spirit of the erroneous population theories and egalitarian policies, there were no disincentives or penalties for having a large family, just as there were no special rewards for restricting family size.

These five factors explain the preferences in rural Chinese families for having at least two children. Croll refers to a survey which shows less than 5 per cent of women preferring to have one child, 51 per cent wanting two children, and as many as 44 per cent wanting three or four. The objective basis for such a preference pattern is explained by another survey which shows that for families with only one or two members, 92 per cent of the households had a per capita income of less than 100 yuan while 8 per cent had more than 100 yuan; the corresponding figures for households with three or four, and six or eight members were 74 and 26 per cent, and 69 and 31 per cent respectively.

From an analytical point of view, the economic motivation can be best understood in terms of children being the source of inter-generational income flows. Both when they are young (but of working age, i.e. above five years old) as well as when the parents are old, children generate positive flows of income from themselves to their parents. This phenomenon characterises most poor countries, especially in the rural sector. In rural China these flows are increased because the parents do not have to meet the full costs of raising children. From the point of view of the population planners, this raises two issues. First, it points to the need to set up corrective interventions in this inter-generational flow of income, so as to make the returns reflect social costs and benefits rather than private ones. Presumably, it could be argued that if parents had to pay 'social' prices for the services of children, then the state would not need to interfere with fertility behaviour patterns through such programmes as the single child family. This price intervention might be justifiable and necessary; however, it is unlikely to obviate the need for further direct or indirect interventions, since even with prices reflecting planners' implicit valuations of labour, food, savings, etc., individuals might still place an extra premium on their future security; on the satisfaction of perpetuating the family name; on the pleasure of having more children about the house; on the social advantages of having more sons. Such extra-economic preferences would vary from couple to couple, and would in any event be extremely difficult to counter through the adjustment of 'prices' affecting inter-generational flows of income.

NEW RURAL REFORMS, NEW DEMOGRAPHIC PRESSURES

The underlying causes of high fertility rates discussed in the previous section operated in the context of the pre-reforms rural China, i.e. in the pre-1979 period. Since the new economic and institutional policies have begun to unfold in the countryside, however, it has quickly become apparent that there are new demographic pressures which the economic and institutional reforms have themselves unleashed. This has sometimes led to the contention that there exists a basic contradiction between the twin policies for achieving a high per capita income growth rate: the 'production' strategy is held to run counter to the 'reproduction' policies. It has even been asserted on occasion that this reflects a flaw in the planning framework. Without subscribing to this simplistic reasoning, let us discuss how the two sets of new policies are related. Before doing so it is necessary to set down some of the main features of the new economic and institutional policies that are being implemented in rural China.

The main emphasis of the institutional reform seems to be to shift away from the three-layered pyramidal structure of the people's commune into smaller team-sized co-operatives of the type which preceded the communes. Within these, while planning functions are still performed by the 'team' or co-operative leadership, the main task of agricultural production is delegated to individual peasant households which are set fixed production quotas. Variations from the quotas are then transformed into small penalties, or relatively larger rewards in the form of retentions of high proportions of the surplus or above-quota production. Land is allocated on a medium-term basis in many cases, and in one version of the production responsibility system, the team's means of production are auctioned off to the (wealthier) members of the team, though the larger implements such as tractors and threshers are obviously retained under collective ownership and management. Peasants are assured by officials that this system will not be changed in the near future; this is meant to allay their risk aversion with regard to making land improvements, or making medium-term investments. Alongside this, the size of the private plot has been enlarged; the range of goods that can be produced on it and bought and sold freely in the markets has been greatly widened; rural and urban market fairs have been encouraged and now flourish in every part of rural China, providing a ready arena for the exchange and sale of goods produced by the peasants on their private or contracted land; the range of sideline activities that private individuals are allowed to engage in has been greatly widened as well, and the limits to the operational size of such establishments has also been vastly liberalised; new private economic initiatives relying on the pooling of private capital and resources between rural households have been sanctioned; a certain (though widening) degree of apprentice employment has been allowed in such and similar enterprises; a significant degree of withdrawal from collective labour has been permitted in those units where the new production responsibility system still calls for collective labour; the strictures on out-migration to the towns have in practice been relaxed; hawking, vending and selling and trading from stalls in towns is allowed; so also is poultry farming and pig raising on a very substantial scale.

The other major policy change of relevance for our discussion is the new price policy: farm purchase prices have been raised substantially, and this has raised the income levels of those peasants who produce a marketable surplus to a very substantial extent, though the progressive structure of the price rise leaves the deficit producers and the marginal surplus peasants relatively untouched. This price rise raises the profitability of agriculture to a marked extent, and permits further intensification of input use more or less across the board in potentially surplus areas. Alongside this is the new policy of encouraging crop diversification away from grain, and letting peasants decide to a greater extent how much of which crop they might wish to plant within the overall constraint of the production quota. The profitability of production thus becomes a real objective for the peasants in rural China, perhaps for the first time since the Revolution.

From these policies and their implications and corollaries stem several effects on the fertility behaviour of the peasants. New demographic forces and pressures have been released, and while it is still too early to judge their strength, it is possible with some accuracy to speculate about their direction. These new pressures are juxtaposed upon the groups of causes of high fertility discussed in the previous section.

The negative impact of erroneous theories of population growth under socialism had already been countered in the 1970s through the introduction of serious family planning and birth control programmes. The new SCFP, however, has no doubt driven home the ideological message if it still needed doing so. However, objective economic conditions on the ground have changed radically, and this has affected factors governing fertility behaviour. Let us first look at the cost of generating labour power within a peasant household. After the reforms, it could be argued that the rejection of egalitarian distribution rules would tend to raise the implicit cost of raising children, since grain which is retained for consumption within the household after meeting the quota would now logically have to be valued at the going market price, rather than the subsidised rates at which the team supplied distribution grains to its members under the previous system. Additionally, labour would not be rewarded any more at the average rate within the team, based on the average value of the workday and the number of days worked by any one worker. Now the land itself is contracted out. Thus for any given household, labour returns would depend on their marginal productivity on the contracted land given the pattern and level of resource endowment of the household. Hence returns to labour, and its opportunity cost, would have to be reckoned in terms of its marginal contributions to output. In land short areas, this could be expected to lower the demand for labour, and therefore for children. (But these factors are countered powerfully by those making for an increase in the demand for labour.)

This new land policy goes hand in hand with that of economic liberalisation, so that while the opportunity cost of peasant labour is reduced, opportunities for its use outside agricultural activities are greatly enhanced. This encourages economic diversification within the household. The demand for labour has increased very noticeably, and to an extent where there are uncharacteristic calls from PLA soldiers to be allowed to return to their peasant homes to take financial advantage of the new opportunities. Since very many of the new activities are such as would easily absorb and benefit from the use of child labour, the demand for children must have increased significantly. Indeed, this is the constant answer one receives to questions enquiring into this problem in the course of field work in rural China. It is probable that the net balance between the increase in the costs of and the returns to additional labour power have swung in favour of the latter thus having an upward impact on fertility. Of course, parents must continue to control their children's earnings in order to benefit from having raised them. In this regard, it is unlikely that the situation has been much altered by the new reforms. On the one hand, one could argue that the increased possibility of migration, and certainly of earning outside the household and the village, would lead to the weakening of parental control over the economic activities of their children. But typically, migration leaves behind ties of dependency (of the migrant on the household) in cases where the livelihood of the former is not assured. On the other side, the weakening of the collective unit is also unlikely to have created any net weakening of control, since the reorganisation of peasant production around the household level is also likely to generate a new pattern of intra-household division of labour embracing the sectoral, seasonal and sexual dimensions, and division of labour is another way of stating the interdependence between participating members.

Added to these new pressures for increasing the size of the household, one could list the legitimate apprehension that with the passage of the collective (of the style of the commune) into history, parents would be ever more dependent upon their offspring for providing them with material support in their old age. Within the commune system, it was still possible that the richer units could institute a pension system; but in the new framework, such social cover would have to be for all persons in a much wider administrative unit, or for none; consequently the likelihood of such pension systems being put in place in rural China in the near future becomes more dim than before. Peasant perceptions in this regard could not be faulted for being unrealistic or subjective.

Having got this far, however, it is necessary to make a few sceptical observations. The first concerns the frequently encountered argument that since the land allocations under the new responsibility systems are related to the size of the household (apart from the size and composition of its labour force), there would be a great incentive for the peasants to increase the size of the family in order to lay a higher claim to team land. Such an argument would be misleading for the reason that land distributions have been linked to the incentive structures for promoting birth control. If a couple has a second child, then far from getting an extra share of the contract land, it is penalised even in terms of its previous entitlement. Moreover, there are no extra allocations of a private plot for second children, nor indeed of housing space. The promised periodic readjustments in the land allocations will only take into account deaths and sanctioned, or 'planned' births. It is possible that there might have been a short interim period where the situation was unclear, and that this might have led to a small and temporary spurt in fertility. But it could hardly be argued to have any secular existence.

The second point is that even to the extent that fertility levels have risen in response to the increase in demand for labour, this effect cannot be expected to last for more than a short period. The reason is that all the new activities and opportunities created by the new reforms constitute avenues which will soon become saturated – just as the market for a good which is import-substituted quickly becomes saturated – and further growth then becomes linked to the trend rate of growth of income within the new framework. Thus, how many million yards of hand-made lace can China absorb at present levels of income? How many glasses of lemonade and sticks of home-made ice cream can the Chinese consume per year? After a rapid growth which soaks up unmet demand, the boom will taper off into normal growth linked to income growth. The conclusion must be that the increase in the demand for labour is also to some extent a transitional phenomenon whose impact on increased fertility will also peter out in the coming few years.

Thirdly, the current debate suffers from the fact that no attempt is made to link altered fertility behaviour to expected future returns from children after they have grown up. That is, if parents shrewdly expected that the boom in labour demand would be relatively short-lived, they would not favour having more children. In ignoring the role of expectations in making assumptions about peasant fertility behaviour, the current argument becomes rather unrealistic and unsound in that it is assumed that peasants assume that their future economic environment will be a simple projection of their present one. There is no easy way to solve this problem and no clear conclusion can be drawn except on the basis of rather untestable assumptions about peasants' expectations. However, it is important to recognise that a problem exists.

In summary, then, it appears that while the demand for labour, and the economic returns to labour, are likely to have increased substantially as a consequence of the new policies, it would be injudicious to assume that this will lead to an immediate, emphatic or longstanding alteration in peasant fertility behaviour in favour of having more children. This is not to deny the probable presence of some positive relationship between fertility and the returns to labour.

However, a more significant argument is that the decline of the collective, and the revival of the household as the basic production unit has led to a corresponding revivification of a peasant–feudal mentality, with peasant parents showing a renewed concern over the perpetuation of the family name, over the number of sons, etc. Even casual observation in the course of field research corroborates this argument, especially in the case of rural households which have prospered in the recent post-reform years. Overall, then, it is likely that peasants might prefer to expand their family size as a consequence of the large increases in the demand for labour, and on account of the revival of traditional social values in the countryside, though it is difficult to draw conclusions about the strength or longevity of this effect.

THE RESPONSE OF THE STATE: SCFP

Changes in population growth rates could determine whether China's attempt at rapid modernisation succeeds or fails. Given the tension between the high desired speed of growth and the new lagged effects making for a higher population growth, the choices of the government are restricted. One of three broad options can be followed. Either the targets for the growth of per capita income can be revised downwards to take into account the demographic pressure; or the new rural reforms can be modified so that they do not lead to an increase in the demand for labour within the peasant household; or finally, the birth control efforts and the family planning programme can be redoubled and intensified. The first two options would involve a negation of the entire economic strategy of the present leadership, and it is clear that the only credible option currently is the third one. Certainly it is the one which has been taken up with vigour and almost on an emergency basis. The adoption and implementation of the SCFP has been monitored closely inside and outside China, and we can therefore dispense with a detailed account of its progress. It is enough for us to note a few important features which have emerged in the short period since it was introduced.

There is a marked difference in the rates of adoption and speed of adoption of the programme between the rural and the urban areas. The latter, led by cities such as Shanghai, have displayed very low rates of net natural increase, and very high rates of subscription to the SCFP on the part of couples with less than two children.[5] This might be explicable in terms of a variety of factors, the main ones having to do with the much lower income-generating possibilities that additional children have in cities, when compared with the diversified economy of the rural areas. Further, parents in towns generally work in establishments which have regular pension systems, so that the other key motivation for a large family, i.e. old age security, is removed. In addition, most cities are faced by housing problems, and unlike the rural areas, there is no direct way of increasing living space upon the birth of another child. Small families are a response to these conditions.

There is also a marked difference in performance by nationality group and by region. For the minority nationalities, the SCFP does not really apply, and the norm remains the previous two-child one in principle, and often an unspecified one in practice. Even when we leave out of consideration regions whose performance is strongly influenced by the high proportion of population from minority nationalities, there still remain wide differences between the performance of provinces. At one end is Sichuan, with extremely low rates of natural increase, and with a high degree of implementation of the SCFP; at the other end is Guangdong in the south, which has displayed the opposite tendencies. It should be noted though that this is typically a drive which might be expected to follow the path of a logistic curve in its advance towards maximum levels of adoption consistent with specific conditions. Viewed in this way, the inter-provincial differences would reflect, apart from differential methods and styles of implementation of the SCFP, different socio-economic conditions. For example, the rural economy of Guangdong is much more diversified than that of the northern provinces. Certainly, the tendency to equate success rates with crude birth rates, or with the incidence of adopters places too great an emphasis on the role of machinery for implementation.

The SCFP preceded the new institutional reforms in the countryside. Thus the early regulation laying down the incentive/disincentive structure for the SCFP ran in terms of work points, and made no mention of the size of the land allocated under quota-contract to the peasant household.[6] With the reforms, however, the regulations have been reframed so as to include the crucial clauses which penalise violators of the SCFP (as also non-adopters who have a second child) with a cut in their land allocation, or by the allocation of no additional land for any child outside the birth plan. In addition the structure for implementation has been greatly strengthened, and in many rural areas it is standard practice for birth plan quotas to be assigned to the leadership of the unit, with a bonus for overfulfilment, and a penalty for not meeting the norms. Success, however, may create its own problems. The experience of some of the big cities shows that where a large majority of the target population does subscribe to the SCFP, the authorities frequently run into serious difficulties in meeting the promises made under the incentive system. Thus, better housing might have been promised for SCF certificate holders, but the large numbers of those eligible for this benefit mean long queues and lengthy delays; so also with school and medical facilities, and the promise of job preference. The implicit result is a weakening of the *de facto* incentive structure. While an identical situation might not hold in the rural areas, it is obvious that the SCFP could prove quite expensive. In the countryside, however, the key element is the private plot and the size of the contract land, and allocations of these really imply redistributions from those outside the SCFP (but eligible to be within it) to the adopters of the SCFP; such a programme, while providing powerful incentives, remains costless with regard to the additional land allocated to SCF certificate holders.

Notwithstanding this, it is apparent that new regulations are frequently very tough on offenders; and increasingly, it is the disincentive side of the regulations which ensures compliance. One reason for this is that with the reforms, the 'profitability' of having children has risen, and hence so must the disincentives to prevent additional births. Moreover, even the incentives contain an implicit punitive effect: the annual flow of incentives could add from a quarter to a third to the income of a household in some communes, but the real problem is in the rule that should the couple have a second child later, they would have to pay back the cumulative sum of benefits obtained to date. Needless to say, few households would be in a position to do this and survive, and it is this inability to repay that allows the local family planning officials to put pressure on the couple to abort their second child.

Alongside this, the structure for implementation has been strengthened. This was perhaps necessary since the weakening of the old collective units. The key element of this is the system of rewards and penalties for the leadership for meeting the quotas of births under the plan for their unit. This device can be very cost effective, to put it in somewhat cynical terms, since the proportion of the unit's population eligible for these particular benefits is very small, in fact not more than a handful of persons. Thus, rewards to the leadership can be very generous without upsetting the budget. On the other hand, the difference made to the income of a unit leader can be significant. The net result is the intensification of the SCF drive through an enthusiastic participation by the leadership in meeting birth targets.

Finally, we noted earlier that the rate of increase of the population rose after 1979 in the course of the two following years. One must be careful in attributing this change to the new reforms in rural China. The reforms might have been a contributory factor, but in the main, the rise reflects the earlier bulges in the crude birth rates that China experienced a generation later. It is not uncommon to encounter communes where the crude birth rate is high or rising despite a very high rate of adoption of the SCFP. Indeed, it may be that the bulge of earlier births helps the SCFP by demonstrating to the peasantry the urgency of the population problem.

SCFP: SOME IMPLICATIONS AND CONSEQUENCES

Throughout this chapter, the radical departure that the SCFP constitutes from normal family planning practice has been justified in terms of its expected impact on the rate of accumulation and, subsequently, on the rate of increase of per capita income. But these results, when they do materialise, reflect only one part of the balance sheet. The SCFP, and especially when considered as part of the larger package of the new rural reforms, also possesses some undesirable consequences and side effects. Once again, the strength of these undesirable effects is difficult to judge at present: some are manifest already but others, while inherent in the logic of the scheme, might not yet have appeared. Further, the authorities clearly recognise that the SCFP, like the production responsibility systems, also creates some problems. But it is officially contended that precisely because the problems have been anticipated, they will also be dealt with appropriately with timely counter-measures. Be this as it may, it is useful to consider the topic at some length, since these are precisely the areas of discussion which, while necessary and extremely important, have so far been substantially ignored. It will also help the reader to form a judgement about whether or not the problems are of a kind which can be tackled at the present juncture by the current leadership of the country. Our discussion is divided into two broad sets of considerations: the first group deals with the implications of the SCFP for inequalities at various levels; the second with some real and potential consequences of the SCFP for the role and position of women.

Inequalities

The first point arises from the unevenness of the adoption of the SCFP between urban and rural areas. We referred earlier to the problem that could be faced by city family planning authorities in providing incentives to SCF certificate holders. While these difficulties are real enough in the case of specific incentives, e.g. housing, it does not follow that city populations do not gain significantly from other elements of the incentive package. This raises the possibility that the SCFP will become a source of increasing inequalities between the two sectors in per capita terms, since the adoption rates are lower, and the incidence of penalties higher in the rural areas. Needless to say, such an effect could be countered to some extent through a suitable incomes policy, though doing so would clearly affect the operation and potency of the incentives themselves.

Secondly, even if we suppose that severe penalties do ensure that the SCF is adopted in the rural areas, it does not follow automatically that this will lead to the peasants receiving all the benefits that the SCF is expected to produce for China. Even if we assume that per capita income in money terms does rise, peasants still have to be able to convert their entitlements into goods. This in turn depends upon the overall rate of accumulation, on the availability of industrial goods in the countryside, and on the prices set for these goods. It is possible that the nominal increase in rural per capita incomes will be higher than the real increase. Further, the implied 'welfare' savings of SCF (namely, schools and hospitals not built, etc.) do not always directly accrue to rural areas. Earlier we reported the official estimate that one-third of the cost of such services was borne by the state, and this saving would clearly not be transferred automatically to the SCF certificate holders. It remains possible then that the surplus or savings generated through the adoption of the SCF in the rural areas will be transferred through the budgetary system into uses which tend to favour income growth in other sectors.

A third implication stems from the fact that the SCF is not intended for implementation (at least as yet) in the areas inhabited by the minority nationalities. Thus, the proportional share of the minorities in the total population can be expected to increase, but unless their share in resource allocation is also adjusted upwards, the inequality in per capita incomes between the minorities and the rest of the Chinese people will also drift upwards. This argument assumes, justifiably, that in the minority areas the marginal returns to labour are below the average returns in present conditions.

The fourth, and perhaps the most disturbing implication is for inter-sectoral differences in the pattern of educational participation. The new production responsibility systems have already created a serious conflict of interest between school attendance and the use of child labour by parents. Field observations testify to this in areas where the more extreme forms of individual household-based responsibility systems are being followed. The simultaneous adoption of the SCFP in such regions is likely to lead to an exacerbation of this conflict through placing an increasing premium on the labour of children in small-sized families. And where the couple ignores the penalties for the second child and expands family size, such an effect is likely to be even stronger since the family will wish to recover these penalties through the economic returns to the second child's participation in remunerative economic activities rather than in economically unrewarding educational ones. The expectation of high returns through adopting this strategy might be part of the motivation for incurring the penalties in the first place. This behaviour would be further encouraged by the fact that the educational and other expenses for the second child would have to be paid for by the parents, rather than by the collective, as in the case of the first child. The longer term implications of this phenomenon are unlikely to be different from those for child cowherds in poor Third World countries, where early participation in the labour force does provide early benefits to the parents but a longer term stagnation of income and opportunities for the child. In sharp contrast, the impact of the SCFP in the urban areas is likely to be the reverse. Here, the full participation of the parents in the labour force is assisted by smaller family size, while the prospects for children to contribute to household income are but a small fraction of those in the countryside. In fact, the future of the urban child is crucially related to educational opportunity and performance. And parents are likely to have a direct interest in furthering this, since if they only have one child their future old age insurance will depend on the economic success of that child. This is partly what explains the rise of private tuition schools in urban China in the last few years, whereas educational participation has dropped somewhat in the countryside. These difficulties are further accentuated by the increased problems that rural school-goers face in competing on 'equal' terms, i.e. taking the same examinations, with their urban counterparts. Recent independent changes in education policies along these lines have already made it more difficult for the rural sector; now, the combination of the new institutional reforms and the SCFP makes it even more likely that these inter-sectoral and inter-class inequalities will be further widened, and at present, it is rather difficult to imagine how specific counteracting policies could be designed or implemented successfully.

The position of rural women

On the whole the implications for rural women appear to be somewhat bleak.[7] This calls for explanation since it would normally be assumed that being freed from the burdens of repeated childbearing would be a great boon. The difference is that the women of rural China passed through this stage in an earlier phase of socialist China's development; the issue now is the reduction of the number of children from say two to three to strictly one. In considering the impact of the SCFP on women, it is necessary first to comment on the realised or potential effects of the new institutional reforms on the position of women, since it is in the framework of these effects that the SCFP generates its own impact.

The main implication of the move towards household-based production systems in the countryside is the increased domestication of women. Since collective labour is replaced by work on the household's contracted and private land, inputs of female labour will be related to their marginal returns rather than the average as in the case of the collective. Women are therefore likely to be relegated to their traditional role of taking charge of the domestic economy, including the private plot. As elsewhere in the Third World, in their 'spare time' they would occupy themselves producing handicraft items, processing foods, or engage in other sideline activities. Of course, it is possible, though not likely to become generalised, that where the male finds some exceptionally lucrative employment in the non-agricultural sector, the female labour power of the household would be used for agricultural activities. But the intra-household sexual division of labour would in this case too be structured unfavourably from the point of view of the women.

Such a relegation of women to the domestic economy, coupled with other reforms aimed at shedding 'extra' labour from factories, is likely to exacerbate the already pronounced sexual division of labour (which operates against the interest of women) in collective enterprises in the rural sector. So also, it is possible that the wider role assigned to private sector non-agricultural (commercial and petty industrial) activities would provide an advantage to men, since these are likely to involve frequent interaction with male-dominated authority structures. This increased domestication of the labour of women will be reflected in a corresponding reduction in the extent of their participation in collective forms of labour, such as do remain. The changing sexual division of labour by type of activity is therefore likely to correspond to one categorised by its social character. The first implication of this is likely to be a weakening in the nature and extent of female participation in the decision-making process at the level of the collective unit. It is pertinent to note in this context that alongside the reforms to the leadership structure of the production teams, the usual positions assigned to women have been somewhat downgraded. Simultaneously, the role of the women's leader becomes overwhelmingly to serve as the instrument of the SCFP and ensure the desired response from women within the unit to family planning initiatives, rather than to fight the other, more serious and difficult, battles of safeguarding women's rights and improving the terms of their participation in the labour and decision-making processes. The women's leader thus forms the interface, the instrument, the agent of the state in its birth control programmes. This is, of course, as it should be since it would be even less acceptable in general to have a male performing this role. Yet, what is disturbing is the extent to which the women cadres spend a disproportionate extent of their time on the question of birth control, while the parallel and attendant issues arising from the implications of the rural reforms and the SCFP for women's position in rural society do not receive the intensive attention that they urgently demand.

It also needs to be remembered that the new rural reforms are part of a larger phenomenon of 'going traditional', where old pre-socialist values are resurfacing, and forming the basis of new lines of authority, new groups of allegiances, and new matrices of interdependencies in economic interests. The dominant factor is kinship. A part of this system of values, which is not new to the lives of the older generation, prescribes a rather clear traditional role to the woman in the household, a role which is likely to prove difficult to contest under the shadow of the old cultural ethos revivified by the reorientations of the post-Mao period. How all this will square with a generation of women who have tried to organise increasingly to fight for equality is at present imponderable.

Let us see how the SCFP interacts with this set of factors from the point of view of women. First, in keeping with the resurgence of traditional attitudes in the countryside and with the increased importance of ensuring a successful career for an only child in the urban areas, there has been a great revival of interest in 'the mothering role of women'. This tends to lead to a situation where women find themselves having to rear children and spend a greater proportion of time than before in associated household tasks. This, in turn, increases the pressures making for the domestication of women. Secondly, it is almost universally true that if a couple is going to have one child, it would like to have a son. This intensified preference for male offspring accentuates pressures on women, and also influences their social position. The major implications of the SCFP for women arise from the clash between the new regulations and the preference of parents (a) for two or three children, and (b) for sons. Let us consider each in somewhat greater detail.

With regard to the preference for more than one child, the problems for women arise not so much from observing (or not observing) the new norm, but in the *manner* by which an increasing number of young women eventually comply with it, i.e. through abortions. There can be little doubt that the drive to implement the SCFP has greatly increased the use of this device of birth control. Abortion is accepted, of course, as a 'last-resort' method of birth control, and as such, its incidence is likely to be high when family planning and birth control services and facilities are weak in an area. But our argument extends much beyond this point. If we consider the national level, the ratio of abortions to live births for China in the mid-1970s was about 1:3, which is higher than that for say, India (at 1:5 to 1:10), at par with that for some European countries, but lower than that for some East European countries, and for Japan in the 1950s. This national average no doubt hides inter-sectoral differences where the urban sector has lower ratios because of better availability of birth control facilities and other social factors. But the disturbing feature is the rising trend that the ratio displays in the rural sector in the last few years. In the absence of systematic data, we must fall back on some field notes for illustrating this argument. In a team in a rural commune in a prosperous part of Yunnan, there were twenty-two births and eight abortions in 1980, the corresponding figures being twenty-two and thirty in 1981, and five and twenty-eight in the first five months of 1982. The ratio of abortions to live births changes dramatically from about 1:2.8 in 1980 to about 1:0.16 by mid-1982.

By way of an explanation, various points need to be made. First, there is a sharply rising trend in conceptions in the team, from a minimum of thirty in 1980 to an annual estimate of about eighty in 1982, a rise which cannot be ascribed solely to a kink in the age structure or to an earlier baby boom in the 1950s or 1960s. The increase in the number of conceptions coincides with the adoption of new economic policies in the region, with the consequent increase in the demand for family labour. Since the cover provided by the family planning services could not be assumed to have declined in effectiveness, it is likely that the rising trend emanates from the desire (on the part of couples) to have larger families. Secondly, this trend is countered very sharply by the SCFP. This exposes the puzzle: why do women get pregnant if in all probability they are going to have to abort the child? In all cases, abortions were of the second (or in some cases of the third) child. The answer lies probably in the expectation that such couples might have had about actually being able to extend their family size beyond the limits prescribed by the SCFP.

This implementation of the SCFP has been variable; local regulations have not everywhere or always been strictly enforced, and this allows the objective possibility of getting away with a second child. However, in the case cited, such expectations met with a very strong response, leading to the high abortion rates observed. This would appear to imply some irrationality on the part of the couples involved. But this deduction would be somewhat hasty. For one, we are dealing with a span of only three years, and it is possible, indeed even probable, that if the official response to a second child remains as it is at present, some lessons will be learnt, and the original expectations adapted. For another, one should note that the couples concerned decided to have a second child in the full knowledge of the array of economic disincentives triggered off by their step. What accounts for the decision to abort later, is not a belated realisation of such disincentives, but the sudden discovery of the range and strength of extra-economic pressures that are simultaneously brought to bear on the women pregnant with a second child. Women's leaders, team leaders, party officials, SCFP workers, neighbours, team or work group colleagues all join in a barrage of propaganda and argumentation directed at the woman, all aimed at making her revise the decision and to agree to an abortion. Frequently, this can involve cases of rather late abortions terminating pregnancies of more than four months duration. This network of extra-economic 'persuasion' was operational even in the period prior to the SCFP. What is new is the intensity of its operation in the present situation, something which emphasises the rather large overlap between persuasion and outright coercion.

The increased intensity of operation of moral pressures is assisted, if not actually triggered off, by new systems of contracts and quotas concerning the number of births allowed in any one unit. Strong incentives are provided to the team leadership to ensure that team members keep within the birth plan. Thus, in the team in Yunnan mentioned earlier, the five team leaders receive a collective bonus of 200 yuan if the team keeps within seven births per 1000 members, and if there are no second births. For every second birth, there is a 10 yuan fine on the leaders. There are separate powerful penalties on the couple which has a second child, and since 1981, there are also penalties imposed on the work group to which the erring couple belongs. The group has a deduction of a total of 1000 work points per second child born within it. The need for collective penalties both on the team membership and the leaders is explicable in terms of the inadequacy of even strong disincentives for the couple. The result is the pattern of conceptions, births and abortions reported earlier.

The other abnormal phenomenon which has surfaced subsequent to the adoption of the SCFP is more distressing. It concerns not second, but even first births. Given the powerful pressures to have sons, as well as the equally powerful ones to restrict family size in accordance with the SCFP, it is not altogether unexpected that there are frequent reports of female infanticide in rural China. This ghastly effect of the SCFP is difficult to quantify, though in some press reports the sex ratio for localities is reported to have been as much as 5:1 in favour of male children. If couples are to have just one child, then they clearly want it to be a male one. Female infanticide, even if sporadic, raises profound doubts about the readiness of the population of rural China for such a radical change as the SCFP demands.

In summary, the implications of the SCFP, especially in the context of the wider rural reforms, are far from encouraging for women in rural China. The subjective factors released by the new socio-cultural ethos lead to a revival of old attitudes which prescribe narrow, domesticated roles for women; the objective socio-economic forces generated by the new policies provide the material conditions which further strengthen these attitudes on the one hand, and accentuate the sexual division of labour on the other; the much increased incidence of abortions poses a threat to women's health; the near coercive nature of the methods of implementation of the SCFP take away powers of decision-making about fertility from the couple to the state; the incentive structures for the leadership create a social and political divide between the leadership and the members of a unit; and the clash between the demands of the SCFP and the strong preference for male offspring leads to a possibility that the inhuman practice of female infanticide will find new life in socialist China. These effects might well be anticipated, but one cannot be optimistic because it is a fact that in most parts of rural China the role of the women's leaders revolves almost exclusively around the implementation of the SCFP, and little time is devoted to countering the various problems mentioned in this section. The negative implications of the SCFP are so significant that one wonders whether women in rural China have been used as instruments for development rather than as the object of development. In the early heady phase of the Great Leap Forward the labour of rural women was socialised at a fantastic rate and it made a profound contribution to a development effort which relied considerably on the device of 'labour accumulation'. Now, in the new strategy, increasingly women's labour is assigned (whether as an unintended effect, or by design) to the domestic sphere. It is to be hoped that this does not become a permanent feature of Chinese socialism.

CONCLUSION

Yet again, China has launched a programme of large-scale social experimentation and the rest of the developing world is bound to monitor its progress with great interest. Will the new economic and institutional reforms in the countryside succeed? Will the SCFP be accepted by the population? Whatever the answers to these questions, there are prior issues that should be posed. Were the rural reforms really necessary from a development point of view? Is the SCFP unavoidable if China is to attain a high growth rate? The answers to these last two questions can be given and interpreted only within a broader framework which specifies and weighs the costs and benefits of major strategic changes. Such a specification clearly requires a statement of the ideological predilections underlying the answers. Consequently, the questions can never have unique answers. Be that as it may, it is arguable that the SCFP, especially in the context of the wider refroms, is something of a Pandora's Box, and is likely to unleash forces which will be difficult to control subsequently. Its negative effects, especially on the role and position of rural women, are already evident. One lesson which the Chinese family planning drive might well learn from the Indian experience is that it is socially dangerous and politically divisive to give local level administrative officials incentives and instructions to meet quotas related to birth control.[8] When this happens the programme tends to degenerate rapidly into an authoritarian system of implementation in which the main ingredient for success is coercion.

Finally, let us reflect briefly on the relationship between the SCFP and economic growth. Is the former really necessary for achieving a respectable performance in terms of per capita income growth? In an earlier section, we gave a negative reply to this question. If we are correct, then the SCFP becomes merely an element in a strategy which places a very high premium on attaining exceptionally high rates of growth of per capita income. In our opinion the objective of exceptionally fast growth is not worth such a high premium, especially given the high social costs associated with the single child family programme. There is a danger to socialist values in separating the means of fertility control from the end of greater well being for all men and women. Whether, on what scale, and for what duration the danger is realised will depend on the judgement of policy-makers as much as on the responses of the rural masses.

NOTES AND REFERENCES

1. See, for example, J. Aird, 'Population Studies and Population Policy in China', *Population and Development Review*, Vol. 8, No. 2, June 1982; L. F. Goodstadt, 'China's One-Child Family: Policy and Public Responses', *Population and Development Review*, Vol. 8, No. 1, March 1982; Liu Zheng *et al.*, *China's Population: Problems and Prospects* (Beijing: New World Press, 1981); Su Wenming (ed.), *Population and Other Problems*, China Today (1), *Beijing Review* Special Feature Series, April 1981; Tien H. Yuan (ed.), *Population Theory in China* (New York: M. E. Sharpe Inc; London: Croom Helm, 1980).
2. A. M. Tang and B. Stone, *Food Production in the People's Republic of China*, Research Report 15, International Food Policy Research Institute, May 1980.
3. Ibid.
4. Ibid. Also see Keith Griffin and Ashwani Saith, *Growth and Equality in Rural China*, ILO/ARTEP (Singapore: Maruzen, 1981), ch. 5.
5. P. Kane, 'The Single Child Family in China: Urban Policies and their Effects on the One-Child Family', paper presented at the International Workshop on the Single-Child Family in China, 17–18 March 1983, Queen Elizabeth House, Oxford.
6. Ashwani Saith, 'Economic Incentives for the One-Child Family in Rural China', *China Quarterly*, September 1981.
7. Elizabeth Croll, 'The Sexual Division of Labour in Rural China', in L. Beneria (ed.), *Women and Development: The Sexual Division of Labour in Rural Societies* (New York: Praeger, 1979), ch. 9; Elizabeth Croll, 'Production Versus Reproduction: A Threat to China's Development Strategy', *World Development*, Vol. II, 1983; Delia Davin, 'Women's Impact on China's Development', in N. Maxwell (ed.), *China's Road to Development* (Oxford: Pergamon Press, 1979); S. W. Mosher, 'Birth Control in a Chinese Village', *Asian Survey*, Vol. XXII, No. 4, April 1982.

8. M. Vicziany, 'Coercion in a Soft State: The Family-Planning Program of India, Part I: The Myth of Voluntarism', *Pacific Affairs*, Vol. 55, No. 3, Fall 1982; A. K. Jain and A. L. Adlakha, 'Preliminary Estimates of Fertility Decline in India During the 1970s', *Population and Development Review*, Vol. 8, No. 3, September 1982; Robert Cassen, *India: Population, Economy, Society* (London: Macmillan, 1978).

6 Commune- and Brigade-Run Enterprises in Rural China: An Overview

KEITH GRIFFIN and
KIMBERLEY GRIFFIN

Agriculture as the foundation and industry as the leading sector: today more than ever before this epigram describes an important feature of China's strategy for rural development. Since 1978 there have been major changes in economic policy and with these changes has come increased priority for commune- and brigade-run enterprises. Indeed, within the Ministry of Agriculture a new division is in the process of being established – the General Corporation of Chinese Commune and Brigade-Run Enterprises – in order to regulate rural industry while encouraging its rapid expansion.

The purpose of this chapter is to describe the present size of the commune- and brigade-run enterprise sector, to indicate a few of its economic characteristics, to estimate its rate of growth in the last few years and to discuss briefly some of the recent changes in policy affecting the sector.[1] This chapter provides an overview of the sector and presents the context in which some of the more detailed points discussed in the following chapter arise. The two chapters should thus be read together.

SIZE AND ECONOMIC CHARACTERISTICS OF THE SECTOR

In 1981 there were 1.3 million enterprises run at the commune or brigade level. These enterprises absorbed over 30 million persons or slightly more than 9 per cent of the labour force employed in the rural communes. The gross sales income of commune- and brigade-run enterprises was 67 000 million yuan in 1981 and the income generated in this sector accounted for about a third of total commune or collective income. This is a measure of the extent to which the communes have been able to reduce their dependence on agricultural activities.

Over three-quarters of the gross sales income of the sector originates in industrial activities. The rest is generated in construction, commerce, transport and miscellaneous occupations. The precise percentage breakdown of gross income for 1981 is as follows:

industry	76
construction	8
commerce and services	6
fishponds and forestry	6
transport and communications	4
	100

In Table 6.1 we include data for the four most recent years (1978–81) on the number of commune and brigade enterprises, employment, gross sales income, net profits and value of fixed assets. It can be seen in the table that the number of enterprises declined by about 200 000 between 1978 and 1981, or by about 13.3 per cent. This occurred as a result of a change in policy favouring mergers, the creation of joint ventures and in some cases the devolution of small enterprises from brigade to team level. Total employment in the sector, however, increased by more than 2 million, or by more than 7 per cent. Gross income rose dramatically, namely by roughly 55.8 per cent, while net profits[2] increased by 25 per cent.

There is in China a general policy to reduce the rate of accumulation, which in 1979 was 34.6 per cent of the national income,[3] in order to increase consumption levels for the mass of the population. Despite this policy, investment in commune- and brigade-level enterprises was exceptionally rapid and consequently the value of fixed assets increased by 63 per cent in just three years.

The data on income, profits and capital assets in Table 6.1 are expressed in current prices and hence the changes in monetary values fail to take into account the effects of inflation. Unfortunately, there is no generally reliable price index for China and consequently it is difficult to convert current value series into constant value series. This did not

TABLE 6.1 *Basic data on commune and brigade enterprises, 1978–81*

	1978	*1979*	*1980*	*1981*
Number of enterprises (million)	1.5	1.48	1.42	1.3
Total employment (million)	28	29	30	30+
Gross income (million yuan)	43 000	49 000	59 000	67 000
Net profits (million yuan)	8800	10 300	11 000	11 000
Fixed assets (million yuan)	23 000	28 000	32 000	37 500

matter very much until recently as it was widely accepted that the rate of inflation was unusually low compared to other countries. For example, between 1952 and 1978 the general retail price index rose only about 0.75 per cent a year. Since then, however, inflation has accelerated and the same index rose nearly 3.5 per cent a year between 1978 and 1981. This is still very low by international standards, but some adjustment (if only a mental adjustment) should now be made when comparing the value figures of one year with those of another.[4]

Let us turn to some of the economic characteristics of the sector. We shall concentrate on three topics: scale, employment creation and efficiency in the use of capital. The relevant information is presented in Table 6.2.

On average, commune- and brigade-run enterprises are small in scale. The typical enterprise employed just under nineteen people in 1978 and just over twenty-three people in 1981. Clearly employment per enterprise increased significantly, but despite the merger movement that took place in that period the workshops and factories in the sector remained rather small. Turnover, too, was relatively modest, but it rose from 28 667 yuan in 1978 to 51 538 yuan in 1981. Clearly this was a substantial increase. Moreover, turnover (or gross output) per worker also increased quite rapidly, namely, from 1533 yuan to 2231 yuan in 1981. By this measure the productivity of labour in the sector rose more than 45 per cent in three years. Even after making some adjustment for inflation, this is an impressive performance. Finally, the scale of enterprise as measured by the value of fixed capital assets is small, rising from over 15 000 yuan in 1978 to nearly 29 000 yuan in 1981. By all three standards, thus, commune- and brigade-run enterprises are on average small-scale establishments.

These rural enterprises, however, have been able to create jobs at very low cost. The easiest way to show this is by calculating the amount of

TABLE 6.2 *Economic characteristics of commune- and brigade-run enterprises, 1978–81*

	1978	*1979*	*1980*	*1981*
Average size of enterprise:				
a) employment	18.7	19.6	21.1	23.1
b) turnover (yuan)	28 667	33 108	41 549	51 538
c) capital assets (yuan)	15 333	18 919	22 535	28 846
Average capital–labour ratio (yuan per worker)	821	966	1067	1250
Efficiency indicators:				
a) capital–output ratio	0.53	0.57	0.54	0.56
b) rate of profit on sales (% per annum)	20.5	21.0	18.6	16.4
c) rate of profit on fixed capital (% per annum)	38.3	36.8	34.4	29.3
Average productivity of labour (yuan per worker)	1533	1689	1969	2231

fixed capital per worker, i.e. the capital-labour ratio. As can be seen in Table 6.2, the average capital–labour ratio in commune and brigade enterprises is very low. In fact, in 1978 it cost only 821 yuan to create a job in one of these enterprises; by 1981 the nominal cost was half again as high, indicating more mechanised methods of production, but the average ratio still was remarkably low. There can be no doubt that expansion of commune- and brigade-run enterprises is an excellent way to create additional employment opportunities in the countryside.

Lastly, let us consider whether capital is utilised efficiently in these enterprises. We have constructed three indicators of capital efficiency: the average capital–output ratio, the rate of return on sales (or gross income) and the rate of net profit on capital. All three indicators suggest that at prevailing prices for material inputs and output the productivity of capital is very high in commune- and brigade-run enterprises. The rate of profit on capital declined significantly over the period examined, but at 29.3 per cent in 1981 it still was high. Indeed, such a profit rate implies that a new enterprise could recover its initial capital outlay in less than three and a half years. Similarly, the rate of return on sales is high, although it too declined after 1978. The third indicator, however, namely the capital–output ratio, has remainded stable. More important, it is remarkably low: the figures in the table imply that it takes less than 600 yuan of fixed capital to produce an annual flow of output of 1000 yuan.

Viewed as a whole, commune- and brigade-run enterprises are ideal vehicles for rural development. They are small in scale and do not require massive investment to begin production. They are an inexpensive way of creating employment in the countryside at a higher level of labour productivity than is at present obtainable in agricultural activities. They yield a high return on capital and thus provide a large and quick pay off to collective savings, thereby encouraging further savings and capital accumulation in rural areas. The fall in profit rates reported in Table 6.2 probably is not very significant. They do not in themselves indicate a decline in capital efficiency, particularly since the capital–output ratio has remained fairly stable, and may reflect little more than a change in the sectoral composition of investment and in relative prices.

INDUSTRIAL ENTERPRISES AT COMMUNE AND BRIGADE LEVEL

As we have seen, industrial and construction activities account for about 84 per cent of the gross income of all commune- and brigade-run enterprises. These enterprises employed two-thirds of the labour force engaged in the sector as a whole. When one compares the industrial and construction activities with non-industrial activities it becomes apparent that the former are much larger establishments than the latter. For example, industrial enterprises on average employ 27.8 workers whereas the non-industrial enterprises employ only 17.2 workers on average. Similarly, the turnover of industrial enterprises is 78 611 yuan on average versus a turnover of 17 930 yuan in the non-industrial establishments. In other words, the average gross income of industrial and construction enterprises is more than four times larger than the other enterprises in the sector. Equally, the productivity of labour is 170 per cent higher in industry and construction than in the non-industrial enterprises. To be specific, gross income per worker is 2830 yuan in industry and construction and only 1040 yuan in the other enterprises.

There are also significant differences between industrial and construction enterprises run at the commune and at the brigade levels. Some of these differences are summarised in Table 6.3

There are a total of 720 000 enterprises engaged in construction and industrial activities, of which 190 000 are located at the commune level

TABLE 6.3 *Industrial and construction enterprises at commune and brigade levels, 1981*

	Commune level	*Brigade level*	*Total*
Number of enterprises	190 000	530 000	720 000
Total employment (million)	approx. 10	approx. 10	20
Gross income (million yuan)	31 300	25 300	56 600
Average size of enterprise:			
a) employment	approx. 52.6	approx. 18.9	27.8
b) turnover (yuan)	164 737	47 736	78 611
Average productivity of labour (yuan per worker)	approx. 3130	approx. 2530	2830

and 530 000 at brigade level. Employment is divided approximately equally between them. In consequence, commune-level industrial enterprises are much larger than those at brigade level. The typical commune-level industrial enterprise employs 2.78 times as many persons as the brigade-level enterprise, namely, 52.6 and 18.9 persons, respectively.

Total gross income of commune-level industrial enterprises in 1981 was 31.3 billion yuan compared to the 25.3 billion yuan gross income of brigade-level enterprises. The average turnover of a commune-run industrial enterprise was 164 737 yuan or about 3.45 times as large as the turnover of a brigade-run industrial enterprise. The differences in labour productivity, however, are not so great, being 3130 yuan in commune-run enterprises and 2530 yuan in brigade-run enterprises, a difference of just under 24 per cent.

In the last four years there has been a change in the composition of output of industrial enterprises at commune level in favour of light manufacturing and greater production of consumer goods. This is reflected in the fact that between 1978 and 1981 the share of light industry in total manufacturing output rose from 45 to 58 per cent while there was a corresponding fall in the share of heavy industry from 55 to 42 per cent. These changes in the output mix followed national trends and priorities and were not peculiar to commune-run enterprises. Nevertheless, these rural industries demonstrated an impressive degree of flexibility, a capacity to adapt quickly to changing circumstances and an ability to grasp new opportunities when they appeared.

The importance of commune- and brigade-run industrial enterprises lies not so much in their contribution to national output as in the contribution they make towards raising the standard of living in rural areas. Commune- and brigade-run industrial enterprises account at present for only 10.8 per cent of total industrial production, yet in the countryside they are an important source of collective income, a major provider of funds for collective accumulation and at least potentially a base on which to create higher productivity employment. Even now, gross output per worker in commune- and brigade-run industrial enterprises is more than six times that in agriculture and this productivity differential is likely to increase still further in future.

RECENT POLICY CHANGES

The commitment of the government to promoting commune- and brigade-run enterprises can be seen in the policy changes that have recently been introduced. Broadly speaking, these policy changes cover four areas: the creation of new forms of enterprise organisation, the introduction of the 'production responsibility system' and new contractual arrangements to commune enterprises, the recruitment of labour and the payment system.

Perhaps the most dramatic change is the proliferation of experiments with alternative forms of organisation. Many communes are being encouraged to consider radically new methods of organising industrial production. Examples include enterprises established jointly by households[5] or groups of individuals or by households in combination with teams, brigades or communes; enterprises established jointly by teams or brigades of the same or different communes; enterprises established jointly by the commune in combination with state enterprises. A common feature of these new forms of organisation is that they cut across the pyramidal and hierarchical structure of the traditional three-tiered commune; any person, household or unit may combine with any other to produce a product for which there is a demand.[6]

There has been a tendency both to decentralise some units of production to the team level and to merge other enterprises into joint ventures or into single production units under the authority of the commune or brigade.[7] The overall policy is to encourage the development of commune enterprises at all levels, to co-ordinate commune and state activities and promote joint ventures but not to encourage activities that compete with state enterprises for energy and raw materials in short supply. That is, enterprises based in communes are expected to exploit locally available resources and not to increase the claims put upon scarce national resources. Thus there is an intention to regulate commune- and brigade-level enterprises more closely, to bring some order into local investment projects and ensure where possible that commune- and brigade-level enterprises complement rather than compete with state enterprises.

Once the establishment of a new enterprise has been agreed it becomes eligible for considerable assistance from the state. For example, the provincial or county government may provide technicians in the early stages and even some raw materials; loans may also be granted from the banks, the government or a state enterprise (for example if the new firm is producing a component for the state enterprise). Joint household enterprises are allowed to hire technicians – a radical departure from past practice when hiring labour was regarded as exploitation – and the general policy as regards employing labour is now being reviewed. It seems likely that in practice hiring of labour in some form or other will become fairly common.

The capital 'market' too is undergoing change. Some joint stock companies are emerging in Sichuan, and also in Shandong province. For instance, in Guanghan county, Sichuan, we visited the Jinan Joint Corporation. This is a joint venture established in 1980 of three xiang (once a single commune) and a number of other units. The Corporation is now responsible for the management of twenty-eight enterprises, most of which were formerly undertakings run at commune level. The Corporation issued shares free of cost to the villages (formerly brigades) and co-operatives (formerly teams) out of which it emerged. It also sells new shares to finance investment. So far shares to the value of 275 000 yuan have been sold. These are marketable to anyone although the great majority of shares have been purchased by villages and co-operatives. Indeed, private shareholders account for only about 1 per cent of the capital and it is the policy of the Corporation to discourage private investors. Nevertheless, the fact that an individual can in principle acquire shares in a collective enterprise in China represents a startling change of policy.[8]

Similarly, we visited Feng Huan Brigade, Zhan Xiang Commune in Qionglai county, Sichuan. The brigade is known as the Phoenix Agricultural, Industrial and Commercial Joint Corporation and is responsible for the management of four companies with an annual turnover of 2.62 million yuan. A Board of Directors elected from among members of the Corporation is in charge of the day-to-day running of the four companies. Shares corresponding to the value of fixed assets of the companies were issued in 1979. Shareholders may be individuals or representatives of one of the five teams from which the Corporation was formed. The Directors are elected by shareholders, each shareholder having one vote regardless of the number of shares owned. Each share costs 100 yuan and enjoys a fixed dividend rate of 20 per cent a year. In 1982, of the 201 households in the five original teams, more than sixty owned more than ten shares and one household owned twenty shares; twenty-five households appeared to own no shares. It is not difficult to see from this example that the new forms of enterprise organisation, and the methods used to finance them, could lead rather quickly to the emergence in the countryside of a class of 'penny capitalists'.[9]

A second set of reforms is concerned essentially with increasing production efficiency at the enterprise level. This is to be done in three inter-related ways. First, some decision-making is being decentralised to the workshop or work group level or in some cases to the level of the individual. Secondly, the responsibilities of the workshop, work group or individual are spelled out in detail in the form of a contract. Such contracts typically specify five items (the five 'fixes') although there is considerable variation from one enterprise to another.

All contracts specify or fix an output quota in physical terms. They then usually specify too the cost of production in value terms. Next, the use of some material inputs is fixed in terms of the quantity that can be absorbed in production. Then the gross income is specified and finally a profit target is fixed. This mixture of physical and value indicators or targets or quotas would appear on the surface to be rather clumsy and 'over-determined', but the purpose is to ensure that the quantity and quality of output are maintained while costs are kept as low as possible.

The contractual obligations are reinforced by a third element, namely, the bonus system. Success is rewarded and failure is punished through bonuses and penalties, and these provide a strong incentive to fulfil and if possible exceed the targets itemised in the contract. A bonus is awarded for overfulfilling each of the five 'fixes', the size of the bonus varying from one industry to another and from place to place, but the bonus usually is quite substantial, i.e. 30–50 per cent. Penalties for not meeting one of the five 'fixes', in contrast, usually are rather low in commune- and brigade-run enterprises.[10] The size of the penalty depends in part on why a given quota was not met, but in practice penalties rarely are greater than 1 or 2 per cent of the shortfall in the target. Looked at as a package, the three elements comprising the production responsibility system as applied in commune- and brigade-run enterprises represent a tendency to place greater reliance on individual and on material incentives to increase production and correspondingly less reliance on collective and on non-material incentives. Whether or not an incentive problem existed in commune- and brigade-level enterprises before 1978, the Chinese evidently believe that the new package of policies will improve labour productivity. Yet the changes must not be exaggerated. Enterprise workers as a whole do put great pressure on individual workers to fulfil their quotas, particularly in sequential process operations.

Another way in which enterprises are attempting to increase their efficiency and profitability is by changing their recruitment policy. There has been a widespread tendency to put greater emphasis on skill or ability when recruiting labour from the production teams for commune- and brigade-run enterprises. Indeed in several communes we visited workers were recruited on the basis of their performance in an examination. This policy is tempered, however, in several ways. First, in order to achieve balanced representation in collective enterprises, the teams may be given a quota of industrial workers which they are invited to fill. Secondly, some priority may be given to poor households or to poor teams in recruiting labour for industrial enterprises. This policy is hardly new and in fact it may be less significant than it once was. In only one commune that we visited, namely, Zu Chiao Commune near Chengdu, Sichuan, was it explicit policy to recruit labour from poor teams into commune-run enterprises. Thirdly, priority in obtaining jobs in collective enterprises sometimes is given to teams which supply raw materials to the enterprise. Presumably the justification for this is that raw materials are purchased from teams at relatively low prices to the consequent benefit of the net income of the processing enterprises. Labour recruitment policies in this case are used to compensate for an 'inequitable' set of relative prices. Finally, in the case of the experimental joint stock corporations that we visited, everything else being equal, priority is given to members of households which own shares in the enterprise.

In practice the recruitment policy adopted varies greatly between communes. For example, in Fu Bao Brigade, Liu Jia Commune near Kunming, Yunnan province, jobs in brigade-run enterprises were allocated among teams in proportion to the profits of the enterprises in which members of the various teams happened to be working. Thus when vacancies occurred in old or newly established activities, a team with members in high-profit enterprises would be given a larger share of the new jobs than a team with members engaged in relatively low-profit enterprises. Suppose, for example, that only one brigade-run enterprise (Enterprise *X*) was generating a profit and that 70 per cent of the workers in that enterprise came from one team, say, Team *A*. Then if a new brigade-level enterprise were established, 70 per cent of the jobs created would be filled by recruiting workers from Team *A* and the remaining 30 per cent of workers would be recruited from Teams *B*, *C*, *D*, etc. in proportion to their contribution to the labour force of Enterprise *X*.

The recruitment policy of the Jinan Joint Corporation is rather different. The original workers in the enterprises managed by the Corporation came from the co-operatives (formerly production teams) out of which the Corporation was formed. New workers, however, tended to be recruited from the three xiang which effectively own the Corporation and from the county seat. Particularly in capital-intensive industries, the Corporation hires townspeople and specifically urban job-waiting (unemployed) youths. The reason for this is that in enterprises which obtain more than half their labour force from among the urban unemployed, liability to pay the corporate income tax and the industrial and commercial tax is waived for three years and one year, respectively. Thus the recruitment policy makes sense from the point of view of a profit maximising firm. On the other hand, by recruiting people from the town the policy undermines one of the original objectives of commune- and brigade-run enterprises, namely, the industrialisation of the countryside and the creation of non-agricultural employment opportunities for the rural population.

The changes in recruitment policy have been accompanied by some changes in the payment system. Increasingly workers in commune- and brigade-run enterprises are paid directly in cash and the older method of payment in the form of work points appears to be in rapid decline. In Sichuan, for instance, the majority of enterprises have already switched to a monthly cash wage system and it is likely that this practice will be adopted soon in most of the other provinces.

The wage level in commune- and brigade-run enterprises typically is 20–40 per cent higher than collective incomes in agriculture. This differential is justified in part by the fact that persons engaged in agriculture have greater opportunities to supplement their income from private sideline occupations (pigs, poultry) and the private plot. Even after taking this factor into account, however, it is clear that in general commune and brigade industries pay their workers somewhat more than can be earned by other commune members. Some enterprises still determine their cash wages with reference to the average income levels of the teams from which the workers have come, but when two payment systems are in operation side by side within a single commune, one for agricultural workers and another for commune industrial workers, tensions inevitably arise. Once the work point system which links agricultural and industrial incomes in the commune is severed, there will be strong pressure within an enterprise to pay all workers an equal wage for equal work. Even those enterprises which continue to pay workers work points, which are then converted to a money wage according to the workpoint value of their team, now pay cash bonuses directly to the workers, and these bonuses may amount to half a worker's monthly remuneration.

As the links between agricultural and industrial incomes within a team become weaker, workers in commune- and brigade-run enterprises are likely to take wage levels in state enterprises as their point of reference. That is, industrial workers in the communes can be expected to compare their remuneration not with incomes derived from agricultural activities but with incomes obtained by urban workers in state factories. This happens already, of course, but it is bound to become more prevalent in future. As a result, commune- and brigade-run enterprises will find – as the Jinan Joint Corporation has found – that by switching from a work point to a cash wage payment system they will ultimately be forced to accept the higher wage levels and the wage structure of state enterprises. This, in turn, may have important implications for the long run profitability and competitiveness of commune- and brigade-run enterprises, for their rate of growth and for the contribution they can make to rural development.

NOTES AND REFERENCES

1. The national data contained in this chapter were kindly provided by Mr Huang Guangxu, the head of the General Corporation of Chinese Commune- and Brigade-Run Enterprises, while supporting provincial information and data from individual communes were obtained on field trips to Sichuan and Yunnan.
2. Net profit is defined as sales income minus costs of production, administrative expenses and taxes.
3. 'Economic Readjustment and Reform', *Beijing Review*, 1982, appendix table VI.
4. For the benefit of readers who wish to deflate our figures by the general retail price index (1952 = 100), we give the index numbers of the most recent years: 1978 = 121.6; 1979 = 124; 1980 = 131.4 and 1981 = 134.6. The reader is warned, however, that other price indices show a much lower rate of inflation, notably, the index of industrial prices and the index of retail prices of commodities purchased in rural areas.
5. In Qionglai county, Sichuan province we came across one enterprise producing silver fungus which was jointly run by eight families.
6. The only restrictions on what these new enterprises may produce are that they may not process cotton or tobacco and as regards other commodities

subject to quota, they may process only the output in excess of the quota. More generally, enterprises located in communes would not normally be allowed to produce goods in competition with the state. These restrictions are not new but have been carried over from the past.

7. In Fu Bao Brigade, Liu Jia Commune in the environs of Kunming, Yunnan province, we encountered a case in which the brigade has taken over a forging and casting workshop from one of its teams.
8. The private purchase of shares in the Jinan Joint Corporation represents an attractive investment since the shares have a dividend rate of 12 per cent whereas the deposit rate of interest is only 4–5 per cent.
9. For additional details on the Jinan Joint Corporation and on the Phoenix Corporation see Chapter 2.
10. In agriculture both the bonus and the penalty usually are 100 per cent.

7 Commune- and Brigade-Run Industries in Rural China: Some Recent Observations

J. L. ENOS

The purpose of this chapter is to report what was learned during a recent visit to China about industrial activities in the communes. Some two dozen enterprises were observed, chiefly in the provinces of Sichuan and Yunnan, and were found to be diverse in terms of the activities in which they were engaged and significant in terms of the output which they produced. The enterprises employed a substantial portion of the rural population and yielded an even more substantial portion of their income. In the communes in which the data for 1981 were gathered, over 40 per cent of the total collective distributed income was generated by industry. This percentage is rising rapidly; at a guess, the figure for 1982 will prove to have been one-third again as high, and the figures for subsequent years will be higher still.

COVERAGE

Before the data are presented and analysed, the universe to which they belong must be identified. Geographically, much of China's industry is located outside the cities, in the countryside. Some of the establishments in the countryside are administered from the centre, some from the provincial capitals, some from the county seats and the remainder by the communes and brigades. Those administered by the last group, the communes and brigades, are not distinguished therefore by geography, nor, as will be seen, by scale of operation or state of technology, but rather by the matter of ownership. The industrial enterprises visited were owned by communes, or by their next smaller division, the brigades: hence the words 'commune and brigade' in the title.

In China, ownership confers on collective bodies – in this case communes or brigades – certain obligations and rewards. The major obligations are to choose the activity to be undertaken, to acquire, mainly from the commune's or brigade's own members, the resources necessary for production, and to administer these in an efficient manner. The major rewards are the incomes that the employees of the enterprises, again mainly the members of the communes or brigades, receive and the profits which are retained by the communes or brigades for the expansion of their existing enterprises, or the creation of new ones.

The locus of decision for the enterprises owned by communes or brigades thus lies in China's primary administrative units. In visiting the enterprises – the processing centres, the workshops, the factories – we were visiting the places where the decisions were made. In talking to the commune's or brigade's leader or party secretary, or to the enterprise's manager, we were talking to those who made the decisions. The enterprises are not only owned by the communes and brigades, they are administered *within them as well*, i.e. they are 'run' by the communes and brigades.[1]

During the visit, a total of twenty-three commune- and brigade-run enterprises were observed, one in the municipality of Beijing, fourteen in the province of Sichuan and the remaining eight in the province of Yunnan. Ownership of five of the enterprises was vested in communes, seventeen in brigades and one in a household. In size, the enterprises ranged from the smallest, which employed two persons on capital equipment valued at 316 yuan producing in 1981 output valued at approximately 900 yuan, to the largest, which employed 230 persons on equipment valued at 3 500 000 yuan and producing in the same year output valued at 2 900 000 yuan.

The enterprises can be identified by the attributes listed in Table 7.1. The enterprises appear in the same order in subsequent tables, being identified there simply by number and chief product. There is a division in each table between those enterprises established before 1981, for which financial data are available for that year, and those established afterwards, for which only data after 1981 are available: four of the total of twenty-three establishments fall in this second, less informative category (enterprises 20–23). Otherwise, the order of enterprises within each table follows the chronological order in which they were visited.

After the first table, summarising the enterprises' characteristics, Table 7.2 gives the sources of their financial capital and other inputs;

Table 7.3 the manufacturers of their capital equipment; Table 7.4 the means by which they acquired the necessary technical knowledge and operating skills; Table 7.5 their level of output and the markets they serve; Table 7.6 their sales revenues and costs; and finally Table 7.7 their employment and four measures of performance – capital per worker, capital: output ratio, return on (fixed) capital, and rate of utilisation of capacity.

Much information is encapsulated in the tables. Were it our purpose to provide as nearly as possible a complete description of twenty-three commune- and brigade-run plants, we would augment the data in the tables with the other relevant facts and impressions gained, but our purposes rather are to note trends in the industrialisation of the Chinese countryside and to identify the controversial issues that are likely to arise in the future. We will therefore let the tables speak for themselves, without further embellishment.

TRENDS IN RURAL INDUSTRIALISATION

The first observation to be made is that the nature of commune- and brigade-run enterprises is changing, to the point where they cannot easily be characterised. Until a few years ago characterisation was simple; observers such as Sigurdson[2] and the American Rural Small-Scale Industry Delegation[3] were able to typify commune- and brigade-run enterprises as those operating at a small scale, utilising a primitive technology, employing resources that were abundant locally but costly to transfer outside the locality, and producing goods either for local consumption or as compoennts to state firms. Yet by 1981 this stereotype of the small, locally oriented enterprise was no longer valid. Perusal of the tables, particularly Table 7.5, reveals that many commune- and brigade-run enterprises now operate at an intermediate scale, utilise modern techniques, employ resources that are scarce and mobile, and serve markets throughout China and abroad. If a characterisation can be made, it would be that rural enterprises are now a part of the national economy. The dualistic nature of Chinese industry is disappearing; the state firms and the rural enterprises are now becoming integrated into a single productive system.

Commune- and brigade-run firms are expanding and modernising, but they have not expanded and modernised to the point where they are as large and as technically advanced as the most advanced state enterprises. The question arises whether or not they will ever reach this

TABLE 7.1 *Characteristics of the enterprises visited*

Enterprise number	*Locus of decision*	*Location*		*Products*	*Initial dates*			*Expansion*
		Province	*Locale*		*Conception*	*Construction*	*Operation*	
1.	commune	Beijing	Yellow Sands Commune	vermicelli	n.a.	1958	1958	1962 (merger) 1979, 1982 (expansions)
2.	brigade	Sichuan	Brigade No. 9, Zu Chiao Commune	garments	n.a.	1979	1979	
3.	brigade	Sichuan	"	fur coats, waistcoats	n.a.	1979	1979	
4.	brigade	Sichuan	"	wheat noodles	n.a.	n.a.	n.a.	
5.	household	Sichuan	"	biogas	n.a.	1977	1977	
6.	brigade	Sichuan	Fang Huan Brigade, Zhan Xiang Commune	bricks	1978	1980	1981	1982 (200 % increase)
7.	brigade	Sichuan	"	distillery	n.a.	1978	1979	
8.	corporation (= commune)	Sichuan	Jinan Joint Corporation	cement	n.a.	1977	1977	1980–2 (2000 to 20 000 m.t./year)
9.	corporation (= commune)	Sichuan	"	fine chemicals	n.a.	n.a.	pre-1981	Jan.–March 1981 (to 100 m.t. fine chemicals); 1983 (to 410 m.t.)
10.	brigade	Sichuan	Shu Guang Brigade, Mi Mu Commune	wheat noodles	n.a.	1976	1977	1979 mechanised (from 75 to 300 m.t.)
11.	brigade	Sichuan	"	tailor shop	n.a.	1966	1966	
12.	brigade	Sichuan	"	gypsum board	n.a.	April 1978	July 1978	

13.	brigade	Sichuan	Chao Tan Brigade, Yuan Men Ko Commune	pre-stressed concrete panels	n.a.	1980	1980	1982 (100% increase)
14.	brigade	Yunnan	Production Team No. 1 Gao Chang Brigade, Gao Chang Commune, Yu Xi county	wheat noodles	n.a.	n.a.	n.a.	
15.	brigade	Yunnan	Long Xu Brigade, Gao Chang Commune, Yu Xi county	metal components	n.a.	n.a.	n.a.	intention to expand
16.	commune	Yunnan	Gao Chang Commune, Yu Xi county	cement	n.a.	1970	1971	see enterprise no. 22
17.	brigade	Yunnan	Gao Chio Team, Pu Chao Brigade, Ala Commune	bricks and tiles	n.a.	pre-1978	pre-1978	
18.	brigade	Yunnan	Fu Bao Brigade, Liu Jia commune	waterpipes, etc.	1960s	1978	1979	1983 (50% increase)
19.	brigade	Yunnan	"	sweet biscuits	1980	1980	1980	1982 (100% increase)
20.	brigade	Sichuan	Fung Huan Brigade, Zhan Xiang Commune	fine chemical	1980	June 1982	1982 (pilot ops.) 1983 (full scale)	Sept. 1981–April 1982 produced chemical fertilizer
21.	brigade	Sichuan	Chao Tan Brigade, Yuan Men Ko Commune	printing shop	1980	May 1981	March 1982	from 39 to 50 employees
22.	Commune	Yunnan	Gao Chang Commune, Yu Xi county	cement	n.a.	1979	end 1981	to full capacity by end 1982
23.	brigade	Yunnan	Fu Bao Brigade, Liu Jia Commune	kraft paper	n.a.	1980	May 1982	to full capacity in 1983

TABLE 7.2 *Sources of capital and other inputs*

Enterprise number	Products	Fixed capital: Amount (Yuan)	Fixed capital: Sources	Materials	Labour: Management	Labour: Workers
1.	vermicelli	118 000+	commune	municipal vegetable authority	local	local
2.	garments	approx. 50 000	brigade	Chengdu Leather Enterprise	local	local
3.	fur coats, waistcoats	approx. 50 000	,,	Chengdu Fur Makers	local	local
4.	wheat noodles	approx. 500	,,	commune members	local	local
5.	biogas	100	household	commune (bricks) county (cement)	local	local
6.	bricks	23 000 (machinery only)	80% brigade, 20% county	clay from brigade, coal from Dai Yi county (72 km away)	local	local
7.	distillery	23 000	province	bricks from brigade	local	local
8.	cement	1 420 000	majority from corporation (formerly commune)	lime from Jian Yo county (120 km), coal from Du Ko city, Sichuan (550 km)	local	local
9.	fine chemicals	110 000	Sichuan State Bank (guaranteed by corporation)	MoS_2 from Honan and Shanxi NH_4OH from county fertiliser factory	Special Steel Plant, Chengdu	local
10	wheat noodles	300	brigade	wheat from brigade members	local	local
11.	tailor shop	316	,,	cloth from brigade members	local	local
12.	gypsum board	200 000	(250 000 working capital from brigade too)	gypsum locally	local	local

13.	pre-stressed concrete panels	57 000	brigade	cement from Chengdu	local	local
14.	wheat noodles	75 000	brigade	wheat from customers	local	local
15.	metal components	approx. 500 000	enterprise	steel from state steel works, approved by Ministry of Light Industry	local	local
16.	cement	600 000	approx. ½ commune ½ province	limestone from commune, coal from state mine, 100 km away	local	local
17.	bricks and tiles	approx. 10 000	production team	clay local, coal Yunnan	local	local
18.	water pipes, etc.	310 000	brigade	iron from state iron and steel complexes in Yunnan	local	local
19.	sweet biscuits	40 000	brigade	wheat, sugar from state marketing boards	local	local
20.	fine chemical	approx. 80 000	brigade (most) county (remainder)	hair locally; hydrochloric acid from Chengdu Chemical factory	local	local
21.	printing shop	n.a.	brigade	Chengdu	local	local
22.	cement	3 500 000	approx. 300 000 province, remainder commune	same as enterprise 16	local	local
23.	kraft paper	approx. 2 400 000	550 000 from province remainder from brigade	waste paper from Kunming, rice straw from county	local	local

TABLE 7.3 *Sources of capital equipment*

Enterprise number	Products	Machine	Cost (Yuan)	Source: Manufacturer	Source: Location	Source: Distance away
1.	vermicelli	electric motors	38 000	n.a.	Beijing	15 km
2.	garments	sewing machines	approx. 5000	n.a.	Chengdu	15 km
3.	fur coats, waistcoats	sewing machines	approx. 5000	n.a.	Chengdu	15 km
4.	wheat noodles	electric motor rollers	200	Tung Tong Electric Mach. Co. (state enterprise)	Chengdu Zen So county, Sichuan	15 km 180 km
5.	biogas	n.a.	n.a.	n.a.	n.a.	n.a.
6.	bricks	2 extruders	23 000	Chengdu Brick Factory	Chengdu	60 km
7.	distillery	2 pots	23 000	hardware factory	Chengdu	60 km
8.	cement	rotary kiln, crusher	approx. 1 million	Jang Yo Mining Machinery Factory	Chengdu	55 km
9.	fine chemicals	reactors, boiler	appr. 20 000 appr. 39 000	Chung King Mach. Factory Chengdu Boiler Factory	Chongqing Chengdu	280 km 55 km
10.	wheat noodles	rollers, electric motor	60 240	Guanghan county electric motor factory	Guanghan, Sichuan Chengdu	26 km 29 km
11.	tailor shop	sewing machines	158 each	n.a.	Shanxi	500 km
12.	gypsum board	crusher boiler	17 600 16 000	machine manu. Chengdu Boiler Factory	Pan Shan commune, Sichuan; Chengdu	30 km 29 km

13.	pre-stressed concrete panels	stressing drum	n.a.	n.a.	n.a.	n.a.
14.	wheat noodles	rollers, mining mach.	n.a. n.a.	n.a. n.a.	Kunming Yu Xi city	160 km 6 km
15.	metal components	lathes, planers, drills, etc.	n.a.	state enterprises, local adaptations	Kunming, Tianjin, (stamping machines)	160 km 2400 km
16.	cement	crusher	n.a.	n.a.	Beijing	2400 km
17.	bricks and tiles	kiln	n.a.	local		
18.	water pipes, etc.	cont. casting, lathes	n.a. n.a.	local state factory, Honan	secondhand from Kunming	 12 km
19.	sweet biscuits	12 waffle irons	n.a.	state factory	Shanghai	1950 km
20.	fine chemical	reactors, boiler	n.a. n.a.	South-west Chemical Factory Chengdu Boiler Factory	Chongqing (secondhand) Chengdu	350 km 60 km
21.	printing shop	rotary and moving bed printers	n.a.	some by factory in Wuhan, Hubei	new and secondhand, local distribution, Chengdu	6 km
22.	cement	kiln, crushers	n.a.	by commune, Heavy Ind. Equip. Factory	Kunming	160 km
23.	kraft paper	Foudrinier machine	300 000	Light Industry Equipment Factory	Guiyang, Guizhou	450 km

TABLE 7.4 *Sources of technological knowledge*

Enterprise number	*Products*	*Main process employed*	*Provision of knowledge by outsiders*		*Acquisition of knowledge by employees*		
			No. of technicians	*Total time on site*	*No. sent away*	*Total time spent away*	*Blue prints, manuals*
1.	vermicelli	filtering			2, to municipal plant 20 km away	2 weeks	
2.	garments	sewing			1, to Chengdu	approx. 1 week	
3.	fur coats, waistcoats	sewing			n.a.	n.a.	
4.	wheat noodles	rolling					
5.	biogas	construction					Yes
6.	bricks	kiln baking	6 from Chengdu, 2 from commune	7 man-months	7; 3 to county, 4 to commune	1 man-year	from C. and B. Ent. Bureau, Chengdu
7.	distillery	distilling	1 from state distillery	3 man-years	6, to state distillery	1 man-year	
8.	cement	rotary kiln	8; 6 from Provincial Research Inst., 2 from Kuan Tan Co.	approx. 1 man-year	28: 8 to Kuan Tan Co; 20 to Provincial Research Institute	3 man-years	Kuan Tan Cement Co., Gansu.
9.	fine chemicals	chemical processes	1, manager	full-time			National Ministry of Mines
10.	wheat noodles	rolling					
11.	tailor shop	sewing					
12.	gypsum board	kiln	4, from Pan Shan county	3 man-months	7, to Construction Research Institute, Chengdu	4 man-months	

13.	pre-stressed concrete panels	stressing					
14.	wheat noodles	rolling milling					
15.	metal components	metal working					
16.	cement	vertical kiln, crushing			15: 1 to Kunming plant, 14 to Provincial Bureau for Construction Materials	1 man-year	Yes
17.	bricks and tiles	kiln					
18.	waterpipes, etc.	casting	1, from Light Industrial Equipment Factory	1 man-month	3; 2 formerly worked in state foundries, 1 in electric motor factory	18 years' experience	
19.	sweet biscuits	waffle baking	1, from Shanghai	2 visits, ½ man-month	2, to Shanghai	1 man-month	
20.	fine chemical	batch chem. reaction	1, with 40 years' experience in Shanghai	now brigade resident			
21.	printing shop	printing	3, retired from Chengdu	full-time			
22.	cement	kiln, crushing			3, to Kunming	1 man-month	
23.	kraft paper	Foudrinier	3; 2 from Kutiyang, 1 from Kunming	2 man-months full-time	30, to paper-making plant, Kunming	7 man-years	Yes, from equipment suppliers

TABLE 7.5 *Rates of output and markets served*

Enterprise number	*Product*	*Yearly rate of output*	*% sold locally*	*Sales outside locality*			*Distance to furthest market*
				% sold	*Distribution channel*	*markets served*	
1.	vermicelli	2000 m.t.		100	municipal retail shop	Beijing	25 km
2.	garments	4000 coats 2000jackets		100	Chengdu Leather Enterprise	Chengdu	60 km
3.	fur coats waistcoats	2700		100	Chengdu Fur Makers	export	60 km
4.	wheat noodles	approx. 200 m.t.	100				
5.	biogas	n.a.	100				
6.	bricks	4 500 000 bricks (1981) 6 000 000 bricks (1982)	approx. 10	approx. 90	direct	own and adjacent communes	20 km
7.	distillery	30 000 litres	approx. 45	approx. 55	Tobacco and Wine Company	Sichuan	200 km
8.	cement	13 000 m.t.	20	80	own	Sichuan, Shanxi, Yunnan, Tibet	1300 km
9.	fine chemicals	160 m.t.		100	General Bureau of Export of Chemical Products, Beijing	export to Phillip Chemical Co., USA	55 km. or 11 000 km
10.	wheat noodles	300 m.t.	100				
11.	tailor shop	approx. 900 Y.	100				

12.	gypsum board	approx. 400 000 Y.		100	own	within Sichuan (90 %) Yunnan, Shanxi, Guizhou, Tibet (10 %)	1300 km
13.	pre-stressed concrete panels	32 400 panels	little	most	own	chiefly Chengdu city	5 km
14.	wheat noodles	approx. 900 m.t.	little	most	own	chiefly Kunming city; some to neighbouring communes	160 km
15.	metal components	approx. 900 000 Y.	little	most	prefectural provincial marketing boards; provincial export body	within prefecture and province; foreign countries	
16.	cement	20 000 m.t.	little	most	own	Yunnan Province	700 km
17.	bricks and tiles	approx. 100 000	100				
18.	water pipes, etc	approx. 60 000 pipes		100	own	Guangdong and Gansu	1100 km
19.	sweet biscuits	160 000 Y.	little	most	own	Yunnan Province	600 km
20.	fine chemical	6 m.t.		100	Sichuan Bureau of Export of Chemical Products	export to West Germany	12 000 km
21.	printing shop	n.a.		100	own	Chengdu	6 km
22.	cement	40 000	little	most	own	Yunnan Province	700 km
23.	kraft paper	approx. 3000 m.t.	little	most	own	Kunming, to corrugated box factory	16 km

TABLE 7.6 *Income and expenses of enterprises (1981 unless stated)*

Enterprise number	Products	Value of sales (Yuan)	Raw(1) materials	Expenses (as % of value of sales)					Net profits	
				Fuel	Interest and depreciation	Wages	Bonus	Taxes	Amount (Yuan)	Distribution
1.	vermicelli	1 240 000	60	n.a.		10	n.a.	n.a.	approx. 240 000	by commune
2.	garments	120 000	sub-contract	n.a.		approx. 60	n.a.	n.a.	40 000	by brigade
3.	fur coats, waistcoats	240 000	sub-contract	n.a.		approx. 60	n.a.	n.a.	90 000	by brigade
4.	wheat noodles	44 000	approx. 55	n.a.		approx. 45				
5.	biogas	n.a.								
6.	bricks	150 000(1981) 220 000(1982)	n.a.	approx. 20	n.a.	37		n.a.	42 000(1981) 50 000(1982)	by brigade
7.	distillery	770 000	n.a.	n.a.		n.a.	n.a.	9	140 000	30% working capital 70% by brigade
8.	cement	1 080 000	10	n.a.	n.a.	11	1	n.a.	83 000	by corporation
9.	fine chemicals	1 500 000	n.a.	n.a.	n.a.	3.6	0.4		21 000	by corporation
10.	wheat noodles	4500		approx. 10		approx 80			400	by brigade
11.	tailor shop	approx. 900		n.a.		n.a.	n.a.			
12.	gypsum board	350 000	approx. 45		n.a.	n.a.	n.a.	n.a.	100 000	by brigade

13.	pre-stressed concrete panels	161 700 (1980)	approx. 25		n.a.	33	n.a.	n.a.	57 000	by brigade
14.	wheat noodles	approx. 90 000		n.a.	n.a.	13	n.a.	n.a.	68 000	by brigade
15.	metal components	863 000	approx. 45		n.a.	25	5	n.a.	160 000	by brigade
16.	cement	1 400 000	32	23	5	15	3	4	250 000	70 % within enterprise 30 % by commune
17.	bricks and tiles	approx. 8000	n.a.	approx. 20	n.a.	approx. 80				
18.	waterpipes etc.	1 782 000	n.a.	n.a.	n.a.	n.a.	n.a.	n.a.	approx. 178 000	by brigade
19.	sweet biscuits	160 000	n.a.	n.a.	n.a.	n.a.	n.a.	n.a.	48 000	by brigade
sub-totals		approx. 10 030 000							approx. 1 720 000	
20.	fine chemical	540 000	n.a.	n.a.	n.a.	n.a.	n.a.	n.a.	n.a.	by brigade
21.	printing shop	approx. 100 000	n.a.	n.a.	n.a.	n.a.	n.a.	n.a.	n.a.	by brigade
22.	cement	2 900 000	n.a.	n.a.	n.a.	n.a.	n.a.	n.a.	n.a.	by commune
23.	kraft paper	1 650 000	18	n.a.	0.6 on province's loan	6	3.5	n.a.	300 000 (1982)	by brigade
sub-totals		approx. 5 200 000							n.a.	

NOTE (1) Raw materials costs include costs of spare parts and miscellaneous items.

TABLE 7.7 *Measures of enterprise performance (1981 unless stated)*

Enterprise number	*Products*	*Total employment*	*Total fixed assets (Yuan)*	*Yearly capacity of equipment*	*Measures*			
					Capital per worker (Yuan)	*Capital: output*	*Return on capital (%)*	*Rate of utilisation of capacity (%)*
1.	vermicelli	100	118 000	2000 m.t.	1180	0.10	approx. 200	100
2.	garments	130	approx. 50 000	approx. 6000 garments	approx. 400	approx. 0.42	approx. 80	approx. 100
3.	fur coats, waistcoats	170	approx. 50 000	approx. 3000 garments	approx. 300	approx. 0.21	approx. 180	approx. 90
4.	wheat noodles	4	approx. 500	approx. 300 m.t.	approx. 12.5	approx. 0.01		approx. 67
5.	biogas	household labour						
6.	bricks	65	approx. 100 000	7.5 million bricks (1981) 22.5 million bricks (1982)	approx. 1550	approx. 0.67	approx. 40	67 (1981) 38 (1982)
7.	distillery	60	approx. 80 000	30 000 litres	approx. 1330	approx. 0.10	approx. 175	100, but only low quality
8.	cement	174	1 420 000	20 000 m.t.	8200	1.31	6	65 (1981) 93 (1982)
9.	fine chemicals	75	110 000	100 m.t.	1470	0.074	190	160
10.	wheat noodles	5	300	300 m.t.	60	0.067	133	100
11.	tailor shop	2	316	1500 Y	158	0.35		60

12.	gypsum board	200	200 000 (650 000 total fixed plus working capital)	approx. 400 000 Y	1000 (3250 total)	0.57 (1.85 total)	50	approx. 88
13.	pre-stressed concrete panels	52	57 000	approx. 35 000 panels	1100	0.35 (1980)	100 (1980)	approx. 93 (1980)
14.	wheat noodles	40	75 000	approx. 1000 m.t.	1880	0.84	91	90
15.	metal components	240	approx. 500 000 (800 000 fixed plus working capital)	approx. 900 000 yuan	2080 (3330 total)	0.58	36	96
16.	cement	approx. 230	600 000	20 000 m.t.	2600	0.43	42	100
17.	bricks and tiles	10	approx. 10 000	approx. 200 000	1000	1.25		approx. 50
18.	waterpipes, etc.	196	310 000	approx. 60 000 (pipes alone)	1580	0.17	approx. 58	approx. 100
19.	sweet biscuits	11	40 000	approx. 160 000 Y.	3600	0.25	120	approx. 100
sub-totals		approx. 1770	approx. 3 720 000		approx. 2100	approx. 0.37	approx. 46	
20.	fine chemical	16	approx. 80 000	6 m.t.	5000	0.15	n.a.	n.a.
21.	printing shop	39	50 000	n.a.	1280	approx. 050	n.a.	n.a.
22.	cement	approx. 230	3 500 000	40 000 m.t.	approx. 15 200	1.21	n.a.	n.a.
23.	kraft paper	170	approx. 2 400 000	approx. 3500 m.t.	approx. 14 100	approx. 1.41	approx. 25	n.a
sub-totals		approx. 455	approx. 6 030 000		approx. 13 100	approx. 1.16	n.a.	

point, i.e. whether or not they will close the size and technology gaps. Commune- and brigade-run enterprises could permanently form a sector with lower capital–labour and output–labour ratios than the state sector, in the Japanese mode, or they could approach the same ratios as the state sector, on the average.

The evidence from our survey of commune- and brigade-run enterprises in Sichuan and Yunnan provinces does not enable us to refute either of these conflicting hypotheses. In terms of potential for closing the size and technology gaps, some communes and brigades seem to have the necessary resources, namely, substantial amounts of capital, accumulated from the profits of existing enterprises or borrowed from higher authorities; skilled manual labour, trained in their own plants or in the technical schools; the ability to hire engineers and managers directly from the state enterprises (e.g. the chemist managing enterprise no. 9 in the tables) or, after retirement, from former engineers and managers wishing to supplement their pensions; and finally, the technology, disseminated by the provincial research and development institutes (as in the case of enterprises no. 8, 12 and 16 in the tables). This potential was translated into actuality in two of the communes visited, one of which had installed a modern rotary cement kiln (enterprise no. 8) and the other a modern paper-making plant (enterprise no. 23). Yet the potential had not been translated into actuality in a third commune, which had adopted a vertical cement kiln, employing an earlier state of the art (enterprise no. 22). Thus in the former two cases the technological gap between the communes and brigades, on the one hand, and the state enterprises, on the other, had been narrowed, whereas in the latter case, it had not. Our guess is that the wealthier communes located in the neighbourhood of the provincial capitals and already experienced in industrial activities will tend to adopt the latest available techniques. Technologically they are not likely to be innovators, however, nor are they likely to build and operate plants beyond the scale already experienced in the state enterprises. The poorer, more remote, inexperienced communes and brigades will tend to lag behind.

The above statements beg the question of whether or not those communes or brigades wanting to install the latest technique will be permitted to do so. This leads to our second observation about rural industrialisation, namely, that the authority of communes and brigades, in terms of their right to make the major decisions affecting their industrial activities, appears to have been steadily increasing. The first events leading to the increase were those that occurred at the centre in the years of 1964–5. It was then that the leaders of the Chinese state formulated the economic policy of the 'Five Smalls', assigning the production of three industrial products – cement, fertiliser and iron and steel – to the counties, the next administrative level above the communes and the lowest whose officials are appointed by the centre.

The production of the remaining two 'Smalls' – agricultural machinery, and electricity from small hydro-electric generating plants – was assigned both to the counties and the communes. For the first time, the communes were told that major industrial activities were to lie, at least partly, within their sphere of operation and, since they already had the right of ownership of the assets they employed, control. To be sure, the development of the rest of modern manufacturing industry was left in the hands of enterprises at still higher levels – the prefecture, the province or municipality, or the centre. In some provinces communes were not permitted to undertake such industrial activities and any commune discovered engaging in industry on more than a communal scale was penalised. This prohibition extended even where there were economic grounds for local industry, such as the ready availability of supplies and markets. A greater degree of local autarchy, although perhaps desirable, was not yet allowed.

The prohibition did not extend to small-scale enterprises supplying the brigade or commune with such industrial goods as building materials, nor even supplying adjacent communes or towns with simply processed agricultural products. The number of these sorts of enterprises grew swiftly from the period of the 'Great Leap Forward', reaching one and a half million in 1978.[4] And in that year the centre took a further step in its encouragement of commune- and brigade-run industry. The leaders of the Chinese state, assembled in the 3rd Plenum of the 11th Central Committee, apparently decided to relax the policy of concentrating industry in the hands of the state enterprises. In what may well be an historic decision, the Party leaders let it be known to the communes that they were freed from the prohibition against industrial production, and could enter into industry on a large scale on their own initiative. Only four fields – cotton textiles, tobacco, iron and steel and armaments – were reserved for state enterprises; all others were open to local enterprise.

It is the blossoming of rural industry, in the few years since the communes and brigades were given permission to cultivate the seeds of industrialisation, that this chapter depicts, and it was the accretion of authority in the hands of the rural residents that stimulated the planting.

The accretion of control by communes and brigades leads to the third observation, namely, that the immediate benefits of rural industrialisation still accrue to the localities. The advantages of rural industrialisation, already enumerated by so many scholars,[5] persist: provision of employment, generation of income, utilisation of skills not given reign in agriculture but inherent in the rural population, dissemination of technological knowledge and exploitation of otherwise unused physical resources. To be sure, these benefits accrue to the rest of the economy as well: there is less pressure for jobs in the state enterprises; income disparities between the cities and the countryside are reduced; the overall technical skill of the population is raised; and total output is increased. Nevertheless, the large numbers of individuals who are provided with work in the rural enterprises and the substantial wages and profits that are distributed amongst them and the other members of the communes and brigades indicate that the major portion of the benefits are retained in the countryside. This is not surprising since substantial control now resides there.

The fourth observation is that there had been in the last year or two a great increase in capital intensity. There are no overall measures of capital intensity available before 1978, but the data cited in the previous chapter indicate that the capital–output ratio for all Chinese commune- and brigade-run enterprises remained virtually constant at 0.53–0.57 through 1981. Our data from the sample of enterprises in Sichuan and Yunnan provinces are consistent with the data for the country as a whole in that there was no apparent rise in the ratio in the same period 1978–81. (What is inconsistent is the absolute value of the capital–output ratio for our sample, which, as the sub-total to column six in Table 7.7 indicates, is approximately 0.37, some 30 per cent below the national average.) But our data, which go nearly one year beyond 1981, indicate a substantial increase in the capital–output ratio after 1981. When the average capital–output ratio for the four plants that came into operation in 1982 is compared with the average of those that came into operation prior to 1982, the increase of the first over the second is seen to be 200 per cent; i.e. the second, at 0.37 is only one-third of the first, at 1.16.

Similarly, the amount of fixed capital per worker was only one-sixth for the older plants as for the younger, namely, 2100 yuan per worker as compared to 13 100 yuan. Almost the same changes are evident when the two cement plants belonging to the same commune are compared (enterprise no. 16, which was operating in 1981 and enterprise no. 22, which began operations in 1982).

The trend to greater capital intensity was observed within existing plants too, where tasks which were formerly carried out by hand are now mechanised. Materials-handling is the chief activity which becomes mechanised, but we also learned of plans to mechanise sand-casting in a foundry (enterprise no. 18) and filtering in a distillery (enterprise no. 7). In both cases of increases in capital intensity, the compulsions behind the moves were stated to be the maximum utilisation of the major pieces of existing equipment and the improvement of product quality. In the foundry, mechanising materials-handling and sand-casting would enable the plant's rate of output to be increased by approximately half, without having to increase the capacity of the furnace. In the distillery, substituting a mechanical filter for filtering by hand through scraps of cloth would improve the clarity of the spirits. It was generally recognised that mechanisation would result in the immediate displacement of workers; but it was also generally argued that the increased profits generated by the enterprise would, when reinvested, create new jobs, in greater numbers than those lost.

These observations of increasing capital-intensity are, of course, not very numerous, and can only be taken as illustrations of what we believe to be a general trend. The communes we visited were more prosperous than the average, with more industrial enterprises, yielding more profits. Poorer communes, with smaller surpluses to invest, may choose to initiate new activities that are no more capital-intensive than existing ones. The statistics we collected cannot prove our point.

The same criticism of insufficient data to support generalisations can be levied at our observations on the productive efficiency of commune- and brigade-run enterprises. The impression we obtained was one of considerable efficiency in the utilisation of capital equipment, very little of which was idle during ordinary working hours, being the hours of daylight for mechanical processes and twenty-four hours per day for continuous processes. Moreover, the design, construction and installation intervals for new plant and equipment seemed, by comparison to other countries of South and South-east Asia, to be quite rapid. But these were just impressions.

A more systematic comparison can be made for cement plants, drawing upon two other reports of Chinese rural industrialisation. The results are summarised in Table 7.8, where the first four observations come from Sigurdson's monograph and the next two from the findings of the American Small-Scale Industry Delegation. The final three observations are of the cement plants we visited. The trends towards greater capital intensity through time and towards higher output per worker emerge clearly in the table.

But more can be learned from the data, particularly if the comparison is restricted to the Dazhai and Nan-Lai plants, on the one hand, and the

TABLE 7.8 *Measures of productivity in various cement plants*

Location	Year of construction	Process	Approximate output (m.t./year)	Quality	Ratios: Capital–Output	Ratios: Output–Labour (tons/worker/year)
1. 'Typical commune'	pre-1970	vertical kiln	200–5000 (1971)	low	n.a.	n.a.
2. Typical region or county'	pre-1970	vertical kiln	10 000–50 000 (1971)	n.a.	n.a.	n.a.
3. Zunhua county, Hebei province	1970	vertical kiln	9000 (1971)	n.a.	0.40	93
4. Lin county, Henan province	1965	vertical kiln	20 000 (1971)	n.a.	0.35	80
5. Dazhai plant, Shanxi province	1967	vertical kiln	20 000 (1974)	Portland; 400 grade; slag	0.46	139
6. Nan-Lai plant, Guangdong province	1970–4	2 vertical kilns	103 000 (1974)	pozzolanic; slag	1.28	187
7. Jinan Corporation, Sichuan province	1980	rotary kiln	20 000 (1982)	500 grade	1.31	174
8. Gao Chang commune, Yu Xi county, Yunnan province	1970–1	vertical kiln	20 000 (1982)	300 grade (5%) 400 grade (70%) 500 grade (20%) 600 grade (5%)	0.43	87
9. Gao Chang commune, Yu Xi county, Yunnan province	1982	vertical kiln	40 000 (1982)	400 grade (30%) 500 grade (70%)	1.21	174

SOURCES Plants 1, 2, 3 and 4: Jon Sigurdson, *Rural Industrialisation in China* (1977), table 39, p. 155; figure 17, p. 157 and table A3–2, p. 326. Plants 5 and 6: American Rural Small-Scale Industry Delegation, *Rural Small-Scale Industry in the People's Republic of China*, table VII–2, pp. 182–3.
Plants 7, 8 and 9: our own field data.

three we visited, on the other. The reason is that the Dazhai and Nan-Lai plants fall within the system of state-run enterprises whereas the Jinan and Gao Chang plants are run by communes, or rather by one commune and one corporation formed by consolidating the industrial enterprises of another commune. The comparison is made more relevant by the statement in the findings of the American Rural Small-Scale Delegation that the Dazhai and Nan-Lai plants were selected by the Chinese officials for study because they represented the best designed and operated small-scale cement plants in the country.[6] Thus our commune-run plants are to be set against the best of the state-run plants of equivalent size.

Were the dates at which the data were gathered also equivalent the comparison would be almost perfect, but the difference in dates may well affect the qualities of the cement being produced. The commune-run plants, today, produce cement of considerably higher quality than did their state-run counterparts in 1974. (Differences in cement quality are reflected by differences in their prices: in the year of our visit to the communes, cement of 300 grade fetched 60 yuan per ton, of 400 grade 65 yuan per ton, of 500 grade 70 yuan per ton, and of 600 grade 75 yuan per ton.) Jinan's and the newer of Gao Chang's plant, producing in the former case all of 500 grade and in the latter 70 per cent of 500 grade cement, attained higher quality than the two state-run plants of eight years previously. It is reasonable to assume that the two state-run plants have raised their quality since then, as did the older of Gao Chang's plant: nevertheless, the new commune-run plants are probably producing cement of superior quality to their state-run competitors at the moment. Otherwise, there seems little to separate the two groups of plants, once allowance is made for scale and age of plant: we can conclude that many commune-run cement plants are no less efficient than equivalent state-run plants, and a few may even have a slight edge.

The final observation is not so much of trends as of the acceleration in a trend already noted. That rural industry is growing in importance has been reported by other scholars; what seems remarkable to the author of this chapter is how very rapid this growth has become. From the sample of enterprises visited some measures of the rate of growth can be obtained. For instance, the second column of Table 7.6 indicates that plants coming into operation in 1982 would add approximately 50 per cent (5 200 000 yuan) to the combined value of output (10 030 000 yuan) of those already in production in the same communes and brigades. The third column in the next table, Table 7.7, indicates that the fixed industrial assets of the communes and brigades visited would very nearly treble in 1982 (increasing from approximately 3 720 000 to 9 750 000 yuan).

Moreover, these two measures of growth do not capture the additional growth that has occurred in 1982 within those enterprises already producing in 1981: as the last column of Table 7.1 reveals, seven of the nineteen existing plants were expanded during the year. Allowing for internal expansion would add at least several percentage points to the rate of growth of the value of industrial output. Such figures, based as they are on a small sample of communes and brigades, can only be taken as indicators of an acceleration in the rate of industrialisation of the rural areas of China. But they do imply an extraordinarily fast pace.

LIKELY FUTURE ISSUES

It is the tendencies observed above that contribute to the strains being engendered through rural industrialisation, strains which may be increasingly felt in the future. Predicting which strains will become most severe, and how they will be visualised, is a hazardous undertaking but nonetheless worth attempting. The first tension that may be felt within the communes is that between profitability of enterprises and 'sunk costs'. In the past, communes and brigades appear to have been very flexible in their allocation of resources, expanding profitable plants and constricting, or even closing down, unprofitable plants. When plants were closed down, the machinery and the workforce usually became the nucleus of succeeding plants. In the communes and brigades visited such events were often recalled. For example, one of the plants manufacturing fine chemicals (enterprise no. 20) had originally been established to produce super-phosphate fertiliser, but in both this and other cases the numbers of employees in the disbanded enterprise and the capital investment were small, and the machinery was relatively unspecialised. Whether or not it will prove feasible to cease operations and transfer resources when the number of employees is much larger (in the hundreds rather than in the tens), and the capital invested in quite specialised equipment is much greater, cannot be answered at this stage. The issue of flexibility, hitherto latent, will then have to be faced.

Associated with the issue of flexibility is that of distortions, meaning by distortions allocations different from those that would result were all resources to flow in response to a system of prices that perfectly reflected the national interest. When decisions are decentralised and made on the basis not only of local prices, which may differ from national prices, but also on the basis of other local considerations such as uninterrupted employment and assured markets, distortions are bound to arise. One consequence of the existence of distortions is a lower national output, when valued at shadow prices, than would be obtained were the allocation perfect. The issue here is that as a larger fraction of China's resources are allocated locally, the number of distortions could increase. In principle, one cannot argue that the overall allocation will be any worse as a consequence, particularly if there are already distortions evident in the state enterprises. Our intuition suggests that there are currently fewer distortions in rural than in state industry, but the balance could swing in the other direction.

Besides the issues of flexibility and distortions, one can imagine arising in the future the issue of control over rural enterprises by different levels of authority. All but one of the enterprises visited were under the control of either communes or brigades, yet one relatively small one (enterprise no. 10) was staffed entirely by a single production team, and one relatively large one (enterprise no. 8) employed nearly 200 persons, on equipment valued at approximately 1½ million yuan, and producing goods distributed as far afield as Tibet. In the former enterprise, the production team might claim that it, rather than the brigade to which it belongs, should have control over its operation and over the distribution of the profits that are earned through its members' endeavours. In the latter enterprise, the state bureaucracy at either the county or provincial level might claim that the scale of the enterprise has become so extensive that it, rather than the commune to which it belongs, should have control. Since the former enterprise is currently very profitable and since the latter will in all probability become very profitable in the next year and those following, substantial amounts of money are at stake. So long as control over the distribution of profits remains where it is now, at either the brigade or the commune, profits will be distributed on a roughly equal basis per capita among a moderate number of contiguous individuals. Were control to descend to the production team, the distribution of profits would still remain roughly equal per capita but would be shared among a smaller number of closely related individuals; in contrast, were control to ascend to the county or province, profits would be expended like general revenues, among a much wider number of individuals. In either eventuality, those members of the commune or brigade not employed in industrial enterprises would suffer a reduction in their collective income and hence presumably would be less willing to set aside funds for rural investment.

With this and the following issue in mind it might be worthwhile summarising what little was learned about the disposition of the profits of commune- and brigade-run enterprises. Subtracting bonuses to the employees of the enterprises, whose inclusion in profits is debatable anyway, there remain three chief uses to which profits can be put: reinvesting them in the enterprises themselves, distributing them to the members of the communes or brigades which own the assets, or allocating them to other investment projects. In the province of Sichuan, one half of the profits of industrial enterprises run by communes and brigades are handed over for collective distribution. Another 10 per cent are allocated to the communes and brigades to meet their overheads, and the remaining 40 per cent are reinvested.

These percentages are averages for the province. The figures for the individual enterprises that we visited varied considerably around these averages. For example, enterprise no. 16 (in Tables 7.1 through 7.7), which is in the process of completing its new cement plant, reserved 70 per cent of its profits in 1981 for its own use, releasing the remaining 30 per cent to the commune. In the same commune enterprise no. 15 turned over all of its profits to help finance the commune's ambitious investment programme in new enterprises. The profits of enterprise no. 18 in 1981 were allocated to collective distribution and to reinvestment within the enterprise in the ratio of 65 : 35, but the allocation in previous years had been weighted towards accumulation, in order to finance investment in a new firm, the paper-making plant listed as enterprise no. 23. There are thus variations from year to year within the same commune or brigade, as well as variations between them.

A methodological issue is what is the appropriate level of authority for any particular enterprise? Economic theory has very little to say in answer to this question. One principle might be that authority should reside at as high a level as is necessary to make every decision that affects the performance of the enterprise. If, for example, resources to run the enterprise must be collected directly from other enterprises scattered throughout a province, provincial authority would be appropriate. In economic language, the level of authority would be determined by the extent of the markets. But if the contact between provincial enterprises were indirect, taking place through the medium of local markets which any firm was free to enter, the level of authority need be no higher than the locality. The economic dictum does not change, just the availability of market institutions. The creation of local markets, open to all, near and far, reduces the economic arguments for raising the level of authority as the scale of an enterprise rises. Creating local markets could even permit lowering the level of authority, in principle, to the work group itself; in this atomistic case, the structure of rural industry would tend towards that of pure competition: the level of authority would coincide with the extent of the ownership and employment of the enterprise. In most of the enterprises we visited the application of such a criterion would leave the authority at its current site.

Even if the level of authority is appropriate for commune- and brigade-run enterprises, these enterprises collectively may lay claim to such a substantial volume of scarce resources, or produce such a substantial volume of scarce products, as to affect the overall allocation of inputs and outputs nationwide. In other words, the rural enterprises may become, and probably have already become, competitors rather than complements to the enterprises run directly by the Chinese state. The issue has therefore arisen as to how commune- and brigade-run enterprises are to be accommodated within the system of national planning.

Planning for all China's industrial enterprises need not differ in principle from planning for enterprises run by the state alone. According to foreign observers of Chinese planning,[7] the provincial authorities issue contracts to the communes and brigades specifying how much of each industrial good they are to supply, and how many scarce inputs they are to receive. The quantities of outputs contracted for by the provinces and the quantities of inputs supplied are previously determined through negotiations between the province and the bodies at the centre. Any above-plan output produced by the communes and brigades can be disposed of at their own discretion.

When there is excess demand for industrial goods some tension exists between the provincial authorities, who want to appropriate all the commune's and brigade's output to meet plan targets, and the communes and brigades, which want to retain a portion to meet their internal needs or to supply independently: such situations have characterised the past and for some products may characterise the future too. But it is conceivable, and for some products likely, that excess supply will emerge. This is especially the case in products like cement, half of whose national output is being currently supplied by commune and brigade enterprises and whose productive capacity appears to be rising rapidly. If there is a supply in excess of the target at the provincial level, the provincial authorities will have to decide to which enterprises the favoured contracts will be issued – to provincial- and county-run enterprises on the one hand, or to commune- and brigade-run enterprises on the other. A new source of tension will be created, over how limited markets are to be allocated among competing suppliers. The greater the excess supply, or 'duplication' as it is called, the greater will be the stress.

The final issue that we see becoming more acute in the future is that of the possibility of increasing inequality in the distribution of income, chiefly between communes, as a consequence of rural industrialisation. The issue will differ depending upon the focus, whether it is on the commune itself or upon all communes in China. Considering the narrower focus, inequalities can and probably will increase within a commune because of the varying profitability of brigade-run enterprises. Members of the brigades with more profitable firms will have higher incomes than members of the brigades with less profitable firms. If inequalities are not to increase, new re-distributive mechanisms capable of reducing disparities between brigades within a commune will need to be employed.

More difficult to handle one suspects will be increasing inequalities in the distribution of income between communes. Here the issue is pre-emption, the seizing of limited opportunities for the greatest profits by those communes already most favoured as a consequence of their accumulation of scarce resources. Those communes with a well-educated population, close to the cities and chief markets for industrial products, with easy access to technological knowledge, and with incomes high enough to be able to set aside funds for investment will be most able to profit from the production of new products or the opening of new markets. The tendency of communes already wealthy to increase their wealth further was observed in our visits; it was noticeable that the closer to a city was a commune, and the higher was its income per capita, the greater was its investment in industrial activities. Since industry generally yields a higher income per worker than agriculture, the more the commune's commitment to industry, the higher the income per commune member. The process is circular – high commune incomes lead to high accumulation, which in turn leads to high investment in industry, which generates higher incomes still. Such is the process by which the wealthier communes are becoming wealthier still, and from which the poorest communes may be increasingly excluded. To be sure, the higher authorities – the counties and the provinces – do try to compensate for the increasing disparities, but such compensation will become increasingly difficult as the industrialisation of the wealthier communes proceeds. All this is not meant to be a criticism of the role of commune- and brigade-run enterprises, which certainly reduce urban–rural inequalities and probably, via the distribution of profits of enterprises within communes and brigades, intra-commune inequalities; it is the possibilities of increased disparities between communes within a region, and between regions, that we wish to raise.

CONCLUSION

From our survey, brief as it was, and restricted in numbers of observations, it would appear as if there are in China two industrial economies, formerly running in parallel but now increasingly as one unit. One economy is highly centralised, responding to decisions made at the centre and at the provincial capitals; the other is highly decentralised, responding to decisions made in the 54 000 communes and the 720 000 brigades. In 1981, the last year for which statistics are available, the centralised economy dominated, accounting for approximately 89 per cent of the value of industrial output. The 11 per cent remaining to the decentralised economy may have been minor in terms of the nation's industry, yet it was responsible for roughly 30 per cent of its commune and brigade members' income.

So rapid is the growth of the decentralised economy that neither of these last two percentages is stable; at a guess, by the time the book containing this chapter is published the share of the decentralised economy in both the total value of industrial output and in the total income of the rural sector will have increased by several percentage points. Moreover, from the amounts of money being accumulated for expansion of industry and from the plans of the cadres in the sample of communes that we visited, it seems as if the phenomenal growth of commune- and brigade-run industry will continue. China may be in the process of creating the world's first modern industrialised economy based in the countryside.

NOTES AND REFERENCES

1. In the official terminology, commune- and brigade-run enterprises are classified as 'rural industries'. Other industries, often located physically in the countryside but run by county or provincial authorities, and by municipal authorities as well, are classified as 'local industries'. Since these terms are not sufficiently descriptive, we shall generally adhere to our term 'commune- and brigade-run enterprises'. See A. Donnithorne, *China's Economic System* (London: Allen & Unwin, 1967).
2. Jon Sigurdson, *Rural Industrialization in China* (Cambridge: Harvard University Press, 1977).
3. American Rural Small-Scale Industry Delegation, *Rural Small-Scale Industry*

in the People's Republic of China (Berkeley: University of California Press, 1977).

4. See Chapter 7.
5. See, for example, Jon Sigurdson, *Rural Industrialization in China* pp. 213–25; American Rural Small-Scale Industry Delegation, *Rural Small-Scale Industry in the People's Republic of China* chs. VIII and IX.
6. Ibid., p. 181.
7. See J. Gray, 'Rural Enterprise in China 1977–79', in J. Gray and G. White (eds), *China's New Development Strategy (New York: Academic Press, 1982) pp. 211*–33; P. Hare, 'China's System of Industrial Economic Planning', in S. Feuchtwand and A. Hussein (eds), *The Chinese Economic Reforms* (London: Croom Helm, 1983), pp. 185–223; and Cyril Lin, unpublished D. Phil. thesis, St Antony's College, Oxford, forthcoming.

8 The New Development Strategy and Rural Reforms in Post-Mao China

AJIT KUMAR GHOSE

The Third Plenary Session of the 11th Central Committee of the Chinese Communist Party, held in December 1978, marked a watershed in China's economic history. A new phase of economic and social development has since been initiated, goals and priorities have been substantially revised, relative weights and inter-relationships of the production sectors (state, collective and private) have been radically altered and a series of structural reforms have significantly modified the production relations within the collective sector, particularly in the rural economy. Most outside observers have been puzzled by these changes, especially by those in the commune system which had so far been almost universally recognised as the crowning achievement of the Chinese revolution.

The dominant view in China is that these changes were necessitated by three basic factors:

(i) an urgency of reducing the rate of accumulation and, correspondingly, of raising the consumption and living standards of the masses;
(ii) a realisation that unemployment and under-employment of labour had reached serious proportions and that the problem could not be effectively handled without modifying the structure of the economy; and
(iii) a recognition that the existing production relations had become a

> fetter on the development of the productive forces in the countryside.

China's development strategy, operative during 1952–78, had been remarkably successful in guaranteeing a minimum level of living to the entire population. But it was also characterised by a very high rate of accumulation and a correspondingly low growth of personal consumption. The current concern for raising living standards stems in part from a genuine desire to raise the level of personal consumption of the population. It also arises from an attempt to solve a persistent problem of the Chinese economy, namely, low returns to investment. This is generally attributed to the fact that the rate of investment was far too high in relation to the availability of skilled manpower and infrastructural facilities and to the persistent over-emphasis on heavy industries leading to over-production in that sector.

Raising the level of living of the masses, however, involves not only alterations in the consumption–accumulation ratio in the state budget, but also the provision of adequate supplies of the consumer goods which would be required to satisfy the extra demand arising from increases in disposable incomes. In particular, production of food and light industrial goods would need to be stepped up. This requires agricultural output to grow at a faster rate than was achieved in the past. Within agriculture, more land would need to be devoted to the production of crops which are used as raw materials in the light industrial sector. Given the virtual impossibility of extending the cultivated area in the short run, this implies a decline in the land area devoted to the production of food grains. A faster rate of growth of food grains production would thus have to be achieved in the face of declining land area. It is in this context that the recent reforms of the rural economy were undertaken. Clearly, the government takes the view that within the framework of the commune system as it had evolved over the period 1958–78, accelerating the growth rate in agriculture and altering the structure of agricultural production were impossible tasks. Among the reasons identified, the most important are 'bureaucratism' in decision-making and 'egalitarianism' in distribution which had become deeply rooted practices in the communes and which discouraged initiative and hard work among commune members.

Added to these imperatives was the pressing need to solve the problem of unemployment and under-employment. Following the failure of rather ill-conceived Maoist attempts to absorb part of the growing urban labour force in rural communes, urban unemploymet emerged as a major problem.[1] At the same time, even the commune system, with its massive capacity to organise labour for capital construction and to develop non-agricultural enterprises on the basis of local resources, could not, in the context of a high rate of growth of the rural labour force, prevent the emergence of significant seasonal unemployment.[2] The government, therefore, gradually came to the view that the problem could not be solved without relaxing some of the constraints on the development of the collective and private sectors of production. Hence the alterations in the relative weights and inter-relationships of the three production sectors. Such alterations, moreover, were expected to help expand production of basic consumer goods in the short run.

The rural reforms in particular are designed to promote the development of the private economy within a collective framework so as simultaneously to resolve the problems of incentives and employment. Perhaps there is an additional motivation behind the reforms, though this has not been explicitly stated. Following the establishment of the commune system, internal migration (rural–rural or rural–urban) had been made virtually impossible.[3] While this prevented the growth of urban slums, so typical of the cities in the Third World, and forced a search for localised development in the communes, it also preserved and even accentuated the rural–urban and regional inequalities arising from differences in the resource–population balance. The recent reforms have the effect of relaxing some of the restrictions on the mobility of labour and thus provide a mechanism for mitigating these inequalities to an extent.[4]

The chapter addresses itself to two sets of issues. The first set concerns the distinguishing features of the new development strategy, the role which the rural economy is expected to play in this context and the extent to which the rural reforms are intended to enable the rural economy to play this role. The second set concerns the nature of the reforms themselves, their immediate consequences and the fresh problems to which they may give rise.[5]

DEVELOPMENT STRATEGIES: OLD AND NEW

Barring brief periods of widespread disruption caused by political upheavals, China's economy grew at a much faster rate than that of most developing countries over the period 1950–78 (see Table 8.1). What is even more remarkable is the fact that this growth was achieved largely through the mobilisation of domestic resources (see Table 8.2).[6] Since

TABLE 8.1 *Growth of national income, gross value of agricultural output and gross value of industrial output, 1950–1981*

	Average annual rate of growth		
	National income	*Agriculture*	*Industry*
1950–2	19.3	14.1	34.8
1953–7	8.9	4.5	18.0
1958–62	−3.1	−4.3	3.8
1963–5	14.5	11.1	17.9
1966–70	8.4	3.9	11.7
1971–5	5.6	4.0	9.1
1976	−2.7	2.5	1.3
1977	7.8	1.7	14.3
1978	12.3	9.0	13.5
1979	7.0	8.6	8.5
1980	6.9	2.7	8.7
1981	3.0	5.7	4.1

SOURCES 1. Dong Fureng, 'Relationship between accumulation and consumption', in Xu Dixin *et al.*, *China's search for economic growth* (Beijing: New World Press, 1982).
2. State Statistical Bureau, *Statistical Yearbook of China, 1981* (Hong Kong: Economic Information and Agency, 1982).

NOTE The growth rates are in real terms. Agricultural output includes output of brigade enterprises, a major part of which is industrial. Output of commune enterprises is included in industrial output.

1958, the year which marked the end of the reconstruction period (first five-year plan) and the launching of the commune movement, the economy has generated extraordinarily high rates of accumulation and investment.[7] The rate of accumulation has hovered around 30 per cent of the national income and the rate of investment has hovered around 15 per cent of the national income (see Table 8.3). Mobilisation of resources took place not only at the level of the state; massive resources were also mobilised at the level of the collective enterprise. It has been estimated, for instance, that about two-thirds of the investment undertaken in the communes was financed by the communes themselves.

The basic mechanisms employed by the state for extracting an investible surplus were discriminatory pricing (or the 'price scissors' as it is called in China) and taxation of industrial and commercial enterprises; agricultural taxes provided only a small and declining portion of the state revenues. Relative prices of agricultural products *vis-à-vis* industrial products were set in such a way that the state-owned industrial

TABLE 8.2 *State budget revenues, 1950–81 (Billion yuan)*

	1950	*1957*	*1965*	*1978*	*1979*	*1980*	*1981*
Total revenue	6.519	31.019	47.332	112.112	110.327	108.523	106.429
Enterprise profits	0.869	14.418	26.427	57.199	49.290	43.52	34.701
Tax revenue	4.898	15.489	20.430	51.928	53.782	57.17	62.946
of which taxes on agriculture	1.910	2.967	2.578	2.840	2.951	2.767	2.811
Foreign borrowing	0.302	0.699	0.006	0.151	3.639	4.301	6.028
Other revenues	0.450	0.413	0.469	2.834	3.616	3.528	2.758

SOURCES 1. Annex A, World Bank Report.
2. *Beijing Review*, various issues.
3. State Statistical Bureau, *Statistical Yearbook of China, 1981* (Hong Kong: Economic Information and Agency, 1982).

TABLE 8.3 *Accumulation and investment (as percentage of national income), 1952–82*

Period	*Accumulation*	*Investment**
1952	22.07	7.4
1953–57	24.2	
1957	24.9	15.2
1958–62	30.8	
1963–5	22.7	
1965	26.3	12.3
1966–70	26.3	
1971–5	33.0	
1975	33.1	15.6
1976	30.9	
1977	32.3	
1978	36.5	15.2
1979	34.6	14.9
1980	31.6	14.8
1981	28.3	11.1

* Investment refers to investment in capital construction undertaken by the state and individual enterprises.

SOURCES 1. Dong Fureng, 'Relationship between accumulation and consumption', in Xu Dixin *et al.*, *China's search for economic growth* (Beijing: New World Press, 1982).
2. *Economic Readjustment and Reform (Beijing Review*, Special Feature Series, 1982), Appendix tables.
3. State Statistical Bureau, *Statistical Yearbook of China, 1981.*

enterprises (particularly those producing light industrial products and farm inputs) made huge profits and these profits were directly transferred to the state.[8] Thus it is the price mechanism, and not taxation, which acted as the major means of extraction of a surplus from agriculture. Over time, relative prices moved in favour of agriculture as costs of production in agriculture rose in consequence of increasing use of modern inputs (see Table 8.4). But labour-productivity in the industrial sector grew faster than the wage rate so that the profits of the state-owned industrial enterprises suffered little. The state was also able to tax away a large part of the profits of collective industrial and commercial enterprises. All this is easily observed from the figures presented in Table 8.2.

TABLE 8.4 *Price indices, 1952–80* (1950 = 100)

	1952	*1957*	*1965*	*1978*	*1979*	*1980*	*1981*
Cost of living of staff and workers	115.5	126.6	139.0	144.7	147.4	158.5	162.5
Retail price index	111.8	121.3	134.6	135.9	138.6	146.9	150.4
Agricultural procurement price index	121.6	146.2	187.9	217.4	265.5	284.4	301.2
Rural market price index	111.0	120.9	192.2	246.0	234.9	n.a.	n.a.
Industrial products sold in rural areas	109.7	112.7	118.4	109.8	109.9	110.8	111.9

SOURCE 1. Annex A, World Bank Report.
2. State Statistical Bureau, *Statistical Yearbook of China, 1981.*

The communes generated additional investible surpluses through both direct and indirect means. Accumulation funds were maintained at the level of communes, brigades and teams. In the case of the communes and brigades, the sources were the profits of the industrial and commercial enterprises run by them. In the case of teams the value of a work point was determined only after accumulation funds had been set aside.[9] It is probable that in some poor communes, accumulation funds existed only in account books. But no one doubts that in a large number of communes, the rates of internal accumulation and investment were very high. Perhaps more importantly, most communes succeeded in mobilising labour on an impressive scale for purposes of construction activities and thus transformed a part of the consumption funds into investment.

This process of accumulation had its counterpart in a relatively slow growth of consumption of the population (see Table 8.5). Radical economic reforms in the immediate post-revolutionary period had virtually eliminated luxury consumption, and this made it possible to guarantee a basic subsistence for all and to ensure a high rate of accumulation at the same time. But even afterwards, an acceleration in the rate of growth of national income usually served to accelerate the rate

TABLE 8.5 *Growth of disposable incomes*

	1952–78	*1957–78*	*1965–78*	*1978–81*
1. Per capita real income: total population	2.59	1.82	2.16	12.85
2. Per capita real income: peasants	2.23	1.99	2.20	14.57
3. Per capita real income: workers and staff members	2.07	1.43	1.92	9.25
4. Growth of real wage rate (in state-owned enterprises)	0.55	−0.58	−0.40	3.93
5. Growth of real per capita collective distributed income (in the communes)		2.35		

NOTE Items 1, 2 and 5 have been estimated by deflating the money incomes by the retail price index. Items 3 and 4 have been estimated by using the cost-of-living index of staff and workers as the deflator.

SOURCE Table 8.4 and Appendix Tables 8.1, 8.2 and 8.3.

of accumulation so that consumption growth was slower than that of national income. It has already been noted that industrial wage rates grew at a lower rate than labour productivity, and this is supported by the data presented in Table 8.6. In fact, the real wage rate in state-owned enterprises recorded a decline over the period 1957–78. The wage policy, therefore, acted as an effective instrument of restraining urban consumption, particularly since during the period 1958–78, the urban private economy was virtually abolished and even the urban collective economy was much reduced in significance (see Appendix Table 8.4). In the communes, distributed collective income grew slowly at least partly because agricultural prices were kept low, sideline production was often discouraged and private plots were abolished in some cases. However, the consumption of the urban population rose faster than real wage rates because of a steady decline in the dependency ratio. The average number of people supported by each urban wage earner was 3.6 in 1952, 3.15 in 1957, 2.06 in 1977, 1.83 in 1980 and 1.77 in 1981.[10] Consumption of the commune members, on the other hand, rose at a rate lower than that of per capita collective distributed income because of a relative decline in incomes from non-collective sources.

The relatively slow growth of consumption, however, could be viewed as a necessity imposed by the slow growth of crop production relative to the population, rather than as a result of deliberate policy. Per capita food grains output registered a growth of 0.4 per cent during 1952–58 and 0.2 per cent during 1957–78; per capita production of edible oil declined during 1952–78 and registered zero growth during 1957–78 (see Table 8.7). It is clear from the estimates of implied income elasticities of

TABLE 8.6 Rates of growth of labour productivity and wage rates in state-owned enterprises

Period	*Labour productivity*	*Wage rate*
1952–7	8.7	7.4
1957–62	−5.4	−1.5
1962–5	23.1	3.3
1965–78	1.7	−0.001
1979	6.4	9.5
1980	2.0	13.9
1981	−1.8	1.1

SOURCES State Statistical Bureau, *Statistical Yearbook of China, 1981* (Hong Kong: Economic Information and Agency, 1982).

TABLE 8.7 *Initial and terminal levels and growth of per capita production of selected consumption items*

			Per capita production			
Item	*Level 1952*	*Growth 1952–78*	*Growth 1957–78*	*Growth 1965–78*	*Growth 1978–81*	*Level 1981*
Grain (kg)	288	0.4	0.2	1.3	0.9	328.5
Edible oil (kg)	7.3	−0.4	0.0	2.2	n.a.	n.a.
Pork, beef, mutton (kg)	5.9	1.6	1.8	1.1	12.5	12.7
Sugar (kg)	0.8	4.4	2.8	1.1	10.5	3.2
Cotton cloth (metre)	6.7	2.2	1.9	2.0	7.7	14.3
Wrist watches (per 1000 persons)	0.0		62.4	19.2	27.3	28.8
Sewing machines (per 1000 persons)	0.1	16.3	12.7	8.5	27.6	10.4
Bicycles (per 1000 persons)	0.1	17.7	9.0	10.0	25.8	17.6

SOURCES 1. *Economic Readjustments and Reform*, (Beijing Review, Special Features Series, 1982).
2. *Beijing Review*, various issues.
3. State Statistical Bureau, *Statistical Yearbook of China, 1981*.

demand for grains and edible oil presented in Table 8.8 that the growth in per capita disposable income, slow though it was, almost certainly created excess demand for these basic consumption items. It was only through the operation of a strict rationing system that the government managed to guarantee a minimum level of food consumption for all.[11]

Since the rationing system made it impossible for the excess demand to have any influence on either the prices or the distribution of most of the food items and cotton cloth, the demand for consumption items such as wrist-watches, sewing-machines and bicycles probably rose faster than would have been warranted by the growth of disposable income. However, the production of these consumption items also grew at a rapid rate (see Table 8.7). It is difficult to suggest that the growth of production of these items was inconsistent with the growth of demand (note the values of implied income elasticities of demand in Table 8.8).[12] Growth of production of industrial consumer goods, such as sugar and cotton cloth critically depends on the growth of crop production. The rates of growth in demand for certain items are also interlinked, e.g. cotton cloth and sewing-machines. It is obvious that a slow growth of crop production limits the growth of consumption not only of such items as food grains but also of certain industrial products. There are, of course, industrial products (for example bicycles, wrist-watches, etc.) whose consumption and production do not depend on the performance of agriculture. Given the comprehensive and effective rationing system existing in China, it was feasible to restrain the consumption of certain

TABLE 8.8 *Implied values of income elasticities of demand for selected items*

	1952–78	*1957–78*	*1965–78*	*1978–81*
Grain	0.17	0.10	0.60	0.07
Edible oil	−0.17	*	1.02	
Pork, beef, mutton	0.70	0.99	0.51	0.97
Sugar	1.88	1.54	0.51	0.82
Cotton cloth	0.87	0.93	0.93	0.66
Wrist-watches		24.45	8.89	2.19
Sewing-machines	7.03	6.98	3.94	2.22
Bicycles	8.17	5.38	4.63	2.10

NOTE These estimates are based on the formula:

rate of growth of per capita income × income elasticity of demand = rate of growth of per capita demand

*undetermined

SOURCES Tables 8.5 and 8.7.

items whose production could not be increased rapidly and yet allow a rapid growth of consumption of those industrial products whose production was wholly independent of agricultural production. But even here there were important constraints. For example, household electrical goods could not be introduced in rural areas on a significant scale until the rural electrification programme made substantial progress. Even in 1978, only 9.9 per cent of the electricity generated in the country was utilised in rural areas and a large proportion of the villages did not have electricity. Thus even in the case of industrial products, the list of items whose consumption could be promoted on a mass scale was not large. A strategy of increasing consumption through the introduction of a whole range of sophisticated industrial products would have required not only efficient demand management but also growing income inequality.

In this context, a comparison of China's experience with that of the non-socialist countries of the Third World is revealing. First, the growth of per capita consumption was in fact higher in China than in most non-socialist countries at comparable levels of development.[13] On the other hand, the proportion of national income devoted to consumption in any given year was much lower in China than in other countries.[14] The implication is that while the primary determinant of the ratio of consumption to national income is the level of income inequality, the primary determinant of the growth of consumption is the growth of national income. A tentative hypothesis is thus suggested: in economies where the supply of basic necessities is limited and inelastic, a reduction in income inequality implies (in the absence of a massive inflow of external resources) a rise in the rate of accumulation and hence an acceleration in the rates of growth of national income and consumption.[15] The converse is also true. Secondly, the tendency of consumption to grow at a rate lower than that of national income is quite general. In non-socialist countries, the tendency arises because growing income inequalities tend to reduce the aggregate income elasticity of consumption. In China, however, the tendency arose because of the operation of some direct constraints on the growth of consumption.

The appropriate ratio of accumulation to consumption is a subject of intense discussion in China today. Many economists feel that the rate of accumulation had been far too high during 1957–78, not only because it 'unduly' restrained the growth of consumption but also because it involved a considerable waste of resources since matching development of manpower resources and infrastructural facilities was not feasible. The implicit presupposition is that the national rate of accumulation was the given parameter in Chinese economic planning.[16] A different case is arguable, however. It can be supposed that the given parameters were the objectives of guaranteeing a minimum level of living to the entire population and of reducing income inequalities. On this assumption, the rate of growth of consumption was determined primarily by the rate of growth of agricultural production. The rate of accumulation was then determined as a residual category. The rate of accumulation, in turn, determined another important ratio – the ratio of investment in heavy industries (producing mainly producer goods) to that in light industries (producing mainly consumer goods). Many Chinese economists have argued that this ratio was unduly high. As the data in Table 8.9 show, the ratio was indeed very high. But it has already been noted that the growth of production of light industrial consumer goods was fairly consistent with that of overall consumption (or disposable income) of the population.[17] To the extent that this observation is valid, the high priority accorded to heavy industry would seem to be a mere con-

TABLE 8.9 *Distribution (in percentages) of investment expenditures (capital construction funds)*

	Agriculture	*Light industry*	*Heavy industry*	*Non-productive*	*Others*
1953–7	7.6	6.8	38.7	28.3	18.6
1958	10.5	7.3	57.0	12.1	13.2
1959	10.5	5.2	56.7	13.2	14.4
1960	13.0	4.0	53.3	13.6	16.1
1958–62	11.4	6.5	54.9	13.4	13.8
1963–5	18.4	4.1	48.0	17.2	12.3
1966–70	11.4	4.7	54.5	11.3	18.1
1971–5	10.3	6.9	52.1	13.4	17.3
1976	n.a.	n.a.	n.a.	14.9	n.a.
1977	n.a.	n.a.	n.a.	16.7	n.a.
1978	10.7	5.4	54.7	17.4	11.8
1979	14.0	5.8	46.8	27.0	6.4
1980	9.6	9.1	41.7	33.7	5.9
1981	6.8	10.0	40.3	41.3	1.6

NOTE Non-productive investment includes investment in housing, public health, public utilities (culture and education) and construction of facilities for administrative organs. Others include investment in banking and insurance, public welfare facilities, etc.

SOURCES
1. Dong Fureng, 'Relationship between accumulation and consumption', in Xu Dixin *et al., China's Search for Economic Growth.*
2. Liang Wensen, 'Balanced development of industry and agriculture', in Xu Dixin *et al., China's search for economic growth.*
3. *Beijing Review*, various issues.
4. State Statistical Bureau, *Statistical Yearbook of China, 1981.*

sequence of the high rate of accumulation. Indeed, this feature underlies another important characteristic of China's heavy industry – its tendency to cater to its own needs. Given the rates of growth in agriculture and in light industry, the heavy industrial sector could not have sustained a high growth rate merely on the basis of demand generated outside the sector itself. While this pattern of development of heavy industry has certainly been somewhat wasteful, it is difficult to see how this could have been avoided.

This last argument, however, is not wholly valid; for while the feasible rate of growth of personal consumption dictates a rate of growth of light industrial production, it merely provides a lower limit to the growth of heavy industries (the upper limit is undetermined). It is arguable, therefore, that social consumption (e.g. housing, education, health care, recreation and culture, etc.) could have been improved at a faster rate than was actually done. As the data in Tables 8.9 and 8.10 show, the rates of non-productive accumulation and investment were not very high during the period 1957–78. There is also some evidence to show that the growth of social consumption in urban areas did not always keep pace with that of population.[18] One valid criticism of the development strategy pursued during the period 1957–78, therefore, is that too much emphasis was placed on the development of heavy industry and too little on the growth of social consumption.

Even so, it should be clear that if one is to argue that the high rate of accumulation was not an economic necessity (given the social objectives)

TABLE 8.10 *Non-productive accumulation (as percentages of total accumulation)*

1953–7	40.2
1958–62	12.9
1963–5	34.5
1966–70	25.5
1971–5	22.6
1976	18.0
1977	25.8
1978	25.9
1979	32.5
1980	34.1
1981	n.a.

SOURCES Dong Fureng 'Relationship between accumulation and consumption', in Xu Dixin *et al., China's search for economic growth* (Beijing: New World Press, 1982).

but was the result of political decisions and ideological biases, one would have to presume that the rate of growth of agricultural production could have been much higher with an alternative policy package. In this context, many Chinese economists have argued that at least three aspects of the pre-1978 agrarian policy acted as constraints on the growth of agricultural production:

(a) inadequate investment,
(b) very slow improvement in the terms of trade for agriculture, and
(c) inappropriate relations of production in agriculture.

The last two of these factors will be examined in the following section. Here we can examine the aspect of investment in agriculture.

Investment in agriculture constituted roughly about 12 per cent of total investment. The industries producing inputs for agriculture received 4–5 per cent of total investment, so that investment in agriculture and supporting industries together constituted 16–17 per cent of total investment in the state budget.[19] To this must be added the substantial investment made by the communes themselves, particularly through the mobilisation of labour for capital construction. As has been noted earlier, such investments accounted for about 66 per cent of total investment in agriculture.

Whether or not this investment was adequate is a question that is difficult to answer. The pace of technological change was certainly impressive (see Table 8.11). In 1952, the proportion of farmland irrigated was only about 20 per cent; in 1978, it rose to 45 per cent. There were very few tractors in use in 1952; in 1978 there were 557 000 large and medium tractors (0.006 per hectare approximately) and 1 370 000 small hand tractors (0.014 per hectare approximately), and 41 per cent of the farmland was being machine-ploughed. Very little fertiliser was being used in 1952; in 1978, 89 kg were being used per hectare. The rate of growth of crop output was not extraordinarily high, but it must be remembered that this growth was achieved almost entirely through yield increases. No less important is the fact that fluctuation in output was very considerably reduced.

Indeed, if the period 1965–78 (1965 being the year when the commune structure was finally stabilised and agricultural production was restored to the 1957 level) is considered, the record in technological change looks much more impressive. The number of large and medium-sized tractors grew at an annual rate of 17 per cent and that of small tractors at 56.8 per cent. Tractor-ploughed area expanded at an annual rate of 7.7 per cent, irrigated area at 2.4 per cent and chemical fertilisers per hectare at approximately 12.4 per cent. This was also a period of rapid expansion in commune- and brigade-run non-agricultural enterprises.

Growth of crop production was impressive too, though it is clear that grains and oil-bearing crops were accorded high priority. Thus, while the area sown under grains increased by 0.8 per cent over the period 1965–78, production increased by 56.7 per cent. In the case of oil-bearing crops, the sown area expanded by 15.6 per cent and output increased by 43.9 per cent. Cotton and sugar crops, however, showed poor results.[20] In the case of cotton, sown area declined by 2.7 per cent while output increased by 3.3 per cent. In the case of sugar crops, although the sown area expanded by 68.7 per cent, output increased only by 54.9 per cent indicating a decline in yields; this was probably because cultivation was extended to marginal lands.

Perhaps the wisdom of according such overwhelming priority to grains and oil-bearing crops can be questioned. But on the whole, the commune system, far from hindering growth and technological change in agriculture, appears to have performed remarkably well. Indeed, the above facts throw into doubt not only the proposition that investment was inadequate but also the proposition that unfavourable terms of trade and inappropriate production relations constrained agricultural growth. It still remains arguable that it had become necessary, by 1978, to change price policies and to abolish certain practices from within the commune system. But the reasons are more convincingly sought in the changing requirements of a dynamic economy than in the errors of the past.

Since 1978, much has been done to increase personal disposable incomes of both peasants and workers. Over 1978–81, per capita real income of the peasants rose by 14.66 per cent per annum and that of workers rose by 9.93 per cent per annum. Simultaneously, the rate of accumulation has declined from 36.5 per cent in 1978 to 30 per cent in 1981; the rate of investment in capital construction has declined from 15.2 per cent in 1978 to 11 per cent in 1981; and the share of non-productive investment in total investment has risen from 17.4 per cent in 1978 to 41.1 per cent in 1981 (see Tables 8.3 and 8.9). Furthermore, the share of light industry in total investment has increased significantly. Production relations in the communes have been substantially modified with the objective of boosting both agricultural and sideline production.[21]

The results so far have been mixed. The available evidence suggests

TABLE 8.11 *Technological change in agriculture*

	Proportion of area irrigated (per cent)	*Proportion of area machine ploughed (per cent)*	*Large and medium tractors in use (No. in '000)*	*Small tractors in use (No. in '000)*	*Chemical fertilisers used per hectare (kg)*
1952	20.0	0.1	1.3	nil	neg.
1957	27.3	2.6	14.7	nil	neg.
1965	30.5	15.6	72.6	4	19.4
1978	45.0	40.7	557	1,373	89
1979	45.0	42.2	667	1,671	109
1980	44.9	41.0	745	1,874	127.8
1981	44.6	36.5	792	2,037	134.5

SOURCE State Statistical Bureau, *Statistical Yearbook of China, 1981* (Hong Kong: Economic Information and Agency, 1982).

that the production structure has not changed fast enough to meet the requirements of increased consumption. Indeed, it is probable that there exists considerable excess demand for certain basic consumption items. Production in both agriculture and light industry has increased faster than in earlier periods but does not appear to have kept pace with the growth of personal incomes (see Tables 8.7 and 8.8). As for the industrial inputs for agriculture, the production of tractors appears to have declined while that of fertilisers has increased rather slowly. In the state-owned enterprises, wages have increased faster than labour-productivity; indeed, labour-productivity has actually declined recently (see Table 8.6). The rate of growth of national income has declined from 12.3 per cent in 1978 to a mere 3 per cent in 1981 (see Table 8.1). And, more significantly, the share of agriculture in state investment declined sharply.

New imbalances, therefore, have been created in the economy and these are causes for worry. No doubt some of these will be corrected in the near future. But how and to what extent they can be corrected depends fundamentally on the production and distributional consequences of the current agrarian policy and rural reforms. To an analysis of these, we now turn.

STATE POLICY TOWARDS THE RURAL SECTOR

Development efforts over the period 1949–78, notwithstanding occasional twists and turns in state policies, brought about fundamental changes in China's rural economy. It was far more integrated into the national economy in 1978 than it had been in 1949. Development of transport and communication networks had ended the traditional isolation of Chinese villages. Flood control projects, irrigation works and soil conservation activities had freed the Chinese peasants from their age-old dependence on the forces of nature. Development of collective institutions brought about a sense of security and unity of purpose, unprecedented in Chinese history, among the peasants; diseases, starvation and malnutrition had become events of the past. Agriculture had come to produce an economic surplus by 1978; rural industries made significant progress and, by 1978, accounted for a substantial proportion of income and employment in the communes.

These very developments, however, brought into existence fresh problems and emphasised the need for a re-orientation of state policies. In the immediate post-revolutionary period, the primary problem was guaranteeing a basic minimum level of food consumption for the population and hence the emphasis was on the growth and stability of food grains production. By 1978, however, this problem was less severe and the question of production of non-food grains (cotton, jute, oil-seeds, sugar-cane, etc.) came to the fore. Throughout the 1950s and the 1960s, a slow growth of production of these crops constrained the growth of the light industrial sector (producing some essential consumer goods). Increased consumption of food, moreover, required a greater emphasis on the production of such items as meat, eggs and fish, and less on grains. In the early phase of development, lack of adequate transport facilities necessitated a degree of local self-sufficiency in the production of food grains. Since soil conditions varied widely, this could hardly be the best way of maximising food production (or overall agricultural production for that matter) in the country as a whole. With the development of transport facilities, the strategy of regional self-sufficiency progressively lost its *raison d'être* and the case for specialisation became increasingly stronger.

There was also a need to reorient the investment programme for agriculture. Initially, agriculture had little economic surplus and large-scale mobilisation of labour for capital construction (small-scale irrigation works, soil conservation projects, etc.) constituted a most effective means of accumulation. The scope for undertaking such activities, however, progressively diminished and the emphasis had to shift from creation to efficient utilisation of assets and from labour-investment to capital-investment. Agricultural production, moreover, increasingly needed industrial inputs and scientific research. In any case, within the communes themselves, a shift of emphasis – from capital construction activities to the development of industries – was taking place and, for a period, significant development of industries at the level of brigades and communes occurred. These industries developed primarily on the basis of local resources and initially catered to the consumption requirements of the commune members and to the input requirements of agricultural production. But a sustained growth of industries needed a continuous expansion of the 'market' and this could hardly be generated internally within the communes. Thus there arose a contradiction between the state-owned industrial enterprises and the commune- and brigade-level industries. There was also the problem of raw materials; beyond a level, commune- and brigade-level enterprises began to compete with the state-owned enterprises for raw materials. For all these reasons, it was only the communes located near towns and cities which could sustain a reasonable rate of industrialisation on the basis of subcontracts received from the state-owned enterprises.

Above all, there was the question of raising living standards in the countryside. It has already been shown that the level of consumption of peasant families rose rather slowly over the period 1957–78 and that the basic underlying cause of this slow growth was a slow growth of agricultural production, particularly food production, in relation to population. Furthermore, the strategy of development on the basis of local resources, while admirable on many counts, tended to accentuate regional inequality in so far as the initial level of development was itself a function of the resource–population balance. There is little doubt that a significant number of communes remained quite poor.

In short, it is difficult to doubt that China's rural economy demanded a reorientation of state policies. The old policies had played their role, and their very achievements had generated new problems which in turn called for modifications of the old policies. On the other hand, new capabilities had developed which made different state policies feasible. The industrial sector generated a growing surplus and the need for extracting a surplus from agriculture declined proportionately. An economic surplus had emerged in the rural sector and capital-investment could increasingly replace labour-investment. The problem of ensuring a minimum level of living for the entire population had been largely solved and attention could shift to a rapid improvement in the levels of living. Production conditions in agriculture had been sufficiently improved to initiate a process of specialisation and diversification.

This is the backdrop against which the changes in state policies, introduced since 1978, have to be viewed. The changes have been wide-ranging; they not only have affected prices, procurement, taxation and marketing policies but also have involved very substantial structural reforms of the communes. The structural reforms, most significant since 1978, will be discussed in the following section. Here we shall focus on the more general macroeconomic policies.

In March 1979, purchase prices for eighteen major farm and sideline products were raised by fairly wide margins.[22] Some of the prices were further increased in subsequent years. The overall purchase price index rose by 22.1 per cent in 1979, by 7.1 per cent in 1980 and by 5.9 per cent in 1981. However, prices of industrial products destined for use as farm inputs (farm machinery, chemical fertilisers, insecticides, etc.) were kept virtually constant (see Table 8.4). There was thus a very sharp rise in the relative prices of farm products. The increases, however, were not uniform for all products; they were higher for raw materials (e.g. cotton, sugar crops, etc.) and sideline products (e.g. livestock) than for grains.[23]

Purchase quotas were fixed in 1979 for a period of five years on the basis of the average output levels of 1971–5. Since the output levels of 1979–81 were significantly higher than those of 1971–5, this amounted to a reduction in the sale quota as a proportion of output, thereby increasing the scope for sale at negotiated prices or in 'free' markets. It also appears that for some poor communes, state purchase quotas have been abolished altogether. The real impact of price increases on the incomes of the communes, therefore, was much greater than appears from the movements of price indices.

The tax burden on rural areas has also been significantly reduced. Areas with per capita grain output lower than the guaranteed minimum level (200 kg of unprocessed grains in rice areas and 150 kg in other areas) have been exempted from paying the agricultural tax. With regard to commune- and brigade-run enterprises the limit of non-taxable annual net profit has been raised from 600 yuan to 3000 yuan. New industrial enterprises (exclusive of tobacco factories, distilleries, wineries and cotton mills) can now operate tax free for two to three years instead of one to two years. In frontier counties or national autonomous areas, such enterprises can operate tax free for five years.

The immediate impact of these measures has been a substantial transfer of resources from the state to the communes. Although the purchase prices were raised, the retail sale prices of grain and edible oil have been held constant and the retail sale prices of other products have not been raised proportionately (and where they have been raised, the government was obliged to provide subsidies to the workers and staff members). This has committed the state to a huge subsidy programme.[24] On grain alone, there is a subsidy of 0.2 yuan per kilogramme; on edible oil, there is a subsidy of 1.6 yuan per kilogramme. The total additional subsidy arising from increases in purchase prices amounted to 8.3 billion yuan in 1979 and 16.8 billion yuan in 1980. For the three-year period 1979–81, total subsidy on basic food items and clothing amounted to 41.6 billion yuan. Secondly, increases in the prices of certain farm products reduced state revenues through a reduction of profits of the state-owned enterprises. Thirdly, state revenues declined as a result of reduction and remittance of taxes in rural areas; tax revenues from rural areas declined by 2.0 billion yuan in 1979 and by a further 2.5 billion yuan in 1980. Fourthly, annual import of grains increased from around 8 million tons in 1975–8 to around 15 million tons in 1979–81.[25] Thus not only have state revenues declined as a result of a decline in tax revenues and in enterprise profits, increased burden of subsidies and imports has also reduced the proportion of state revenues which can be used for investment purposes.

While such a resource transfer, therefore, automatically reduces the state's capacity to invest, it cannot by itself increase either investment or consumption at the level of the communes. For the latter to happen, the production sectors have to respond in particular ways. Consumption can increase only if the production of consumables increases simultaneously. Similarly, investment can increase only if increased volumes of investment goods are available. The government's strategy, as has already been noted, has been to increase consumption by stimulating the growth of light industry. Production of farm inputs, on the other hand, has tended to decline.[26] The general thrust of the post-1978 agrarian policy has thus been to increase the consumption of the rural population at the expense of investment in agricultural production. The development objective itself has changed, and when this is the case, the question as to whether or not past price policies were right is only of historical interest.

THE COMMUNE SYSTEM IN TRANSITION

Evolution of the commune system: a brief historical sketch

The commune system has long been considered to be the best achievement of the Chinese revolution by outside observers; it has appeared to them as the most appropriate institutional framework for solving the typical problems (poverty, under-employment, lack of an investible surplus, etc.) of an underdeveloped agrarian economy. Given its ability to ensure a basic minimum level of living for the rural population, its capacity to mobilise labour on a massive scale for capital construction, its success in generating a high degree of distributional equity and its dynamism in terms of both agricultural growth and rural industrialisation, the commune system has justifiably been judged as vastly superior to any institution known to be in existence in the developing world.

The story of the evolution of the commune system in China is well known and need not be retold here.[27] The following brief account is only intended to place the recent reforms in their proper context. Following the implementation of the radical land redistribution programme in the immediate post-revolutionary period, peasants were quickly organised – first into mutual aid teams, then into primary agricultural producer co-operatives and then into advanced agricultural producer co-operatives. By 1956, the bulk of the peasantry belonged to the advanced producer co-operatives (each with an average membership of 150–200 farm households). In 1958, some 740 000 producer co-operatives were merged into 23 630 people's communes (each with an average membership of over 5000 households). These huge organisations were at that stage viewed as the basic production and accounting units in agriculture.

The jump in scale, however, was too rapid and soon problems emerged. Both the peasants and the local cadres were too ill-equipped to make the commune a success as a production unit. Problems of planning, administration and accounting proved too difficult. To these were added the unusually bad weather conditions (in 1960 and 1961) and the failure of many of the Great Leap Forward programmes to promote rural industry. Agricultural production slumped and a reorganisation was urgently needed.[28] The reorganisation process was initiated during 1962–3.[29] The average size of the communes was much reduced and the number of communes rose from 23 630 to more than 74 000. A three-tier system was also introduced. Small production teams (29–50 households) were established as basic production and accounting units. Several production teams formed a production brigade and several production brigades formed a commune. The tasks and responsibilities of these three levels of organisation were defined clearly. Teams were responsible for organising production: both farming and sidelines (raising pigs, managing orchards, etc.), for allocating labour, for distributing incomes to members, for paying taxes to the state, for fulfilling the quota of sales to the state and for maintaining collective reserves (accumulation funds, welfare funds and contingency food reserves). Brigades were responsible for co-ordinating activities which required pooling of resources of several teams, for instance, capital construction activities, development of small-scale processing enterprises, etc. They were also responsible for organising basic social services (e.g. primary education and health services) and represented the lowest level of party organisation. Communes were responsible for promoting relatively large-scale industries, for organising transportation, credit and marketing facilities and for providing higher level social services (e.g. secondary education, hospital services, etc.). They also represented the lowest unit of government and an important level of party organisation. Commune officials were entrusted with the responsibility for collection of taxes, maintenance of public security, providing leadership and direction to commune activities, implementation of policies and programmes of the government and monitoring their effects, collection of data, providing extension services, and so on. Effectively, communes represented an amalgamation of three units – political, administrative and economic.

This three-tier system remained largely unchanged till 1978, though some readjustments in the size of units occurred. In 1978, there were 52 781 communes, 692 307 brigades and 4 816 000 teams. During the Cultural Revolution, efforts were made progressively with some success to raise the level of accounting and production management. In 1978, sixty-two communes, 72 000 brigades and 4 629 921 teams functioned as production and accounting units.

The internal organisation of the teams underwent more substantive changes. In the early days of the co-operative movement, payments for work were made according to a piece rate system and member families were allowed to retain small private plots and livestock (including pigs and poultry). When communes were established in 1958, private plots were abolished, private sideline production was discouraged and time-rate systems of payment were emphasised. These tendencies were reversed during the period of adjustment (1962–3) when private plots were reintroduced. But again during the early part of the Cultural Revolution (1968–71) time-rate systems were emphasised, private sideline production was restricted and private plots were reportedly abolished in some cases. By 1978, these had been reversed again and many of the practices of the 1962–3 period were reintroduced.

Through all this turmoil, the commune system performed remarkably well in solving the basic problems of China's rural economy. As has already been discussed, growth of production was significant and the technical conditions of production were transformed. The development of rural industries was on a significant scale.[30] Although the level of direct personal consumption of the rural population rose rather slowly, substantial progress was made in such areas as housing, health care, education, transport and communications facilities and in the provision of such basic amenities as electricity and clean water. The living conditions of an average rural person were incomparably better in 1978 than they had been in 1957. And all this was achieved without generating the sort of social inequalities which characterise much of the Third World.

Politics, government and the economy: inter-relationships

The commune, as it existed till 1978, was a political unit, a government organ and an economic enterprise all rolled into one. Consequently, there was no clear distinction between political work, administrative tasks and economic activities, and they always interfered with each other. In principle, this is not necessarily undesirable and it certainly proved workable. But in practice, it seems, certain problems were increasingly encountered. Often enough a single commune official had political, administrative and economic responsibilities and this made an efficient discharge of any of these responsibilities extremely difficult. For example, welfare services and monitoring work might suffer during busy farming seasons, production plans might be based on political or administrative considerations without due attention to local technical conditions of production, and so on. The very development of the communes (implying an expansion in the range and scale of activities) tended to make these difficulties increasingly serious.

Given the hierarchical relationship between the three levels of the commune structure, the scope for interference by the commune officials into the activities of the teams was wide. Usually, the output targets, sales quotas and input allocations for the teams were decided at the level of the communes and were then relayed through the brigades to the teams, though such practices were not sanctioned by the Party. Given the lack of an identity of interests between the commune officials (who were salaried people) and the team members, such decisions tended to be rather arbitrary in many cases. The teams, therefore, were obliged to carry out decisions in the making of which they had not participated. Furthermore, the communes often commandeered the resources (including labour power) of the teams without compensation, although this was strictly forbidden.

This structure, undoubtedly, facilitated the fulfilment of certain quite commendable objectives, and probably came into existence because of its efficacy in this regard. In China of the 1950s and 1960s, the entire population could not be guaranteed a decent minimum level of subsistence without careful centralised planning and its effective implementation, and this required a fusion of political, administrative and economic powers. Similarly, massive mobilisation of labour for capital construction could hardly have been feasible without the 'leader-follower' relationship between the communes and the brigades and between the brigades and the teams.

In recent periods, however, the objectives and requirements of development had begun to shift. In particular, the objective of increasing production had replaced that of ensuring a floor to the level of production and the objective of an efficient utilisation of productive assets had replaced that of creating such assets. Furthermore, many of the old constraints (e.g. transport and communication) were no longer binding and new opportunities (e.g. inter-team, inter-brigade, inter-commune or inter-regional joint economic enterprises) presented themselves.

It is in this context that one of the boldest experiments since 1958 – that of a functional separation between politics, government and the economy – is now being conducted.[31] As a first step, the communes were reorganised to some extent and efforts were made to establish the production teams as autonomous units. In many cases, the level of accounting was moved back to the teams, as can be seen from the data in Table 8.12.

Furthermore, steps were taken to prevent 'requisition or use of the labour power, land, draught animals, machinery, funds, products and other materials of a production team without compensation'. The *Draft of the Revised Constitution of the People's Republic of China* stipulates the re-establishment of township (xiang) governments and retains the people's communes as collective economic organisations which no longer function as a level of political power or administration.[32] This will not change the ownership of the communes, brigades and teams with regard to their enterprises and other collective property. The name of the commune may still be retained, or the communes may be reorganised into other suitable organisations. These measures are to be introduced in limited areas as experiments and, on the basis of experiences accumulated, will then be introduced throughout the country.

Three counties (Guanghan, Qionglai and Xindu) in Sichuan had

TABLE 8.12 *Accounting units, 1978 and 1981*

	1978		*1981*	
Total no. of communes	52 781		54 371	
No. of communes functioning as accounting units	62	(0.12)	31	(0.06)
Total no. of brigades	692 307		718 000	
No. of brigades functioning as accounting units	72 000	(10.4)	35 754	(4.98)
Total no. of teams	4 816 000		6 004 000	
No. of teams functioning as accounting units	4 629 921	(96.14)	5 899 000	(98.25)

SOURCE Data supplied to the delegation by the Chinese Academy of Social Sciences and State Statistical Bureau. Figures in parentheses are percentages.

begun experimenting with these methods before they were sanctified by the constitution. First-hand information is available on two experimental communes – one each in Guanghan and Qionglai counties. In both these cases, party organisation and government have been separated from the commune; the same has occurred at the level of the brigades. From an administrative point of view, each commune is now a *xiang* and each village (usually a brigade) is now a *cun*. A division of tasks and responsibilities has been worked out. The party organisation is in charge of implementing state policies and of monitoring and studying the situation. The local government is in charge of organising and supervising tax collection, education, health care, cultural events, sports, women's affairs, family planning, etc. The leaders of communes, brigades and teams remain responsible for the management of production (industrial, agricultural and sideline) and commercial activities.

These changes have prompted changes even in the sphere of organisation of economic activities. In the case of the Zhan Xiang commune in Qionglai county, one of the brigades (Feng Huan) had been turned into a corporation in February 1980 – it was renamed as Phoenix Corporation. The brigade's five teams have been merged together to form a company which is in charge of production of grains and oil-bearing crops. Three other companies have also been organised: one in charge of industrial production, one in charge of commercial activities and one in charge of sideline production (including production of commercial crops). These three companies do not have a permanent labour force and draw their workers from the first company which rewards them according to work points thus earned. The corporation can raise revenues by selling shares to individual households, groups of households or companies and distributes a certain percentage of the profits to shareholders. It is run by a general conference, consisting of shareholders, workers and managers, which has the power of electing, appointing or dismissing officials. Professional management personnel (not members of the companies) sometimes sign contracts, which specify profit targets, raw materials, labour and capital equipment, with the corporation. The relationships between the corporation and the companies and that among the companies are purely contractual. The ex-commune, which has effectively turned itself into a giant corporation, now provides general guidance and technical assistance and issues instructions on targets for certain specific products. The xiang government issues production plans for grains and oil-bearing crops.

Somewhat different developments have taken place in a commune in Guanghan county. An ex-commune was first divided up into three communes (with three xiang governments) which then placed the important industrial enterprises under the management of the giant Jinan Corporation, established in October 1980. The ex-brigades were turned into joint companies which retained control of some of the erstwhile brigade enterprises and the ex-teams were renamed as co-operatives which retained the responsibility for agricultural and sideline production. The corporation, if requested, provides technical assistance of various types to the joint companies and the co-operatives, and it can establish joint ventures in co-operation with them. It raises funds for establishing new enterprises through a sale of shares, transfers a part of the profits to the joint companies and co-operatives, recruits workers from the co-operatives and pays cash wages.

These examples give us an idea of the type of experiments now under way and the extent to which the old commune structure is planned to be dismantled. As a general rule, contractual relationships, both vertical and horizontal, are replacing the hierarchical relationships, dictated by political–administrative considerations, among different levels of collective production units. Economics, and not politics, is now in command.

Collective and private production: modes of co-existence

A small private economy has always existed alongside the collective economy in production teams ever since the three-tier commune system was established during 1962–3. All members of a team have access to small private plots which are allocated on a per capita basis. Households are also allowed to engage in private sideline production (such as pig raising, poultry, handicrafts, etc.). Products of such private activities were exchanged in the rural fairs which have existed throughout the period. State policy concerning such production activities has gone through some twists and turns. During a phase of the Cultural Revolution (1968–71) private plots were abolished in some cases and private sideline production was discouraged.[33] Towards the end of 1978, both private plots and private sideline production were declared as essential adjuncts to the collective economy. Since then, several important policy measures have been implemented which have led to a considerable increase in the importance of private production in the rural economy.

Throughout the period 1962–78, private plots accounted for 5–7 per cent of the cultivated area owned by a production team. Subsequent reforms made it permissible for a production team to distribute up to 15 per cent of its total cultivated area in private plots.[34] An equally significant measure has been the lifting of all restrictions on the types of products which may be produced on the private plots. In the pre-1978 period, no major crops could be grown on them; they were generally used to produce vegetables and fodder. These restrictions no longer exist.

All restrictions on private sideline production have also been removed. Previously, for example, there were limits on how many chickens or hogs a family could keep, which animals could be privately owned, and so on. Now there are only some very general rules which govern the nature and extent of sideline production. These are: (a) that sideline production should not damage the nation's resources; (b) that sideline production should not affect collective production unfavourably; and (c) that sideline production should not lead to private trading and speculation. Evidently, these rules are so general as to be almost impossible to implement in practice. Even more significant are the newly created facilities and incentives for private sideline production. Banks have been instructed to issue loans to households for sideline production, government extension agencies have been instructed to provide technical know-how and assistance to households willing to undertake sideline production, and the marketing co-operatives have been instructed to assist peasant households in marketing sideline products.

Two other general measures have added to the significance of the above measures in boosting the private economy. The first concerns a new rule for collective labour. Previously, the entire working population in a team was obliged to devote a minimum number of labour days in a year to collective production.[35] Now only one working member from each household is required to engage in collective labour. This means that in the case of labour-rich households, one or more working members may wholly withdraw from collective labour and devote themselves to private production. Secondly, expanded opportunities for exchange in the rural fairs and establishment of urban 'free' markets have created new possibilities for specialisation and commodity production.[36] Such trends are already discernible. Small-scale poultry or dairy farms, handicraft enterprises, etc., owned and operated sometimes by a single household and sometimes jointly by a few households, are beginning to make their appearance.

The combined effect of all these measures has been a substantial expansion of the private economy in relation to the collective economy.[37] For the country as a whole, the value of output from private sideline activities as a proportion of the gross value of agricultural output increased from 16 per cent in 1978 to 20 per cent in 1981. The importance of sideline occupations as a source of household income has increased even more significantly as can be seen from the following table. In some areas, private sideline production has already become the major source of household income. For example, in Sichuan province, income from sideline production constituted 53.6 per cent of a total per capita income of 183 yuan in 1981.

It is clear that the private economy today differs from that which existed prior to 1978 in several quite fundamental respects. Before 1978, the role of the private economy was limited to providing the household with a few minor consumption items (vegetables, milk, meat, etc.) and sometimes with a little extra cash. Sideline activities, moreover, were generally undertaken by the non-working members of the peasant household so that their scale tended to vary directly with the dependency ratio.[38] Today these activities can be undertaken by both working and non-working members of a household and are increasingly oriented towards specialisation and commodity production. Added to these are the newly introduced support facilities (bank loans, extension services and marketing networks), increased size of private plots, absence of restrictions in terms of choice of products and the possibility of establishing joint enterprises by groups of households. Clearly, the scale of sideline activities need no longer be constrained by the availability of either funds or idle family labour. Joint enterprises, it should not be forgotten, can act as a camouflage for labour hiring. It is difficult to resist the conclusion that the private economy has emerged as a potential force of differentiation among the peasantry and may thus seriously erode the basis of the collective economy.

TABLE 8.13 *Distribution of average per capita income by sources*

Source	*1978*	*1981*
	%	%
Collective sector	66	52
Private sideline occupations	27	38
Miscellaneous (remittances, state subsidies, etc.)	7	10

NOTE Bonuses received for overfulfilment of targets and quotas are included in collective income.

SOURCE State Statistical Bureau, *Statistical Yearbook of China, 1981* (Hong Kong: Economic Information and Agency, 1982).

There seem to have been two basic motivations behind the recent measures. The first is to increase the supply of certain consumption items, the demand for which was bound to increase as a result of increases in personal disposable incomes. This is clearly necessary if the increases in money incomes are to translate themselves into increases in real consumption. What is not clear is why such increases could not be achieved by expanding collective sideline activities. Secondly, surplus labour had emerged as a serious problem in most production teams; it was estimated to have been between 30 and 50 per cent in the country as a whole. Expansion of private sideline activities are being viewed as an effective means of utilising this surplus labour. But again, one wonders why this could not be done through expanding collective sideline activities; after all, a major constraint on the expansion of collective sidelines in the pre-1978 period was precisely a slow growth of the market (i.e. slow growth of personal disposable incomes). It is unlikely that the rate of growth of demand for sideline products, achieved during 1978–81 as a result of sudden changes in prices, procurement and taxes, can be sustained over a long period. As the growth of demand decelerates, the problem of surplus labour may reappear, perhaps in the form of open unemployment this time.

Agricultural production under collective management: the responsibility system

The term 'production responsibility system', originally coined during the period of readjustments (1962–3) in the commune structure,[39] used to refer to a distributional principle which effectively amounted to a piece rate system of allocating work points to the workers in a collective production unit (usually a production team). The system was virtually abolished during the period of Cultural Revolution when so-called 'egalitarianism' was promoted as the socialist principle of distribution. Egalitarianism referred to two basic rules. First, the system of payment was basically a time–rate system. At the beginning of an agricultural year, workers were graded according to work abilities; workers in each grade were entitled to a fixed number of work points per day of work.[40] This usually remained unchanged throughout the year. For accumulating work points, therefore, what mattered was the number of days a worker was formally at work rather than the actual amount and quality of work accomplished. Secondly, the bulk of the collective income tended to be distributed on a per capita basis. In 1978, for example, on a countrywide average, about 72 per cent of the distributed collective income was distributed on a per capita basis.

Additional restrictions, intended to generate a high rate of accumulation in the production units, were also sometimes imposed. In some provinces, for example, there was a rule that the value of a work point could not exceed 1.5 yuan. There was also a rule in some areas that the per capita grain ration for the peasants could not exceed 600 jins (= 300 kg). Thus even in developed communes and production teams, consumption of the peasants tended to be unduly restrained and the link between the material prosperity of the collective and that of individual peasants was considerably weakened or even totally severed.

Such practices, to the extent that they existed, could be expected to produce serious disincentives for work. It is to combat these ill effects of egalitarianism that the production responsibility system was reintroduced in 1979. However, it soon assumed forms which altered, quite fundamentally, not only the method of distribution but also the production process itself. Indeed, the presently dominant form of responsibility system can, with justice, be called an antithesis to the very concept of collective production.

The existing forms of responsibility system can be classified into the following two basic categories:

(a) Contracts without linkage to output: In this case the production teams (or brigades and communes when these are accounting units) enter into contracts with either small work groups or individual labourers for certain specific tasks, usually seasonal or time-bound (e.g. weeding or transplanting). Hence the absence of any linkage to output. Certain standards are set for ascertaining the satisfactory completion of the tasks, and the tasks themselves carry a fixed number of work points. The system thus approximates a piece rate system.

(b) Contracts with linkage to output: Here the reward for labour depends on the level of output achieved. The system has the following three basic forms:

(i) Contracts along specialised lines: In this case, the collective land is divided into small parcels and the parcels are contracted out usually to groups of workers but sometimes to individual workers for production of special items (e.g. vegetables, flowers, forestry products, aquatic products, etc.). The contract for each work group specifies the quality and levels of certain inputs and the output targets for different crops. If these targets are fulfilled, the work group concerned is allotted a pre-determined number of work points. Over-fulfilment is rewarded in the form of additional work points and under-fulfilment is punished by a deduction of work points according to certain established norms. The entire output is handed over to the production team which distributes the collective income according to work points. The work groups are left to their own devices for distributing the group incomes among individual workers.

(ii) Contracts with households with fixed input and output targets and work points (*bao chan dao hu*): the operational principles of this system are similar to those of the system described above except that the land in this case is parcelled out to individual households. Land is allocated partly on a per capita basis and partly according to the number of workers in the households.

(iii) Contracts with households with fixed input targets and delivery quotas (*bao gan dao hu*): this system is in essence equivalent to a fixed-rent tenancy system. Collective land is parcelled out to individual households, in most cases partly on a per capita basis and partly according to the number of workers in the households. The production team fixes not production targets but delivery quotas (which are used to pay taxes, to fulfil state purchase quotas and to retain collective reserves) and the level of application of material inputs. All output in excess of delivery quotas is retained by the households and there is no collective distribution of income. The households thus have a considerable freedom in the choice of product mix and an incentive to maximise output. The most distinguishing feature of this system is that neither the value of labour nor the distribution of income is determined at the level of the accounting unit. The value of labour, being linked to the value of output, can obviously vary across households.

The relative importance of these different forms of responsibility systems (as in June 1982) can be seen in Table 8.14.

Various permutations and combinations of these four basic systems are observed in practice, as the following data (Table 8.15) for Sichuan and Yunnan provinces illustrate.[41] This variety of forms is explained by the fact that, as a rule, the choice of the form is left to the accounting units themselves and most units have been experimenting with different forms with a view to identifying the most suitable one. The state has only set the following guiding principles (frequently referred to as 'three

TABLE 8.14 *Forms of responsibility systems*

Responsibility system adopted	*Percentage of accounting units*
(a)	8
(b)(i)	5
(b)(ii)	12
(b)(iii)	75

NOTE The figures are approximate estimates.
SOURCE Data supplied by the Chinese Academy of Social Sciences.

constants and four unifications'): no change of ownership, no change of accounting level, no change in the system of distribution at the level of the accounting unit, management under the unified leadership of the accounting unit, a unified plan of production, a unified arrangement of the labour process (division of labour between agriculture, industry and sidelines), and a unified management of assets (farm implements and machinery, draught animals, irrigation systems, water conservancy projects, etc.). The accounting units must also retain the responsibility for paying taxes, for fulfilling state purchase quotas and for maintaining collective accumulation funds, welfare funds and contingency grain reserves. They remain responsible, moreover, for assisting the deficit households and five-guarantee families.

In view of the current emphasis on developing diverse systems to suit diverse local conditions, it is remarkable that the household contracting system has acquired such an overwhelmingly dominant position. In the country as a whole, about 87 per cent of the accounting units are practising this system. *Bao gan dao hu* alone is being practised by about 75 per cent of the teams. This picture is corroborated by the data for Sichuan and Yunnan provinces. Past trends indicate, moreover, that those practising *bao chan dao hu* are inclined to shift to *bao gan dao hu* rather rapidly. Once again, therefore, a uniform system is seemingly being promoted throughout the country. It is only the highly developed communes (usually located near the cities) which appear to have been able to resist the change.

Clearly, the most significant consequence of the introduction of responsibility systems has been the re-emergence of the household as the basic unit of production in the Chinese countryside. This implies a fundamental change in the labour process: control over labour allocation has passed, to a large extent, from the collective on to individual households. In the case of *bao gan dao hu*, even the valuation of labour is

TABLE 8.15 *Responsibility systems in Sichuan and Yunnan*

Responsibility system adopted (July 1982)	*Percentage of accounting units*	
	Sichuan	*Yunnan*
Contracting without linkage to output	1.32	6.8
Contracting with work groups or individual labourers		
(a) along specialised lines	0.38	5.4
(b) not along specialised lines	9.45	1.8
Bao chan dao hu	17.06	1.4
Bao gan dao hu	64.46	63.8
Contracting grain areas to households (either *bao chan dao hu* or *bao gan dao hu*) and commercial crop areas to labourers (may or may not be along specialised lines)	3.35	
Contracting agricultural production to households (*bao gan dao hu*) and sidelines to labourers along specialised lines		20.4
Irrigated fields contracted to work groups (may or may not be along specialised lines) and unirrigated fields contracted to households (*bao chan dao hu* or *bao gan dao hu*)	3.97	
Responsibility system not adopted	0.01	0.4

SOURCE Data supplied by the Chinese Academy of Social Sciences.

no longer a matter of collective choice. Thus the laws governing the distribution of land and other productive assets among peasant households have once again emerged as principal determinants of production patterns, labour process and income distribution.

Under the household contracting system, it is usually the households who bear the costs of current inputs; they receive credit from the team for the purpose. The teams retain control over the distribution of modern inputs such as chemical fertilisers, pesticides, etc. These are allocated to the teams by the state; teams allocate them to households in accordance with landholding. As for draught animals and farm machinery, these are contracted out by the teams to individual labourers who provide services to households on demand for a fee, earn work points and are rewarded by the teams. The teams also impose certain restrictions concerning the use of land and labour on the households: no land-leasing or labour-hiring is allowed and unauthorised construction on collective land is forbidden. Furthermore, the teams reserve the right of periodic reallocation of land.

But any fundamental change in the production system always generates pressures for further change and some of the above regulations are in the process of being relaxed. Moreover, there are some genuine anomalies. For example, timeliness and speed of completion of particular operations significantly influence land and labour productivities and hence influence the value of labour under the *bao gan dao hu* system. Dependence of peasant households on hiring of services of draught animals and farm machinery, therefore, is bound to lead to conflictual situations. Similarly, when land is allocated partly on a per capita basis and partly according to the number of workers in a household, the worker/land ratio will vary across households. Pressures for equalisation of the worker/land ratio through land-leasing or labour-hiring, therefore, are likely to exist. Hence a ban on land-leasing and labour-hiring tends to give rise to an anomalous situation.

Thus, attempts strictly to implement the restrictive regulations by the teams would either be unsuccessful or, if successful, would prevent an optimal combination of factors of production. There would, therefore, be an understandable tendency for the teams to relax controls or simply to ignore violations of the rules. Signs are already there. In some teams, draught animals have been sold to individual households on an instalment basis. In many areas, peasants can buy and sell draught animals in 'free' markets. Many households in richer areas are reported to have bought small tractors. It would be most surprising if the households did not have informal arrangements for buying and selling of chemical fertilisers and for hiring of labour.[42] Pressures are also likely to be generated for setting unreasonably low output targets and delivery quotas since few households would be willing to risk paying penalties for underfulfilment. If inequities in the allocation of work points existed under the old system, there is no reason why similar inequities may not exist in the allocation of land and material inputs today. Although there is the provision for periodic reallocation of land by the teams, to attempt such reallocation too often would be impractical and would tend to negate the very incentives the household contracting system is supposed to provide. All this seems to suggest that the new system can lead to significant peasant differentiation. Above all, it is doubtful if labour mobilisation on a significant scale for capital construction, a basic strength of the old system, would be at all feasible under the new system.[43]

Against these disadvantages is the fact that the household responsibility system does provide strong incentives to peasant households for maximising output. As individual initiatives are brought into play, productive efficiency is likely to increase in the short run. Long-term growth, however, depends on a different set of factors: accumulation, investment and technological change. The emergence of the household as the basic production unit, the expansion in private commodity production and the possibilities of peasant differentiation may cause a sharp discontinuity in the trajectory of these variables. It is generally held in China today that as forces of production develop, the objective need to raise the scale of production will provide compelling reasons for the peasants to move towards a collective mode of production. But could it not provide compelling reasons for them to demand greater scope for private accumulation? Or could not the peasants begin to condition the development of the forces of production in such a way as to suit the requirements of small-scale production?

The commune system in transition

The structural reforms of the commune system were initiated with a view to countering the disincentive effects of 'bureaucratism' and 'egalitarianism' on the rural labour force. Attempts to overcome 'bureaucratism' have inspired functional separation of political units, administrative organs and economic enterprises within the commune structure – a measure which is likely to have expanded the area of decision-making for the peasant masses. Attempts to overcome 'egalitarianism', however, seem to have resulted in a considerable weakening of collective institutions. The peasant household is fast emerging as the basic unit of agricultural and sideline production and there is a distinct trend towards a growing privatisation of the labour process. These facts give rise to a whole range of issues concerning the future course of development in rural China. It is not possible to deal with these issues at an empirical level; the changes are too recent for that to be feasible. Some preliminary observations can nonetheless be made.

It appears that growth of agricultural production has significantly accelerated in the wake of the rural reforms. Some notes of scepticism need to be added, however, before a causal relation between the reforms and growth is automatically assumed. First, the reported growth rates of crops are very high, sometimes too high to be credible. For example, over the period 1978–81, grain output is reported to have increased by 6.6 per cent in spite of an (approximately) 4.7 per cent decline in the area under grains. Growth rates for commercial crops have been reported to be much higher: 37.0 per cent for cotton, 95.6 per cent for oil-bearing crops, 45.7 per cent for silkworm cocoons, 40.5 per cent for sugar-cane and 35.4 per cent for sugarbeet. These growth rates represent such a sharp break from the historical trends that it needs to be ascertained that no statistical illusions are involved. Secondly, all the reports suggest that it is the poorer production teams which have achieved relatively higher rates of growth in crop production. If this is accepted, then it has to be believed that teams had remained poor not so much because they lacked resources but because they had an incompetent leadership. Even if this is true, it certainly is not self-evident and needs to be established through investigations.

The observed trends in some indicators of technical change in agriculture over the period 1978–81 strengthen the scepticism regarding a causal relation between the reforms and agricultural growth. It can be seen from Table 8.16 below that investment in modern inputs was most significant during 1978–9 and has since been declining. It seems quite reasonable to suppose that the short-lived spurt in investment was due to the changes in relative prices, taxes and procurement (effected in 1978) rather than the reforms (initiated in 1979).

Even if it is accepted that the reported rates of growth in crop production are true and that they are primarily attributable to the structural reforms, it has to be remembered that they have been achieved at the cost of privatising labour and production processes to a significant extent. This fact, moreover, has to be viewed in conjunction with the fact that the private economy itself has been considerably expanded. These features, which have significantly increased the power of the market forces, have important implications for social inequalities and division of labour, and hence, in the long run, for accumulation, technical change and growth.

The expansion of the private economy has certainly helped increase employment and output of some basic consumer goods in the short run. But it has also created conditions for a widening of intra-regional inequalities, and these conditions are likely to be reinforced by the

TABLE 8.16

	Rate of growth over the period		
	1978–79	*1979–80*	*1980–81*
Large and medium tractors in use	19.7	11.7	6.3
Small hand tractors in use	21.7	12.1	8.7
Chemical fertilisers used per hectare	22.5	17.2	5.2

SOURCE State Statistical Bureau, *Statistical Yearbook of China, 1981.*

partial privatisation of the collective economy itself. On the other hand, it could be argued that these measures are likely to reduce inter-regional and rural–urban inequalities since they overcome to some extent the disadvantages arising from a lack of mobility of labour. In fact, the measures can conceivably have the effect of encouraging internal migration since it is no longer necessary for every able-bodied person to participate in the collective economy. The newly created provisions for self-employment in the urban service sector and the proposals for the establishment of small urban centres throughout the country point in the same direction.

The reforms are also likely to lead to a sharper division of labour in rural areas, not only because expansion of the private economy has increased the scope for specialisation in private production but also because of the growing separation of activities within the collective economy. For example, separation of commune and brigade enterprises from agricultural production and the abandonment of the Maoist idea of a 'peasant-worker', contracting out collective land to households or work groups along specialised lines, and attempts to create specialised co-operatives (such as marketing cooperatives) within the communes will all have the effect of separating the different component parts of the production and distribution processes and will correspondingly sharpen the division of labour.[44] These different component parts, therefore, are likely to experience different rates and types of technical change. In crop production, for example, land-augmenting technological change is likely while in processing activities labour-augmenting technologies may prove more attractive. In principle, however, a sharper division of labour should raise the productivity of labour.

As for accumulation, it seems plausible to suppose that labour accumulation on a significant scale will no longer be feasible, though other forms of collective accumulation will continue to exist.[45] Labour accumulation, of course, is irreplaceable. Private accumulation can now exist to a limited extent, but its effects are as yet uncertain. What is certain is that it cannot generate significant capital construction in rural areas. Thus while the state's capacity to invest has declined, the need for state investment in rural areas is likely to have increased.

It is clear from the above observations that the institutional reforms were intended not merely to combat 'egalitarianism' but to alter fundamentally the pattern of development in rural China. For combating 'egalitarianism', it was not necessary either to expand the private economy or to introduce *bao gan dao hu*. Since these measures have been adopted, the post-1978 developments cannot provide a basis for judging the validity of the claim that 'egalitarianism' had hindered agricultural growth in the past.

CONCLUDING OBSERVATIONS

Maoist China developed an economic system which was geared to maximising accumulation. This tendency reflected itself not merely in the realised values of such budgetary parameters as the rates of accumulation and investment but also in the structure of production itself. The differential growth rates achieved in the three major production sectors – heavy industry, light industry and agriculture – underline the fact that growth of consumption was much slower than that of national income, given the autarchic environment in which development took place.[46]

Yet it would be absurd to suggest that growth and accumulation *per se* were the basic objectives of Maoist policies. In fact, Mao and his associates were always prepared to sacrifice growth for the sake of realising certain valued social objectives. The most important of these involved guaranteeing a minimum level of living to the entire population and this in a country which, by contemporary standards, was one of the poorest and most backward in the world. The institutional framework which, through a process of trial and error, developed after 1949 was clearly designed to ensure that accumulation neither involved excessive compression of consumption nor led to a widening of social inequalities. It is only in this context that the hallmarks of the Maoist system – reliance on local resources and collective efforts, emphasis on labour accumulation, localised self-sufficiency in staple foodgrains, and almost complete absence of internal migration – can be adequately appreciated. Available facts leave no room for doubting that the Chinese masses enjoy a level of material life and a degree of social security which are unequalled in most other parts of the Third World.

Ironically, it was the concern with social objectives which produced a high rate of accumulation and hence a high rate of growth. For it made the rate of growth of agricultural production a binding constraint not on the growth of national income but on that of personal disposable incomes.[47] It is perhaps arguable that the rate of growth of agricultural production might have been higher had the institutional framework of agriculture been different. But the argument is misplaced; it amounts to proposing that the social objectives could and should have been sacrificed to some extent for the sake of growth.

Undoubtedly, the emphasis on social objectives extracted a price. The excessively high rate of accumulation had led to a lop-sided industrial structure and low investment efficiency; consumption of the peasent population remained low and labour productivity in agriculture stagnated; unemployment and under-employment began to plague the system; and although intra-regional inequalities were drastically reduced, inter-regional inequalities remained significant.[48] The current impatience and concern, both of the leadership and of the population, with these problems are wholly understandable, if not fully justified. But it would be unfortunate if they tend to obscure the real strengths of the old system. Equally, it would be incorrect to overlook the fact that it is the achievements of the old system which make the contemplation of a new development strategy possible.

State policies in a dynamic economy cannot remain unchanged over time. It has been argued in this chapter that even if the social objectives of development had remained unchanged, some reforms of the Maoist economic system would have been necessary. The post-1978 reforms, however, are not of this nature. Their genesis cannot be traced to growing inadequacies of the old policies. Rather the reforms reflect the fact that the social objectives of development have been radically altered. In this sense, the reforms represent a political choice and cannot be fully explained in economic terms.

The post-Mao development strategy began by attempting to raise the level of consumption in the short run. On the one hand, a significant transfer of incomes from the state to individuals was effected through a drastic revision of wage and price policies. On the other hand, both production and imports of consumables were stepped up. The result has been a sharp increase in the share of consumption in national income and a corresponding decline in the rates of accumulation and investment. The rates of growth of national income and consumption, therefore, will almost certainly be lower in the future than they have been in the past.

Even the short-run growth of consumption, however, could not be sustained without stepping up the growth of agricultural production. A recognition of this led to the implementation of important structural reforms of the commune system. The reforms, originally intended to counter 'bureaucratism' and 'egalitarianism', appear to have altered rural institutions quite fundamentally; some of the Maoist social objectives are apparently being sacrificed for the sake of short-run growth. The hallmarks of the emerging system are almost polar opposites to those of the earlier system – individual initiative in place of collective effort, specialisation and exchange in place of self-sufficiency, capital investment in place of labour investment, mobility in place of immobility of labour, and so on. Preliminary analysis suggests that the distinguishing features of future development in rural China are likely to be increased intra-regional inequalities, reduced inter-regional and rural–urban inequalities, increased internal migration, sharper division of labour, land-augmenting technological change in crop production and labour-augmenting technological change in other activities, lower rates of internal accumulation and investment and increased need for state investment in rural capital construction.

There is a considerable risk, perhaps deliberately chosen, in all this. With reduced overall capacity of the state to invest and the increased need to invest in light industry, it will not be easy to maintain an adequate rate of investment in the production of farm inputs and in rural capital construction. There may thus be a temptation to assign an increasingly bigger role to private accumulation. But unless private accumulation is properly controlled, some of the cherished socialist goals will be in jeopardy. And if agriculture fails to sustain the momentum of growth, it will be difficult to prevent the emergence of unacceptable social inequalities through an inflationary redistribution of incomes.

APPENDIX TABLE 8.1 *Annual average per capita disposable money income, 1952–82*

	Total population	*Peasants*	*Workers and staff members*
1952	76	62	148
1957	102	79	205
1965	125	100	237
1975	158	124	324
1978	167*	134	316
1979	197	160	406
1980	236*	191	444
1981	266*	223	463

* Author's estimates

SOURCES 1. *Economic Adjustments and Reform* (*Beijing Review*, Special Feature Series, 1982), Appendix Tables.
2. *Beijing Review*, various issues.
3. State Statistical Bureau, *Statistical Yearbook of China, 1981.*

APPENDIX TABLE 8.2 *Average distributed collective income, 1957–78*

	Annual distributed collective income per capita (yuan)[a]
1957	40.5
1975	63.2
1977	65.0
1978	74.0

[a] Distributed collective income is income distributed, in cash or in kind, to production team members out of net income of the team. It excludes income earned by team members from non-collective sources – private plots and other activities – as well as income from sales of manure by households to the collective and those wages in collective enterprises that are paid directly in cash to individual workers.

SOURCE Annex A, World Bank Report.

APPENDIX TABLE 8.3 *Wages of staff and workers in state-owned enterprises, 1952–81*

	1952	*1957*	*1965*	*1978*	*1979*	*1980*	*1981*
Average annual wage in state-owned enterprises (yuan)	446	637	652	644	705	803	812

SOURCE State Statistical Bureau, *Statistical Yearbook of China, 1981.*

APPENDIX TABLE 8.4 *Labour force and employment, 1952–81 (millions)*

	1952	*1957*	*1965*	*1978*	*1979*	*1980*	*1981*
Total Labour Force[a]	207.29	237.71	286.70	398.56	405.81	418.96	432.80
Employment by Institutional Sector							
Workers and staff, of which	16.03	31.01	49.65	94.99	99.67	104.44	109.40
State organisations[b]	15.80	24.51	37.38	74.51	76.93	80.19	83.72
Urban collectives	0.23	6.50	12.27	20.48	22.74	24.25	25.68
Commune workers	182.43	205.66	235.34	303.42	305.82	313.71	322.27
Urban self-employed	8.83	1.04	1.71	0.15	0.32	0.81	1.13

[a] Includes those awaiting permanent jobs, most of whom are in temporary jobs.
[b] Includes state farms.
SOURCE State Statistical Bureau, *Statistical Yearbook of China, 1981.*

Appendix Table 8.5 *Increase in national income for each 100 yuan of investment (yuan)*

1953–7	35
1958–62	1
1963–5	57
1966–70	26
1971–5	16
1976	−10
1977	26
1978	34
1979	29
1980	23

Source Dong Fureng, 'Relationship between accumulation and consumption', in Xu Dixin *et al.*, *China's search for economic growth* (Beijing: New World Press, 1982.)

Appendix Table 8.6 *Relative rates of growth of light and heavy industries*

	Average annual rate of growth	
	Light industry	*Heavy industry*
1950–2	29.0	48.9
1953–7	12.9	25.4
1958–62	1.1	6.6
1963–5	21.2	14.9
1966–78	8.3	11.8
1952–78	9.1	13.6
1979	9.6	7.7
1980	18.4	1.4
1981	14.1	−4.7

Sources State Statistical Bureau, *Statistical Yearbook of China, 1981.*

NOTES AND REFERENCES

1. For evidence and discussion, see Feng Lanrin and Zhao Lükuan, 'Urban unemployment in China', in *Social Sciences in China*, No. 1, 1982.
2. That significant disguised unemployment exists in the communes is indicated by the following facts. Cultivated land area per agricultural worker declined from 9.35 mou in 1952 to 5.07 mou in 1978 (see Zhang Shuguang, 'Reform the economic structure and increase the macro-economic results', in *Social Sciences in China*, No. 1, 1982). Mechanisation, as we shall see later, had progressed significantly over this period. The proportion of commune workers engaged in collective industrial activities was only 9 per cent in 1978. Labour productivity in agriculture was no higher in 1978 than during the First Five-Year Plan period. (See Yang Jianbai and Li Xuezeng, 'The relations between agriculture, light industry and heavy industry in China', in *Social Sciences in China*, No. 2, 1980).
3. Policies in this respect in fact moved from one extreme to another, but viewed over the whole period 1952–78 there was very little net migration from rural to urban areas. For evidence and discussions, see Zhang Zhehou and Chen Yuguang, 'On the relationship between the population structure and national economic development in China', in *Social Sciences in China*, No. 4, 1981, and Feng Lanrin and Zhao Lükuan, 'Urban unemployment in China', in *Social Sciences in China*, No. 1, 1982.
4. Indeed, plans for building settlements in sparsely populated areas and developing small urban centres throughout the country are currently being considered.
5. This study relies on data acquired either from official publications or directly from Chinese officials and academics in the course of a research trip undertaken in July–August 1982. As is well known, some problems arise when using these data, especially for purposes of international comparison. For a discussion of some of these problems see D. H. Perkins, 'Research on the economy of the People's Republic of China: a survey of the field', *The Journal of Asian Studies*, Vol. 42, No. 2, February 1983.
6. In this respect, China differs radically from countries such as South Korea or Brazil, which also achieved high growth but relied on massive inflows of foreign resources.
7. Accumulation refers to that portion of the net income of the material production departments which is used to expand reproduction, to develop non-productive capital construction and to build up stocks of materials. Investment refers to funds allocated for new productive capital construction; it excludes funds used for non-productive capital construction, funds used as circulating capital, funds used for replacement purposes and funds used for technical innovations. Estimates of accumulation and investment, as reported by the State Statistical Bureau, exclude those undertaken by the collective units out of their own resources.
8. For some evidence on profitability in light industries see Hi Jianzhang, Kuang Rilan and Zhang Zhouyuan, 'Reform of the economic structure requires industrial pricing based on production price', in *Social Sciences in China*, No. 1, 1981.

9. The percentage distribution of gross income of the communes for China as a whole in the year 1978 was reported to be as follows:

production and management costs	34.88
taxes	3.35
collective reserve	9.30
of which	
accumulation fund	6.76
welfare fund	1.63
distributed collective income	52.59

SOURCE State Statistical Bureau, *Statistical Yearbook of China, 1981.*

The share of production and management costs tends to vary directly and that of taxes tends to vary inversely with the level of gross income. The share of distributed collective income, however, shows a remarkable stability.

10. See *Daily Report: China*, 22 March 1982.
11. The problem is underlined by the fact that the average per capita grain ration was actually below the level of 1957 during most years of the period 1958–78. See Yang Jianbai and Li Xuezeng, 'The relations between agriculture, light industry and heavy industry in China', in *Social Sciences in China*, No. 2, 1980.
12. Chinese sources claim, however, that many light industrial products including bicycles and sewing-machines were in short supply. See, for example, Yang Jianbai and Li Xuezeng, ibid.
13. Cf. The World Bank, *World Development Report, 1980* (Washington, DC 1980). It is particularly interesting to note that in India, a country comparable to China in many respects, the rate of growth of per capita private consumption over 1964/65–1977/78 was only 0.56 per cent in real terms. See Centre for Monitoring Indian Economy, *Macro Framework of Indian Economy* (Bombay, 1979).
14. This is merely another way of saying that the rate of accumulation was higher in China than in most developing countries. Again a comparison with India is interesting. The ratio of consumption to national income in China and India was as follows:

    China – 1952: 0.79, 1957: 0.75, 1965: 0.73, 1978: 0.63
    India – 1964/65: 0.88, 1977/78: 0.78

15. Consumption of necessities cannot be affected by income redistribution since the supply is fixed. Redistribution in favour of the poor, however, will reduce luxury consumption. Hence total consumption must decline. The argument appears to contradict conventional theory which holds that higher income inequality permits higher savings.
16. This means that the national rate of accumulation was a politically

determined parameter. This is indeed the view held by a majority of Chinese economists today. See, for example, Xue Muqiao, *China's Socialist Economy* (Beijing: Foreign Languages Press, 1981), and Xu Dixin *et al.*, *China's Search for Economic Growth* (Beijing: New World Press, 1982). It has been argued that over-accumulation is a common characteristic of all centrally planned economies and its explanation is to be sought in the institutional and political superstructure of these economies. Cf. Mario Nuti, 'Socialism on earth', in *Cambridge Journal of Economics*, Vol. 5, No. 4, December 1981.

17. The average annual rate of growth of gross output (at constant prices) over the period 1952–78 was 9.1 per cent in light industry and 13.6 per cent in heavy industry (see Appendix Table 8.6). Two points are immediately clear. First, the rate of growth of light industry in China compared favourably with that in most countries of the world. Secondly, the investment–output ratio was much lower in light industry than in heavy industry. In fact, the very high investment–output ratio in heavy industry was probably responsible for the very high investment–output ratio in the economy as a whole (see Appendix Table 8.5).
18. A good example is urban housing. A recent survey of 182 major cities shows a decline in average per capita floor space over the period 1952–78. See Liang Wensen and Tian Jianghai, 'Final products: a new point of departure', in *Social Sciences in China*, No. 4, 1980.
19. Cf. Liang Wensen, 'Balanced development of industry and agriculture', in Xu Dixin *et al.*, *China's search for economic growth* (Beijing: New World Press, 1982).
20. Cf. State Statistical Bureau, *Statistical Yearbook of China, 1981*. Significant amounts of oil-bearing crops and cotton had to be imported in order to maintain a modest growth in the production of edible oil and cotton cloth (see Table 8.7).
21. A vigorous family planning programme is also being implemented, but its impact will be felt only in the long run.
22. The eighteen major farm products include grains, oil-bearing crops, cotton, livestock, eggs, aquatic products, sugarbeet, sugar-cane, hemp, ramie, silkworm cocoons, timber, bamboo and hides and skins. For each of these products, there is a state purchase quota fixed at the beginning of the year. For grains, cotton and oil-bearing crops, there is a second purchase quota for which prices paid are 30–50 per cent higher. Purchase prices refer to these two types of prices. All above-quota purchases by the state are at negotiated prices. Private sale of cotton is forbidden. Grains and oil-bearing crops can be sold in rural fairs or urban 'free' markets only after state purchases have been completed, i.e. after the expiry of the date by which state purchases have to be completed.
23. Cf. State Statistical Bureau, *Statistical Yearbook of China, 1981.*
24. See *Beijing Review*, 25 October 1982.
25. See *Daily Report: China* (US Department of Commerce: Foreign Broadcast Information Service), 4 January 1983. Reportedly imports of other farm products such as cotton, soyabeans etc. have declined.
26. The rate of growth of production of selected items of farm inputs since 1978 has been as follows:

	1978–9	*1979–80*	*1980–1*
Chemical fertilizers	22.6	15.6	0.6
Large and medium tractors	10.7	−22.2	−46.0
Small tractors	−2.1	−32.4	− 8.7

SOURCE State Statistical Bureau, *Statistical Yearbook of China, 1981.*

27. For detailed and competent discussions, see Jürgen Domes, *Socialism in the Chinese countryside* (London: C. Hurst and Co., 1980) and the World Bank Report, *China*, Annex A, Washington DC 1981. For some interesting insights with regard to the collectivisation process, see Yan Lin, 'The necessity, possibility and realisation of socialist transformation of China's agriculture', in *Social Sciences in China*, No. 1, 1982.
28. The nationwide average per capita grain ration declined quite sharply; it was 203 kg in 1957, 198 kg in 1958, 186.5 kg in 1959 and 163.5 kg in 1960. See Yang Jianbai and Li Xuezeng, 'The relations between agriculture, light industry and heavy industry in China', in *Social Sciences in China*, No. 2, 1980. It is now known that famine conditions prevailed in some parts of China over the period 1959–61.
29. The basic document which outlined the method of reorganisation is called 'Regulations on the work of the rural people's communes, revised draft, Sept. 1962' popularly known as '60 regulations'.
30. By 1978, commune- and brigade-run enterprises accounted for about 27 per cent of the total income of the communes. Cf. State Statistical Bureau, *Statistical Yearbook of China, 1981.*
31. See 'The decision on some questions concerning the acceleration of agricultural development', published in *Beijing Review*, 24 March 1980.
32. See *Beijing Review*, 19 July 1982.
33. Similar efforts by the Gang of Four were largely unsuccessful.
34. Originally, this measure was intended to be applicable only to those teams which had not adopted the 'household responsibility system'. In practice, however, most production teams have expanded the share of area under private plots.
35. The norm varied across teams. In general, adult women were required to perform 200 days of collective labour. For adult men, the general norm was more than 200 days, but it varied depending upon the physical abilities and health conditions of the labourers.
36. At present, there are about 30 000 rural fairs and about 2300 peasant markets in urban areas throughout China.
37. It will be argued in the following sub-section that in many areas the collective economy itself has been privatised to a great extent.
38. This is why private sideline activities tended to have an equalising influence on the distribution of income among peasant households.
39. See '60 Regulations'.
40. Within each grade, women workers were usually allotted less work points per day than men.
41. For examples of other variants, see Jürgen Domes, 'New policies in the

communes: notes on rural societal structures in China, 1976–1981, in *The Journal of Asian Studies*, Vol. XLI, No. 2, February 1982, and G. E. Johnson, 'The production responsibility system in Chinese agriculture: some examples from Guangdong', in *Pacific Affairs*, Vol. 55, No. 2, 1982.

42. Efforts were reportedly being made to promote 'mutual aid teams', but these may act as camouflage for labour-hiring. Conditions of Chinese peasants today are far less precarious than they were in the 1950s. And even under the old commune system, households often made informal arrangements for transfer of work points.
43. Cf. James E. Nickum, 'Labour accumulation in rural China and its role since the Cultural Revolution', in *Cambridge Journal of Economics*, 1978, Vol. 2, pp. 273–386.
44. According to a recent report, peasant households who switched from crop production to specialised activities numbered about 70 million at the end of 1982. This excludes those households (about 30 million) whose working members are employed in commune- and brigade-run enterprises. Of the 70 million, about 17.6 million engaged in animal husbandry, flower growing, fish breeding, etc., about 1.27 million engaged in private commerce and the rest engaged in service trades such as supplying seeds and fodder, providing an agrotechnical service, servicing farm implements and transportation. See *Beijing Review*, 28 March 1983.
45. Since 1979, the annual contribution to accumulation funds maintained by the communes has in fact declined in both absolute and relative terms. This is rather worrying though it is too soon to say if it represents a long-term trend.
46. In principle, consumption could have been increased faster by exporting heavy industrial products and by importing consumables.
47. A comparison with India helps to keep things in perspective. Since, in India, there was no attempt to guarantee a minimum level of living to the entire population, the level of consumption was not determined by the level of agricultural production to the same extent as in China. Consequently, India had a lower rate of accumulation and hence a lower rate of growth.
48. Again it should be borne in mind that many of these problems exist in a large number of Third World countries which have traversed a totally different growth path.

9 Epilogue: Rural China in 1983

KEITH GRIFFIN

In the summer of 1983 we returned to China for additional work in Beijing, Shaanxi province, the Chongqing municipality of Sichuan and Wuhan, the capital of Hubei province. Our research centred on three major issues: recent changes in agricultural production and rural incomes; the effects of economic reforms on income distribution in the rural areas; and the consequences of the new strategy for rural development on long-run rates of capital accumulation. We shall comment on each of these topics in turn, presenting our most important findings briefly and then relating these findings to those based on the data collected in 1982.

PRODUCTION AND INCOMES

Agricultural output has increased substantially since the economic reforms were introduced. Comparing 1978 (the last year of the old policy regime) with 1982 (the most recent year for which data are available), it is evident that progress has been made across a very broad front (see Table 9.1). Moreover, output has increased steadily from one year to the next – there was a slight fall in fisheries output in 1979 and a fractional decline in farm output in 1980 – and this progress is expected to continue in 1983.

The most general measure of production performance is gross agricultural output value (GAOV). Between 1978 and 1982 GAOV increased by a third in constant price terms or by about 8 per cent a year. Crop production was the slowest growing sub-sector and its share of total agricultural output fell from 67.8 per cent to 62.7 per cent over the

TABLE 9.1 *Agricultural production, 1978–82*

	1978	*1982*	*Percentage increase*
Gross agricultural output value (index)	100	133.4	33.4
Crop production (10 000 tons)			
all grains	30 477	35 343	16.0
cotton	216.7	359.8	66.0
oil-bearing crops	521.8	1181.7	126.5
sugar-cane	2111.6	3688.2	74.5
sugarbeets	270.2	671.2	148.4
Pork, beef and mutton (10 000 tons)	856.3	1350.8	57.7
Per capita output (kg per head)			
grain	318.5	350.5	10.0
cotton	2.3	3.6	57.6
oil-bearing crops	5.5	11.7	115.9
pork, beef and mutton	9.0	13.4	49.7
fish	4.9	5.1	5.2

SOURCE State Bureau of Statistics, *Selected Statistics of China 1983*, Beijing, June 1983 (in Chinese).

period. Livestock expanded rapidly as did the output from sideline occupations. In per capita terms there was significant growth in all sub-sectors, with the expansion of oil-bearing crops, cotton and meat products being especially rapid.

Four factors account for the rapid growth of production since 1978. First, the weather has generally been good. The reforms have been blessed by favourable climatic conditions and this has given them an excellent start. Secondly, as described in Chapter 3, agriculture has benefited from much improved terms of trade. Thirdly, the government has changed its policy toward local grain self-sufficiency and has encouraged regions to exploit their comparative advantage. This in turn has led to changes in cropping patterns and the allocation of land, to a more diversified composition of output and to higher incomes. The area devoted to growing food grains has declined by 6 per cent whereas the area used for cash crop production has risen by 30.1 per cent.

These first three reasons for higher output have nothing to do with institutional change. The first is good luck and the next two are macroeconomic policy reforms which could have been introduced quite independently of the production responsibility system. The Chinese, however, believe that the institutional reforms have had the effect of raising the 'enthusiasm of the masses'. It is hard to know precisely what this means or how much weight to give to it, but it does seem that there is a fourth explanation for higher output that has something to do with the application of labour to production. That is, it is probable that the new responsibility system has affected incentives in such a way that the peasantry now works longer hours than before, works with greater intensity per hour than previously and also works with greater intelligence, imagination and creativity. It is impossible to quantify this effect with the existing data, but our observations in the field nonetheless suggest that it is real.

Whatever the explanation, there can be no doubt that per capita incomes in the rural areas have increased dramatically. Indeed, because of the improved terms of trade, they have increased much faster than production (see Table 9.2). Money incomes have more than doubled and income generated by private household activities has increased 187 per cent in only four years. As a result, private income in 1982 accounted for

TABLE 9:2 *Per capita income and consumption in rural areas, 1978–82*

	1978	*1982*	*Percentage increase*
Income per head (yuan)	133.57	270.11	102.2
of which,			
distributed collective income	89.53	140.12	56.5
household private income	35.79	102.80	187.2
other income[1]	9.25	27.19	193.9
Living space per head (sq. metres)	10.17	13.41	31.9
Consumption per head (jin[2])			
wheat and rice	245	384	56.7
cooking oil	3.94	6.86	74.1
meat	11.51	18.10	57.3
poultry	0.50	1.56	212.0
eggs	1.59	2.85	79.2
fish	1.68	2.63	56.5
synthetic cloth (chi[3])	1.24	4.59	270.2

NOTES [1] Other income includes government transfer payments, remittances and wages earned in state enterprises in urban areas.
[2] 1 jin = 0.5 kg
[3] 3 chi = 1 metre

SOURCE State Bureau of Statistics, *Selected Statistics of China 1983*, Beijing, June 1983 (in Chinese).

38 per cent of total household income as compared to 26.8 per cent in 1978.

Much of the additional income has been spent on improving housing conditions, that is, on building new houses, repairing existing houses and adding new rooms to existing houses. In consequence, living space per head has increased by nearly a third. The peasantry also has used its higher income to improve its diet. Consumption of the superior food grains of rice and wheat has risen by more than a half and consumption of animal protein has risen between 57 per cent (in the cases of fish and meat) and 212 per cent (in the case of poultry). Finally, the peasantry has used its additional income to become better clothed. This is particularly notable in the case of synthetic cloth, purchases of which have increased 270 per cent.

One result of the higher average standard of living in rural areas has been a sharp fall in the incidence of rural poverty. In Chapter 1 we reported that there were 221 'chronically poor counties' in 1978, i.e. counties with an average distributed collective income per head of 50 yuan or less. By 1982 the number of such counties had fallen by more than two-thirds to seventy-two. In other words, only 3 per cent of the total number of counties are now classified as chronically poor. This does not imply, of course, that 3 per cent of the population are poor in the statistical sense of being malnourished. On the contrary, the arguments presented in Chapter 1 apply today with even greater force and at a guess it is likely that no more than 1 per cent of the population live below a poverty line of 50 yuan per capita.

INCOME DISTRIBUTION

Egalitarianism has become a dirty word in China and is used to describe the policies advocated by the Gang of Four. The emphasis now is on increasing production and the government is prepared to accept some increase in the degree of inequality in order to achieve this. Indeed, it is widely believed throughout China that the degree of inequality in the distribution of income has in fact become greater. There are reasons, however, to doubt that this is so.

First, incomes in urban areas have risen far more slowly since 1978 than incomes in the countryside and consequently there has been a pronounced reduction in rural–urban inequality. Secondly, although data are lacking to prove it, the greater opportunities for regional specialisation may well have led to a reduction in inter-provincial income inequalities. Thirdly, the responsibility system has been implemented in such a way that the initial impact effects have almost certainly led to a reduction in inequality at the local level. There are three such effects that deserve consideration.

First, and most important, a significant proportion of the land allocated to households under contract is distributed on an equal per capita basis. In Shaanxi province, for example, 60–70 per cent of the land is allocated on a per capita basis and 30–40 per cent on a per worker basis. In Qian county, Shaanxi – which until 1982 was classified as a chronically poor county – the guidelines laid down for commune leaders by county officials are as follows:

(i) Where the amount of land available for allocation is less than 2 mou per head, 60 per cent should be distributed on a per capita basis and 40 per cent on a per worker basis.
(i) Between 2.0 and 2.5 mou per head, the division should be 50–50. and
(iii) Above 2.5 mou per head, 40 per cent should be on a per capita basis and 60 per cent on a per worker basis.

These guidelines ensure that there will be a very equal distribution of collectively owned land (and hence of income) and that the poorer the locality in terms of land per head, the more equal will be the allocation of land. Thus in Team No. 3, Zhang Jia Bu Brigade, Qian Ling Commune of Qian county, there is 2.19 mou of collective land per head and we found that this land is indeed allocated on a 50–50 basis.

In Feng Fuo Brigade, Feng Fuo Commune of Liquan county, Shaanxi there is only 1.4 mou of cultivated land per capita. Half of this land is allocated to households under contract on a per worker basis and the remaining half is distributed (partly as a private plot and partly as a grain plot) on a per capita basis. This would appear to be a less even distribution than would have applied had Feng Fuo Brigade been located in Qian county. It is important to note, however, that Feng Fuo is a rich Brigade – its per capita income in 1982 was 360 yuan – and 48 per cent of the brigade's income originated not in agriculture but in brigade-owned enterprises. Thus the scarcity of land was more than compensated by the development of manufacturing activities.

This first point confirms our observations in 1982, but there is a second point which we failed to notice then. Under the old work point system the range in earnings typically varied from ten work points per day for a first-class male worker to six work points for a second-class female worker.

That is, the best paid males earned two-thirds more than the worst paid females. Under the new contract system, that fraction of the land allocated on a per worker basis seems to be more evenly distributed among workers than were work points. In the Chongqing municipality, for example, the two communes that we visited (Jiou Long and Ge Le) did not distinguish between male and female workers but gave the same amount of land to each. In Hubei province a distinction typically is made, but male workers receive only 25 per cent more land than females, a narrower differential than prevailed under the work point system. The greatest differential that we encountered in the field was in Team No. 3 of Zhang Jia Bu Brigade, previously mentioned, where a first-class male worker received 2.8 mu under contract and a second-class female worker 1.7 mu. This is a difference of 64.7 per cent in favour of the male and approximates the differential typical of the work point system.

In general, however, the rules used to allocate land on a per worker basis would appear to result in a more even distribution of income among households than the rules formerly used to allocate work points. Women are treated more equally today and households with a disproportionate number of female workers are less disadvantaged than they once were.

Thirdly, it was argued in Chapter 2, rather tentatively, that the stronger is the collective economy, the higher is income per head and the lower is the proportional contribution of the private economy. A corollary of this proposition is that the existence of the private sector does not worsen and possibly improves the distribution of income. That is, the distribution of total income (collective plus private) may be more equal than the distribution of collective income alone.

This proposition remains no more than an hypothesis, but the data in Table 9.3 on Shaanxi are suggestive. The units of observation vary from a brigade to the all China average and hence one must be very cautious in drawing conclusions from the figures. Even so, it does appear that within the province of Shaanxi the notion that the private sector plays an equalising role cannot be dismissed out of hand.

One must not push the argument too hard, however, for the relationship between the level of income and the proportion originating in the private sector clearly is not monotonic across the whole of China. Other provinces may be quite different from Shaanxi. In Hubei, for instance, per capita rural income in 1982 was 286 yuan while the percentage derived from private economic activities was 51.4. Similarly, it is possible that communes near major cities enjoy more private sector opportunities than less advantageously situated communes. Thus

TABLE 9.3 *The private sector in Shaanxi province, 1982*

Unit of observation	*Total rural income per head (yuan)*	*Private sector income as percentage of total*
Qian county	186	58
Shaanxi province	218	41
China	270	38
Feng Fuo Brigade, Feng Fuo Commune, Liquan county	360	34
Yuan Ja Brigade, Yan Xia Commune, Liquan county	530	21

SOURCE field notes.

average rural income in the Chongqing municipality was 287 yuan in 1982, of which 56.4 per cent was generated in the private sector. Despite these important qualifications, however, it remains possible that the loosening of constraints on the private sector has resulted in a more equal distribution of income than would otherwise have occurred. If so, contrary to common opinion, the institutional reforms may have had a favourable impact on the distribution of income at the local level.

In Appendix Tables 9.1 and 9.2 we reproduce data from Yuan Ja Brigade, Yan Xia Commune, Shaanxi. This brigade is hardly typical: there are no teams, the brigade is the basic accounting unit, contracting is on a seasonal basis only and two-thirds of the brigade's output originates in brigade-owned enterprises and sideline activities. It is the richest brigade in Liquan county and is regarded as a model for its cattle breeding farm. Still, for what they are worth, the data in Appendix Table 9.2 indicate that private sector activities certainly have not led to increased inequality (since the coefficient of variation on distributed collective income per head and total income per head are almost identical) and they may have led to a slight reduction (since the range of highest to lowest collective income is marginally higher than the range of total income per capita). Thus such evidence as exists so far is not consistent with the view that the private sector in rural China is a force for polarisation of incomes.

RELATIONS OF PRODUCTION

Government policy is permissive. People are given an opportunity to become better off if they are capable of doing so and the government is prepared to accept differences in income if they should emerge. We have seen, however, that in practice rural China remains a remarkably equal society and no statistically reliable evidence exists to show that the degree of equality has diminished since the reforms were introduced. Those who believe the contrary have had to rely on anecdotal evidence.

This anecdotal evidence should not be dismissed out of hand for it is possible that rare instances of spectacular rises in the fortunes of an individual household may indicate the direction in which the wind is blowing. What is uncommon today may become more common in future. If in fact income inequality and social stratification do become serious problems in the years ahead, the explanation probably will lie with changes in the relations of production, and it is therefore worthwhile to explore the changes in some detail.

For most practical purposes there is now only one system of farming in China, namely, *bao gan dao hu*. In Qian county, Shaanxi, all the production teams have adopted this form of the responsibility system; in Shaanxi province, 95 per cent of the teams have adopted *bao gan dao hu*; in the Chongqing municipality, Sichuan (which covers twelve counties and seven other districts with a total population of 10.5 million), 97.4 per cent of the households use this contracting arrangement; and in China as a whole about 90 per cent of peasant households have switched to *bao gan dao hu*. Thus China has moved very quickly from collective farming to a peasant farming system. The peasant household, however, remains an integral part of the collective economy: the land still belongs to the collective, the production plan still is prepared at the team level and individual quotas are set at team level and implemented through contracts between households and teams. The peasants clearly are not free to 'go it alone'.

Nonetheless, households have a great deal more freedom than they did five years ago, and the boundaries to their freedom are still expanding. Consider first the rules governing employment of labour. On 1 January 1983 a policy was introduced which permitted employers to hire up to seven apprentices or assistant workers; and in April 1983 the limit was raised to ten. Anyone wishing to employ more than ten persons is expected (but apparently not required) to form a private co-operative enterprise. The regulation is intended to apply mainly in the cities, perhaps as a way of reducing urban unemployment, but in principle it applies in the rural areas too, both in sideline activities and in agriculture.

The limit of ten persons applies to seasonal as well as semi-permanent employment and it is seasonal employment which, in fact, has expanded most as a result of the new regulation. In Qian county, for example, seasonal labour migrates from the southern to the northern part of the county to help with the wheat harvest. Formerly this migration was organised on a collective basis (one team entering into agreement with another), but it is now done entirely on an individual basis. In Hubei province the regulation is interpreted rather flexibly: employers may exceed the limit of ten employees provided they are seasonal labourers and the workers are employed for no more than half a month. Most seasonal labour bottlenecks, however, are broken by households exchanging labour for little or no payment as a form of mutual help.

Permanent hired labour is still rare. Labour-weak households, however, do sometimes hire people, often relatives, to help them farm collective land received under contract. In addition, households which have increased their acreage by bringing previously uncultivated or waste land under cultivation sometimes need to hire extra workers. But in general there is little hiring of permanent labour in the agricultural and livestock sectors. When it occurs it is mostly in specialised households, for example, in households which specialise completely in raising chickens or which have taken over a small collective enterprise and produce bricks and tiles under contract. Research in one county in Hubei, for instance, showed that only 0.03 per cent of the households hired labour.

When the labour is hired by a peasant household the wage is determined by mutual negotiation and agreement, not by regulation. Observations in Shaanxi suggest that the negotiated wage is never lower than the average distributed collective income per worker in the locality. It is possible, therefore, that incomes in the collective sector constitute a floor to wages in the tiny private sector.

Let us next consider the rules governing the use and transfer of land. In principle labour and land can be adjusted to one another in a peasant farming system either by labour-weak households hiring workers to help farm their land or by labour-strong households hiring land to employ more fully their relatively abundant labour. The position in China today, in this as in other matters, is a little unclear. The general rule seems to be that households cannot own land, or rent or transfer it to or from another household. In practice these rules are not rigidly enforced. This is especially true as regards land transfer.

In most cases, if a household wants to give up a piece of land, it must return the land to the collective for reallocation to another household. Land is not normally transferred directly from one household to another. There are exceptions, however, and this rule is currently under discussion. Moreover, if two households wish to exchange or swap land of equal size, they are allowed to do so. This may occur, for example, in order to reduce fragmentation or to reduce the distance between a peasant's house and the fields for which he is responsible under contract. Such swaps, done with the approval of the team, probably affect no more than 1 per cent of the collectively owned land under cultivation.

In some areas, we were told, land has been directly transferred from one household to another. The receiving household then assumes responsibility for handing over the grain quota to the team and for making the required contribution to the team's accumulation and welfare fund. In addition, the receiving household may supply the original household with grain for subsistence consumption. This payment is of course equivalent to a rent and is determined by mutual agreement. Such cases, though, are rare. Most households wish to maintain their right to cultivate collective land and prefer to hire people to work for them rather than hire out part of their land, particularly given the uncertain legality of renting collective land to others.

Land allocated to households by the collective is theirs to cultivate for the indefinite future. In principle land should be reallocated from time to time as the demographic profile of a household changes, the amount of land being increased as the size of the household expands and the number of workers rises and, conversely, as household size and labour power contracts. Frequent reallocations of land would increase uncertainty of tenure and discourage peasants from investing in the land. To overcome this problem most teams seem to have retained some collective land as a 'reserve' or for 'emergency purposes' and have promised households that there will be no change in their entitlement to collective land under contract for at least three years and in some communes for at least five years. In Feng Fuo Production Brigade, for example, 300 mu have been retained by the collective and are used partly to increase allocations to households which increase in size, partly to have land available for ex-members of the army when they return from military service, and partly to increase the amount of land allocated to poor households to bring them nearer to the average income of the brigade. Thus it is hoped that the existing distribution of land among households will remain largely undisturbed for five years or more.

So far we have been concerned with the allocation of cultivated land owned by the collective. In some regions, particularly in hilly or mountainous areas, there is land which at present is uncultivated or unused which potentially could be put to economic use. Where such land exists households, with the approval of the collective, are encouraged to develop it. In the Chongqing municipality this land is known as 'private land'.

Most 'private land' is in forest areas and is used by peasant households as fruit orchards or tea gardens or to grow mulberry bushes to feed silkworms. There is no limit on the amount of private land a collective can have, although there is a limit of 15 per cent on the amount of collective land that can be used as private subsistence plots. Equally, there is no limit on the amount of private land an individual household may cultivate. Households can, of course, hire labour to help clear the forest, plant trees, etc., and to assist with cultivation and harvesting. It is impossible to know how much newly cleared land for specialised production is held in the form of private land, but a rough calculation for the Chongqing municipality suggests that a figure of 2.4 per cent may not be too far off the mark. Whatever the precise figure, it is evident that private land is a new phenomenon in China. Although formal ownership remains with the collective, a household which brings barren land into cultivation is likely *de facto* to enjoy lifetime security of tenure and to have full rights to the income generated on its private land. Such land is not subject to production quotas although the household may be required to make a contribution to the collective accumulation fund. The latter can be regarded as analogous to a land tax.

In some cases the possibility of developing barren land can lead to a substantial increase in household income and to a change in social status. Consider, for instance, the case of the Wei family in the Chongqing municipality.

Mr Wei is an experienced tea grower and in 1981 he assumed responsibility for cultivating 20 mu of tea under contract from his team. He mobilised four other members of the commune and signed a contract for five years. Formally, the five workers take care of the tea garden jointly, but in fact Mr Wei employs his four partners on a semi-permanent basis and pays them wages. In addition, there is another worker from Mr Wei's household, making a total of six semi-permanent workers.

Then in 1982 Mr Wei opened up another 13 mu of barren land and planted it to tea, raising the total area of the tea garden to 33 mu. This new land, too, is farmed under contract and thus is not formally private land. Mr Wei, however, has invested his own funds in the tea garden and in processing facilities and, in addition, has borrowed 5000 yuan from the state bank in order to provide electric power for mechanised tea processing and to construct a tile roof over the processing plant. Given this heavy investment it is likely that Mr Wei has in fact established a right to permanent tenure of the land although, since it is held under contract, he has not established a right to all the income produced on the land. The tea garden hence is neither private land nor collective land; it is something in between.

In 1982 there were thirteen people employed in the tea garden: Mr Wei and one other worker from his household of four persons, his four 'partners' and seven seasonal workers employed for approximately 120 days each. Mr Wei, thus, has ceased to be an ordinary Chinese peasant and has become a fairly large employer on an agricultural enterprise with sizeable fixed assets. In 1982 the income of his household was 4000 yuan – or 1000 yuan per capita – and the prospect for large further rises in future was favourable.

Economic and social differentiation also can occur as a result of changes in the rules regulating the ownership of productive assets. In China today there are very few restraints on peasant ownership of the means of production. Households are free to acquire tractors, vehicles and other items of capital equipment, either by purchasing them from state enterprises or from the collective. These purchases usually are by individuals, but peasants sometimes pool their funds to buy, say, a tractor and these 'groups' may then use the tractor on their own land or hire it out to others. Indeed, many cases have been known of peasants renting tractors from a commune and then hiring themselves and the machine out to their neighbours.

Private savings and investment in capital equipment undoubtedly have risen sharply in recent years although most capital assets still are collectively owned. Accurate estimates unfortunately are not available, but an informed guess in Beijing is that 70–80 per cent of the means of production (excluding land) are publicly owned. It is obvious that as the share of private ownership rises the possibility that capital assets will become a source of inequality increases, either because savings rates among households differ or because the return on peasant investments differ, some investments turning out to be highly profitable and others showing a loss. Once the risks of investment are borne by individuals rather than by the society at large, the dispersion in profit rates among projects is almost certain to be translated into a dispersion of incomes among households.

In the past, households were not allowed to acquire large pieces of capital equipment or even hand tractors; they were restricted to owning small implements and tools. Practice today varies slightly from one region to another but the general picture seems to be the following: there are no controls on the ownership of livestock; there are no controls on the ownership of relatively small items of capital equipment, including especially hand tractors; it is expected that large pieces of capital equipment such as combine harvesters and irrigation pumps will remain in collective ownership, although there is no outright prohibition of private ownership. Control is exercised indirectly, for example, by providing loans to purchase hand tractors but not for the purchase of large tractors and trucks.

In Shaanxi, households are allowed to buy whatever they like and purchases may be made from state enterprises, the collective or the open market. Loans are available from state banks to help peasants buy all kinds of equipment. Such loans usually are for three years and the rate of interest charged to private borrowers is approximately the same as that charged to collectives, namely, 4.8–5.0 per thousand per month. Moreover, the collectives are encouraged to sell their livestock, draft animals and small implements to individual households, often under an instalment plan. The money from such sales is kept for the time being by the collective in the form of idle bank balances, although it is expected that in due course these balances will be used to promote collective industrial and other activities.

The provincial authorities encourage the brigades and communes to assign responsibility for the maintenance and management of large and medium-sized pieces of equipment to households under contract. These and other collectively owned assets such as orchards, fish ponds and workshops are assigned to the household which offers the most favourable contract, and when there is competition among several households, the contract may be auctioned. When collective assets are sold, the price is negotiated between buyer and seller. If there is more than one potential buyer the sale usually goes to the highest bidder. There are exceptions, however, especially when it is the policy of the team to ensure an even distribution of its assets among all households. In some cases, in fact, the buyer is chosen by drawing lots!

It should be clear from the above that changes in the relations of production do contain a latent possibility of greater income inequality and social stratification. The potential is, nevertheless, only latent and as we have seen, there is no evidence yet of increased inequality. Moreover, the rules governing access to land, the hiring of labour and ownership of the means of production are not immutable. The Chinese are observing the situation carefully and it is likely that if serious problems emerge the rules will be altered or counteracting measures introduced. Hence it is best, perhaps, to continue to regard the current period as one of experimentation, albeit on a national scale.

Leaving all this aside, it is natural to ask what is the worst that could happen if current policies continue and if inequalities do come to the surface. The truth is that we do not know, but in my judgement the fundamentals are so favourable as regards access to land, credit, non-agricultural employment opportunities and health and educational services that rural China would continue to be a remarkably equal and fair society.

CAPITAL ACCUMULATION

But would it be an economically progressive society? That depends on whether modernisation and growth can be sustained for, say, another ten years or more. And this, in turn, depends in large part upon the level of investment and its composition. Thus to answer the question it is necessary to consider the five sources of capital accumulation in the Chinese countryside: investment by the state, labour-investment by the commune, investment financed out of the profits of commune- and brigade-level enterprises, investment financed out of the teams' collective accumulation fund and household savings and investment. Let us consider each of these in turn.

Unfortunately, we were not able to obtain accurate information on trends in state capital construction in rural areas, and consequently we can only give a few general impressions. In Hubei province we were told that investment by the state for agricultural purposes has increased since the reforms were introduced. This is particularly true of investments in hydro-electric power, water conservation works and rural communications and transport. In Shaanxi province, in contrast, state investment seems to have remained constant in money terms and hence to have fallen in real terms. There has, however, been a change in the pattern of investment, relatively more being allocated to the hilly and poor regions in the northern and southern parts of the province and less to the richer central area. This is a deliberate change in policy intended to improve the regional distribution of income. In the Chongqing municipality, state investment in the rural areas probably has declined slightly. One cannot draw any firm generalisations from this, but it is a reasonable working hypothesis that if anything state rural capital accumulation may have fallen somewhat in China as a whole. This hypothesis is at least consistent with national policy decisions to reduce aggregate investment in order to raise consumption levels quickly.

Next let us consider labour-investment by communes, brigades and teams. China is known throughout the world for its success in mobilising seasonally unemployed and other 'surplus' labour for investment in rural areas. At its peak in the 1970s construction activities probably accounted for more than 20 per cent of the time of the rural labour force and more than 100 million workers. An enormous amount of work was completed – field terracing and levelling, irrigation and flood control projects, tree planting, road and bridge building, etc. – which changed the face of the Chinese countryside. Some of this work was of poor quality and required frequent repair and maintenance, and although the opportunity cost of the labour employed was low, the return on investment was long delayed and disappointingly meagre.

The new reforms have reduced the emphasis formerly placed on labour-investment. Peasant efforts to combat floods and other disasters are still organised on a collective basis, of course, and there still are many large-scale projects concerned with water control, and road and railroad maintenance. There is no doubt that the amount of such activity has declined in some provinces, e.g. Hubei, and in many communes, particularly communes located in the more economically advanced areas. In Shaanxi there was a decline in the number of very large construction projects after the introduction of the economic reforms, but there was an offsetting increase in the number of small projects undertaken by groups of households, especially tree planting projects. In 1982 labour-investment in Shaanxi probably was equivalent to ten or twenty days per head or roughly 30 yuan per capita. Given that the distributed collective income per capita in that year was only 99.1 yuan (and total income per capita 218.3 yuan), this was not a bad effort.

In general, large construction projects, e.g. reservoirs and major roads, are financed by the state. Medium-sized projects often receive a subsidy from the state but most of the cost must be borne by the local beneficiaries. In such cases, households which benefit directly from the project are expected to supply labour gratis, while labour supplied by non-beneficiary households is paid the standard wage. Small projects with highly localised benefits are financed locally, either by production teams or even groups of households. Collectively sponsored projects are still organised by the commune or brigade, but the labour is obtained directly from households. A brigade, for instance, may require each household to supply one able-bodied person for a project, but the person supplied need no longer be a member of that household. That is, if the household wishes, it may hire the labour from elsewhere to provide a worker for a public works project. This privately paid worker might, of course, represent a contribution from a household which is a direct beneficiary of the project and hence the household would not be compensated by the brigade for the (hired) labour it supplies. This new rule may be efficient, in that it ensures that labour is withdrawn from activities where its opportunity cost is lowest, but it is bound to undermine the sense of solidarity and communal participation that used to be such a striking feature of the commune system. And in the long run it is likely greatly to reduce the amount of labour-investment that is undertaken.

Richer communes, however, rely relatively little on labour-investment to achieve high rates of capital accumulation. The engine of growth in their case is more likely to be the reinvested profits of commune and brigade-run enterprises. Let us therefore consider what has been happening to this source of investment since the reforms were introduced.

The basic data are reported in Appendix Tables 9.3 and 9.4, which bring up to date and partially supersede Tables 6.1 and 6.2 of Chapter 6. As can be seen in Appendix Table 9.3, the net profits of commune- and brigade-run enterprises remained practically stationary between 1980 and 1982, while fixed assets rose by 23.6 per cent and gross output value by 23.2 per cent. The wage bill, in contrast, increased by 31.1 per cent and the average annual wage rose from 396.67 yuan in 1980 to 501.60 yuan in 1982, or by 26.5 per cent. Associated with these changes was a sharp fall in the profitability of commune- and brigade-run enterprises (see Appendix Table 9.4). Between 1978 and 1982 the rate of profit on fixed assets fell steadily from 38.3 to 29.5 per cent and the rate of profit on output fell from 17.3 per cent in 1980 to 14.2 per cent in 1982.

It is evident, therefore, that there has been a squeeze on the profits of commune- and brigade-level enterprises. This squeeze has come from several sources. First, as part of the reform package, the prices paid for raw materials and energy have increased. This is merely another way of saying that agriculture's terms of trade have improved. Secondly, there has been an increase in levels of taxation paid to the state. In a sample of enterprises from the Chongqing municipality, for instance, taxes rose from 4 million yuan in 1978 to 22 million yuan in 1982 whereas profits after taxes increased from 23 to only 28 million yuan. Thirdly, there has been a change in accounting conventions which has raised the rate of depreciation slightly and hence has reduced the funds available for expanded reproduction.

Fourthly, there has been a change in the wage payments system which has resulted in a rapid increase in average wages. In the past, workers in commune- and brigade-run enterprises received work points just like agricultural workers. These work points ultimately were converted into income at the rate appropriate to the team from which the worker was drawn. That is, the wages of commune non-agricultural workers were closely linked to the productivity of labour in the agricultural sector. Today, however, that link has been broken. Wages are paid in cash and the wage rate depends in varying degree upon the success of the individual commune- or brigade-run enterprise in which a person happens to work, the skill of the individual worker and wages paid in broadly comparable state enterprises.

This change in the payments system has had two effects: (i) income differentials between agricultural workers and workers in commune- and brigade-run enterprises have widened considerably; and (ii) real wages in collective enterprises have risen rapidly, with the result that profit rates have fallen. This can be illustrated with data from Jiou Long Commune in the Chongqing municipality. In 1978 the average annual income per worker was 407 yuan in agriculture and 540 yuan in commune- and brigade-run enterprises. By 1982, average income per worker in agriculture had risen to 579 yuan, a rise of 42 per cent. In commune-run enterprises, in contrast, the average annual income of a worker had increased to 1023 yuan and in brigade-level enterprises incomes rose to 1036 yuan. That is, wages in commune- and brigade-run enterprises rose more than twice as fast as agricultural incomes and consequently the income differential in favour of enterprise workers increased from less than a third in 1978 to nearly four-fifths four years later.

Not only has there been a relative fall in profits, there has also been a fall in the proportion of profits used for capital accumulation. This is a deliberate act of policy and is one of the methods that has been used to increase consumption standards of the peasantry quickly. In the Chongqing municipality, for example, the division of net profits after taxes in 1982 was as follows: 40 per cent was retained by the commune- and brigade-run enterprises for reinvestment; 30 per cent was turned over to communes for investment in new enterprises; 18 per cent was used by the communes to subsidise prices paid to agricultural producers for their output; and 12 per cent was turned over to the teams to enable them to increase the distributed collective income of their members. That is, 30 per cent of net profits was used to raise household incomes either indirectly through price subsidies or directly through a higher distributed income.

The combined effect nationally of a falling profit rate and a lower reinvestment ratio has been to reduce the rate of increase of fixed assets in commune- and brigade-level enterprises. Indeed, between 1978 and 1982 the rate of fixed asset formation declined precipitously even in current price terms, namely, by about two-thirds. In 1979, fixed assets increased by an impressive 21.7 per cent; the following year the rate fell to 16.4 per cent and then to 15 per cent in 1981; finally in 1982, the rate of investment collapsed to only 7.5 per cent. By that time commune- and brigade-run enterprises had ceased to be a powerful engine of rural development.

In the relatively poor communes, of course, commune- and brigade-run enterprises never had been terribly important. Most investment had been financed by the teams' collective accumulation funds. It is instructive to consider, therefore, what has been happening to collective accumulation at the team level since the economic reforms were introduced.

There are two dimensions to this question. One concerns the stock of productive assets and the other the annual flow of collectively financed investment. We have indicated above (p. 315) that many teams have begun to sell their assets to individual households or groups of households. In most cases the money thus obtained has not been reinvested but has been held in the form of idle balances. As a result there has been a decline in the stock of collectively owned means of production. In some cases this decline has been very rapid. For example, we visited Team No. 3, Zhang Jia Bu Brigade, Qian Ling Commune in Shaanxi province. In 1981 the team owned one hand tractor and fourteen draught animals and cattle. By 1983 all these assets had been sold and the team had become completely decapitalised! Indeed, in Qian county, Shaanxi, of which Team No. 3 is a part, 13 per cent of all the production teams now own no collective assets and the team as a unit for production and accumulation has virtually ceased to exist.

In principle, it would be possible to adopt a strategy whereby teams sold off their draught animals and small items of collectively owned capital equipment, while both reinvesting the proceeds in larger pieces of equipment in which economies of scale are important and generating new investment through the collective accumulation fund. Such a strategy would permit a change in the composition of collectively owned assets while ensuring that the stock of productive assets continued to increase.

Unfortunately, however, this has not been done. Assets are being liquidated and not replaced and the rate of collective investment has been reduced. Everywhere we went, be it a rich commune in the Beijing municipality (Luguoqiao Commune), the 813 communes in the

Chongqing municipality, or the provinces of Hubei and Shaanxi, we were informed that the rate of collective accumulation had fallen. This was partly a consequence of the spread of *bao gan dao hu* and the accompanying shift of responsibility for agricultural investment from the team to the household, and partly a result of a policy decision to increase distributed collective income at the expense of collective accumulation.

In a few cases we were able to quantify the reduction in the rate of collective accumulation, and these figures are reported in Table 9.4. As can be seen, in only one case did the rate of accumulation actually increase and this was in Feng Fuo Brigade, a brigade which practised *bao chan dao hu*, had a strong sense of collective identity and was expanding rapidly. It is in every sense a model brigade. In the other three cases, alas, the rate of collective accumulation appears to have fallen by two or three percentage points since the reforms were introduced and as a result only about 10 per cent of net collective income now is used to enlarge the collectively owned means of production.

There is, however, a ray of hope. Collective accumulation is recognised by the authorities as a problem and discussions are underway as to what policies should be followed in future. These discussions appear to centre on three issues: (i) the attitude to be adopted towards sales of collectively owned assets; (ii) the purposes of collective accumulation in a farming system in which *bao gan dao hu* predominates; and (iii) the proportion of collective income that should be retained for collective accumulation. These clearly are the key points that need to be resolved if collective accumulation is to have a well-defined role in a reformed economic system.

Be that as it may, there is no doubt that the private sector is expected to shoulder more responsibility for rural savings and investment.

TABLE 9.4 *Collective investment as per cent of net collective income*

Unit	*1978*	*1982*
1. Feng Fuo Brigade, Feng Fuo Commune, Liquan county, Shaanxi	16.9	18.0
2. Shaanxi province	12.8	10.2
3. Jiou Long Commune, Chongqing municipality, Sichuan	12.1	10.3
4. Ge Le Commune, Chongqing municipality, Sichuan	13.1	9.8

NOTE In the case of Shaanxi province, contributions to the collective welfare fund are included in the definition of collective accumulation.

Unfortunately, lack of data makes it almost impossible to assess accurately how well households have responded to the challenge. In general terms, however, several points are clear. First, private savings of households have definitely increased and the savings rate frequently exceeds 25 per cent of total income. Secondly, a high proportion of these savings are channelled to housing and the purchase of consumer durables and only a relatively small proportion is used for investment in fixed productive assets. This pattern of expenditure may be due in part to uncertainty by households in the continuation of present policies and not to a strong preference for consumption at the expense of investment. That is, it can be argued that peasants are reluctant to invest in machinery for fear that if policies change they will lose their capital. There is no evidence to support this hypothesis, but it is plausible and at least is consistent with the observation that a high proportion of the savings that do not go into housing and consumer durables are used to increase bank balances or reduce indebtedness. Whether increased private bank balances lead to more productive investment elsewhere is unknown.

Thirdly, productive investment by households often consists of purchases of assets from the production teams, as has been explained. This transfer of ownership does not represent an increase in the stock of the means of production in the countryside, since what the household gains the team loses. This is especially true, as is the case at present, when the teams do not reinvest the sales receipts or transfer them to the brigades but merely accumulate cash balances. Thus to the extent that households purchase existing assets from teams and these collective assets are not replaced, the long-run rate of capital formation is not accelerated and the prospects for growth and agricultural modernisation are not improved.

Mr Dai Zhen Ru of the Agricultural Commission of the Chongqing municipality believes that private investment in productive assets, i.e. in implements and draught animals, etc., accounts for 8–12 per cent of total household income. A sample survey of households in Qian county, Shaanxi enables us to be a little more precise. There it was estimated that 21.6 per cent of household income in 1982 was devoted to 'accumulation'. This would seem to be an impressive figure, but when the total is disaggregated the proportion saved is not quite so impressive (see Table 9.5).

In fact, only about 7.3 per cent of household income is used for direct investment in agriculture; 5.9 per cent is used to improve housing conditions and purchase consumer durables and 8.4 per cent represents

TABLE 9.5 *Household savings in Qian county, Shaanxi, 1982*

	Percentage of total household income	*Percentage of total household savings*
Housing and consumer durables	5.9	27.3
Acquisition of agricultural implements	3.1	14.4
Purchase of draught animals	4.2	19.4
Increase in cash balances	8.4	38.9
	21.6	100.0

an increase in cash balances. Much of the latter, perhaps, is working capital and will be used in the course of the agricultural year to buy fertiliser, seeds and other current inputs. In other words, only 33.8 per cent of the reported savings is used for directly productive investment; the remaining two-thirds is used for rather different purposes. It is too early to say whether the increase in private investment since the reforms is sufficiently large to compensate for the fall in collective accumulation and in investment financed by commune- and brigade-run enterprises. If the private investment effort turns out to be disappointing, the authorities may have to consider raising the quotas specified in the production contracts with households or raising the contributions from households to the collective accumulation fund.

What, then, are the likely overall effects of the economic reforms on long-run rates of capital formation in the Chinese countryside? Our analysis suggests that state investment is likely to remain roughly constant, that labour-investment is likely to fall but that there may be an offsetting rise in the efficiency of such investment, that investment financed from the profits of commune- and brigade-run enterprises will fall, and that collective accumulation by production teams will decline. In other words, investment financed from commune and state sources will almost certainly contribute less to growth in future than in the past. The rate of investment by households, on the other hand, clearly has increased since the reforms were introduced. It is possible that this represents only a transitory rise in savings out of an unanticipated increase in real incomes, as the permanent income hypothesis would predict. If so, private savings and investment can be expected to fall once the transition to a new economic system is completed. Equally, however, one cannot totally discount the possibility that private savings will remain at their present level or even increase if political uncertainty diminishes. Whatever happens to private savings, it is likely that the productivity of investment will increase. There are likely to be fewer projects in which investment is wasted and more projects which take full advantage of local opportunities for high gains from small capital outlays.

On balance, I would guess that the rise in private investment and in the average productivity of investment will not fully offset the fall in collective investment. There is thus a danger that long-run rates of capital formation and of agricultural growth may decline slightly. This, however, is not inevitable. If the need arises, corrective steps can be taken, but only if the authorities are alert to the danger. It is important, therefore, that trends in capital formation be monitored closely, for if there is a serious weakness in the reform package it may not be reflected in the relations of production but in the forces of production.

APPENDIX TABLE 9.1 *Household income in Yuan Ja Brigade, Yan Xia Commune, Liquan county, Shaanxi, 1982 (yuan)*

Household	*Population*	*Labour force*	*Distributed collective income*	*Private income*	*Total income*
1	4	2	1909.80	310	2219.80
2	7	4	2904.00	950	3854.00
3	4	2	1920.60	280	2200.60
4	5	2	1397.70	1700	3097.70
5	4	2	1515.90	920	2435.90
6	7	4	3093.10	900	3993.10
7	4	2	1601.10	1200	2801.10
8	6	2	1248.90	300	1548.90
9	4	2	2605.80	800	3405.80
10	5	3	3030.90	1200	4230.90
11	5	2	1556.10	500	2056.10
12	4	2	1309.20	250	1559.20
13	4	2	1785.30	800	2558.30
14	4	2	2126.10	1600	3726.10
15	4	3	2928.90	450	3378.90
16	4	2	2021.10	500	2521.10
17	6	3	2503.80	190	2693.80
18	4	1	516.30	1100	1616.30
19	4	1	538.20	140	678.20
20	3	2	1509.20	150	1659.20
21	3	2	1620.30	180	1800.30
22	4	2	1643.70	600	2243.70
23	2	1	531.00	140	671.00
24	4	2	1524.60	160	1684.60
25	4	2	1644.60	600	2244.60
26	4	2	1702.80	220	1922.80
27	3	1	895.80	300	1195.80
28	5	2	1746.30	230	1976.30
29	3	2	1453.55	120	1573.55
30	3	2	1665.90	130	1795.90
31	3	1	1148.10	100	1248.10
32	3	2	1923.00	140	2063.00
33	4	2	1633.80	130	1763.80
34	3	2	1634.40	120	1754.40
35	3	2	1579.40	95	1674.40
36	5	2	1713.90	1100	2813.90
37	5	3	2600.70	1200	3800.70
38	4	2	1695.00	125	1820.00
39	6	2	1957.40	170	2127.40
40	5	2	2633.40	800	3433.40
41	8	2	1675.20	210	1885.20
42	8	3	3034.20	320	3354.20
43	7	3	2480.10	260	2740.10
44	9	4	3885.30	310	4195.30
45	6	3	2316.60	280	2596.60

Appendix Table 9.2 *Per capita household income in Yuan Ja Brigade, 1982 (yuan)*

Household	*Distributed collective income per head*	*Private income per head*	*Total income per head*
1	477.45	77.50	554.95
2	414.86	135.71	550.57
3	480.15	70.00	550.15
4	279.54	340.00	619.54
5	378.98	230.00	608.98
6	441.87	128.57	570.44
7	400.28	300.00	700.28
8	208.15	50.00	258.15
9	651.45	200.00	851.45
10	606.18	240.00	846.18
11	311.22	100.00	411.22
12	327.30	62.50	389.80
13	439.58	200.00	639.58
14	531.53	400.00	931.53
15	732.23	112.50	844.73
16	505.28	125.00	630.28
17	417.30	31.67	448.97
18	129.08	275.00	404.08
19	134.55	35.00	169.55
20	503.07	50.00	553.07
21	540.10	60.00	600.10
22	410.93	150.00	560.93
23	265.50	70.00	335.50
24	381.15	40.00	421.15
25	411.15	150.00	561.15
26	425.70	55.00	480.70
27	298.60	100.00	398.60
28	349.26	46.00	395.26
29	484.52	40.00	524.52
30	555.30	43.33	598.63
31	382.70	33.33	416.03
32	641.00	46.67	687.67
33	408.45	32.50	440.95
34	544.80	40.00	584.40
35	526.47	31.67	558.13
36	342.78	220.00	562.78
37	520.14	240.00	760.14
38	423.75	31.25	455.00
39	326.23	28.33	354.57
40	526.68	160.00	686.68
41	209.40	26.25	235.65
42	379.28	40.00	419.28
43	354.30	37.14	391.44

Appendix Table 9.2 (*Contd.*)

Household	*Distributed collective income per head*	*Private income per head*	*Total income per head*
44	431.70	34.44	466.14
45	386.10	46.67	432.77
Average	419.91	110.36	530.26
Ratio of highest to lowest income	5.67:1	15.24:1	5.49:1
Coefficient of variation	0.30	0.85	0.31

Appendix Table 9.3 *Basic data on commune- and brigade-run enterprises, 1978–82*

	1978	*1979*	*1980*	*1981*	*1982*
Total number of enterprises (million)	1.50	1.48	1.42	1.33	1.16
Total employment (million)	28	29	30.0	29.7	31.1
Wage payments (million yuan)	n.a.	n.a.	11 900	13 000	15 600
Net profits (million yuan)	8800	10 300	11 800	11 300	11 900
Gross output value (million yuan)	n.a.	n.a.	68 200	72 200	84 000
Fixed assets (million yuan)	23 000	28 000	32 600	37 500	40 300

Source Ministry of Agriculture, Department of Commune and Brigade Enterprises.

APPENDIX TABLE 9.4 *Economic characteristics of commune- and brigade-run enterprises, 1978–82*

	1978	*1979*	*1980*	*1981*	*1982*
Average size of enterprise:					
(i) employment	18.7	19.6	21.1	22.3	26.8
(ii) turnover (yuan)	n.a.	n.a.	48 028	54 286	72 414
(iii) capital assets (yuan)	15 333	18 919	22 958	28 195	34 741
Average capital–labour ratio (yuan per worker)	820	965	1088	1264	1296
Efficiency indicators					
(i) capital–output ratio	n.a.	n.a.	0.48	0.52	0.48
(ii) rate of profit on output (% per annum)	n.a.	n.a.	17.3	15.7	14.2
(iii) rate of profit on fixed capital (% per annum)	38.3	36.8	36.2	30.1	29.5

SOURCE Ministry of Agriculture, Department of Commune and Brigade Enterprises.

Index